# Freud on a Precipice

# Freud on a Precipice

## How Freud's Fate Pushed Psychoanalysis over the Edge

Robert Langs

JASON ARONSON
Lanham • Boulder • New York • Toronto • Plymouth, UK

Published by Jason Aronson
An imprint of Rowman & Littlefield Publishers, Inc.
A wholly owned subsidary of The Rowman & Littlefield Publishing Group, Inc.
4501 Forbes Boulevard, Suite 200, Lanham, Maryland 20706
http://www.rowmanlittlefield.com

Estover Road
Plymouth PL6 7PY
United Kingdom

British Library Cataloguing in Publication Information Available

**Library of Congress Cataloging-in-Publication Data**

Langs, Robert, 1928–
    Freud on a precipice : how Freud's fate pushed psychoanalysis over the edge/Robert Langs.
        p. cm.
    Includes bibliographical references and index.
    ISBN 978-0-7657-0600-3 (cloth : alk. paper)
    ISBN 978-0-7657-0721-5 (electronic)
    1. Freud, Sigmund, 1856–1939. 2. Psychoanalysis—History. 3. Freud, Sigmund, 1856–1939—Psychology. I. Title.
    BF109.F74.L365 2009
    150.19'52092—dc22

                                                                    2009027421

Printed in the United States of America

♾™ The paper used in this publication meets the minimum requirements of American National Standard for Information Sciences—Permanence of Paper for Printed Library Materials, ANSI/NISO Z39.48-1992.

# Contents

Introduction                                                      vii

**Chapter One**    Is Freud to be Trusted?                          1

**Chapter Two**    Paradigms and Archetypes                         9

**Chapter Three**  A Tale of Two Paradigms                         31

**Chapter Four**   The Descendants of Freud's Two Paradigms        43

**Chapter Five**   Freud in Conflict                               75

**Chapter Six**    Psychoanalytic Detective Work                   87

**Chapter Seven**  Freud's Early Traumas                          115

**Chapter Eight**  The Ultimate Trauma                            143

A Personal Note                                                  179

References                                                       185

Index                                                            191

About the Author                                                 197

# Introduction

Gradually it has become clear to me what every great philosophy so far has been: namely, the personal confession of its author and a kind of involuntary and unconscious memoir.

—Frederick Nietzsche (2003, p. 37)

On July 7, 1898, Sigmund Freud forwarded several newly written chapters of his masterpiece, *The Interpretation of Dreams* (Freud, 1900), to his friend, colleague, correspondent, and critic, Wilhelm Fliess. In the letter accompanying this material, Freud wrote the following: "It was all written by the unconscious, on the well known principle of Itzig, the Sunday horseman. 'Itzig, where are you going?' 'Don't ask me, ask the horse!' At the beginning of a paragraph I never knew where I should end up" (Freud, 1954, letter 92, July, 7, 1898 p. 258).

All writing is unconsciously motivated, but here Freud alludes to a unique kind of automatic writing in which the part of the mind I call *the deep unconscious wisdom system* takes over (Langs, 2004, 2006) and the conscious mind can do little more than step aside and not get in its way. Much to my surprise, many sections of this book were written in this manner.

This odd phenomenon took over as soon as I sat down to write the first chapter of the book, which is chapter two in the present version. Quite arbitrarily, I decided to forgo the outline I had made and began with an unplanned exploration of archetypes and paradigms. I had only the vaguest reason for making this decision in that I sensed that these two concepts, which deal with universal configurations and world views, would be among the backbones of the book. As I began to write, one idea spontaneously followed another; the chapter took on a life of its own. The key points I ended up making had never crossed my mind before. I was stunned by what was happening and found it enormously rewarding to watch my mind dance that way. After years of conscious struggle and frustration, it seemed that my wise deep unconscious mind had decided to reward my efforts to forge what I mistakenly thought was a new paradigm of psychoanalysis (Freud had been there almost a century before me) with a fertile patch of creativity I did not know I possessed. And it continued to gift me this way throughout the writing of the book.

I share this with you because your staying with a book like this, which has been crafted by tapping into deep unconscious wisdom, depends on your being able to by-pass your natural, in-built conscious resistances against receiving this kind of alien but essential knowledge and taking it in deep unconsciously as well. Freud said as much in another context:

> Just as the patient must relate everything that his self-observation can detect, and keep back all the logical and affective objections that seek to induce him to make a selection from among them, so the doctor must put himself in a position to make use of everything he is told for the purposes of interpretation and of recognizing the concealed unconscious material without substituting a censorship of his own for the selection that the patient has forgone. To put it in a formula: he must turn his own unconscious like a receptive organ towards the transmitting unconscious of the patient. He must adjust himself to the patient as a telephone receiver is adjusted to the transmitting microphone. . . . So the doctor's unconscious is able, from the derivatives of the unconscious which are communicated to him, to reconstruct that unconscious, which has determined the patient's free associations. (Freud, 1912b, pp. 115–116)

I am, then, asking you to play analyst to my patient. And I do this because one of the unexpected insights I came upon in drafting this book is that *the conscious mind—i.e., the conscious system—*is universally opposed to and all but unable to grasp and accept the ideas offered in this book. By virtue of the evolved design of the emotion-processing mind, such openness flies in the face of its fundamentally defensive, denial-dominated operations (Langs, 1996, 2004, 2006). In a few words, your conscious mind doesn't want you to read this book. But your deep unconscious mind does!

You can see why I ask that you open your deep unconscious system to the ideas I shall be offering. And given that the unconscious part of the human mind is far wiser than the conscious mind, if I may say so, there are great rewards awaiting you if you find a way to do it. But therein lies the rub: How is it to be done? Asking you to decode your dreams or to notice their tone after reading portions of this book seems impractical. But beyond that, all I can do is hope that you'll find a way for your unconscious mind to tune into my unconscious mind, which will mean that you'll read on instead of putting this book aside in deference to your conscious, obliterative needs.

In envisioning the structure and goals of this book, my initial idea was to develop some ideas that I had presented in a recent book, *Beyond Yahweh and Jesus: Bringing Death's Wisdom to Faith, Spirituality, and Psychoanalysis* (Langs, 2008). I had argued there that one reason that religion has failed in its promise to bring peace to the world is that it needed a grounding in human psychology of a kind that only psychoanalysis could have given it. I held Freud personally accountable for not coming to the aid of religion and decided to take a cursory look at his personal history for the unconscious reasons he failed to do so. I was able to identify some seldom discussed, but likely secreted early life traumas that seemed relevant to the choices he made and let it stand at that.

But the subject of Freud's early life would not go away. I searched the literature for more on the topic and found indications that his early-life traumas had affected not only his attitude towards religion, but the very manner in which he gave form to psychoanalysis. I learned that the exact dates in 1897 during which he decided on the fundamental propositions of his new psychology were well documented and that there was considerable material that had a bearing on the direction he took his emerging psychoanalytic thinking.

Frankly, I had not appreciated how momentous this turning point in the history of the human mind actually was. In shifting from a reality-centered theory of emotional life—his so-called *seduction theory*—to a fantasy-centered theory with the Oedipal constellation as its centerpiece, Freud marked a change in direction that has shaped the thinking of psychoanalysts and humankind about emotional life and the emotion-processing mind to this very day. With that realization in mind, I decided to retell the story of Freud's creation of psychoanalysis in my own way. It was only during the writing that I came to see that I was basing my efforts on Freud's first theory or paradigm of psychoanalysis and not, as was the case with other writers and present-day psychoanalysts, on his second line of thought. This meant that I was mapping new territory—a realm that Freud had more or less abandoned—and I was eager to see what the terrain looked like.

Three basic goals emerged in the course of writing this book:

First, I needed to show that Freud's shift from reality to fantasy constituted a basic change in the philosophy and psychology of the human mind—that it was in fact a major paradigm shift. For several reasons, this was no easy task. There are overlaps between his two theories and each has tended to borrow from the other; in addition, Freud and his followers never entirely gave up his seduction hypothesis (Good, 2006). It was shadowy situation, but my deep unconscious mind was equal to the challenge and it showed me a surprising way to make my point. In a manner that is typical of the emotion-processing mind, what my conscious mind had missed, my deep unconscious mind saw as clear as a bell.

That done, my second task was to show that compared to his second theory, which is in use to this day, Freud's first theory is far more biologically sound, cogent, predictive, powerfully configured, relevant to the essentials of human psychology and the human condition, unconsciously validatable and thus more reliable, and more complete and relatively unmarred by the hidden errors common to conscious-system forms of psychology. In the context of a qualitative science, presenting this point in a fair and incisive manner also was fraught with difficulty. After all, it is well known that the second paradigm has many valid features: It has sponsored an enormous amount of meaningful research and has generated many insights into the human mind and its development that have all the earmarks of clear, useful thinking. On top of that, variations on Freud's inner-need theory of the mind are accepted today as gospel by all but a handful of mental health professionals and lay people the world over (Good, 2006). And as if that wasn't enough to overcome, I had discovered that Freud's second theory of the mind operates archetypically as a walled-off, closed system that is strongly fortified against all challenges.

I pondered this problem for a while, waiting for an inspiration. And once more, my deep unconscious wisdom system came to my rescue. It showed me a way to carry out this unwelcome but vital task. But as I did so, the insights that came to me were of the kind that would make this book far more controversial than I had planned. I found it necessary to develop the most severe critique of Freudian psychoanalysis I have written and had little joy in doing so. Still, I was not about to suppress what I saw and understood—being popular but wrong-headed is not my forte.

My last task was to see if I could discover, and trace the effects of, one or more early-life traumas that had unconsciously motivated Freud to turn away from the empowered world of reality to the lesser world of fantasy and inner needs. I had already learned that there was very little to go on and a great deal of uncertainty when it came to known family traumas. The death of his brother Julius when Freud was nearly two years of age was the only widely known traumatic event that Freud wrote about directly and with some frequency. Nevertheless, I was quite certain that this consciously remembered trauma could not fully account for Freud's errant flight from reality. This meant that I needed to take on the mantle of a psychoanalytic detective and try my best to track down Freud's family secrets. I had come across a small body of literature (Anzieu 1959; Schur 1972; Balmary 1979; Sulloway 1979; Krull 1986; Vitz 1988; Rizzuto 1998; Good 2006) crafted by writers who had tried to wring out these secrets from unnoticed clues in the Freud family archives and in the encoded messages embedded in Freud's writings—mostly the latter. My task was to evaluate these writings and their conjectures, and to add to them extensively by using the process of trigger decoding that I had developed in forging the adaptive approach which bore many markers of Freud's first paradigm.

Here for once my conscious mind came to my aid. I had the distinct advantage over others of having developed a validatable method of decoding dreams and other forms of narrative like the Oedipal myth which enabled me to detect encoded clues to Freud's early-life traumas that are embedded in Freud's massive writings, clues that others had missed. Even so, this was another chancy situation. Throughout his life, Freud seems to have been caught up unconsciously in the inevitable struggle between the encoded revelation of his personal secrets and outright concealment. Like all humans—and here I speak of another archetype (Langs, 2004, 2006)—his communicative resistances most often won the battle. And seeing that it was Freud who was resisting, these efforts to make matters obscure were ingeniously crafted.

Picture a forest with miles and miles of trees—Freud reported one thousand dreams and I'd estimate at the very least another one thousand or more anecdotes, case histories, parapraxes, jokes, and the like. Now picture Freud in a trance state going randomly to about a dozen of these trees, boring a small hole in each of their trunks, inserting an encoded clue to his early-life traumas, and resealing the holes so the bark will soon grow over them. Now go find those trees, get hold of those missiles, and decode each of them.

This would in fact have been an impossible task were it not for my having discovered a few tricks of my own—ways to identify these trees and with the help of Freud himself, knowing how to properly decode the camouflaged messages they hold close to their bosoms. I found as many of these missiles as I could and proceeded to decode them, only to discover that a single, largely unrecognized but likely trauma dominated the revealed picture. That postulated trauma became the main contribution to the final section of this book.

I had prepared a *pro forma* outline for this book and had expected to expand it into my first book specifically devoted to Sigmund Freud's personal life and his psychoanalytic thinking as it was unconsciously affected—and to a large extent, derailed—by the tragedies of his personal life. Little did I know that even though I have published forty-six psychoanalytic books, writing this book would be a voyage of unforeseen discoveries along unforeseen lines of insight. I have done all I can to pass this gift of revelation on to you, my persistent reader. For both our sakes, I hope I have succeeded!

# Chapter 1

# Is Freud to be Trusted?

"I no longer believe in my *neurotica.*" So wrote Sigmund Freud to his friend and colleague, Wilhelm Fliess, on September 21, 1897 (Freud, 1954, letter 69, p. 215). Freud had lost his bearings; his pathway into the human psyche had taken him to a dead end.

A little more than three weeks later, in another letter to Fliess, Freud wrote:

My self-analysis is the most important thing I have in hand.... Only one idea of general value has occurred to me. I have found love of the mother and jealousy of the father in my own case too, and now believe it to be a general phenomenon of early childhood..... If that is the case, the gripping power of Oedipus Rex, in spite of all the rational objections to the inexorable fate that the story presupposes, becomes intelligible.

—(Freud, 1954, letter 71, October 15, 1897, pp. 221, 223)

Freud had found another path, a way forward that he soon called *psycho-analysis,* and he would follow its twists and turns for the rest of his life.

For better or worse, these seemingly simple pronouncements have had a profound ripple effect. Their ramifications have affected mental health professionals the world over; have determined how people in general view the human mind; have deeply influenced each of our individual lives; and have in their own way generated a turning point in the history of the world.

How was it that so much was at stake?

In the first letter cited above, Freud tells Fliess that he has changed his mind about a clinical finding that until then he had believed to have been a great discovery, namely that adult neuroses like the hysteria he observed in his women patients were caused by their having been seduced as young

1

children by their fathers. Filled with regret that he no longer understood the key source of emotional ills and that he had lost his chance for fame and fortune, Freud sent years of clinical study down the drain because he no longer believed the tales his patients told him.

In the above noted second letter, Freud informs Fliess that he believes that he's back on track. He has come to realize that reality is a minor player in the drama of neuroses; that the starring role belongs to fantasies and wishes, especially forbidden incestuous wishes. Look not to others but to yourself for the roots of your cursed neurosis—that was his new mantra.

There is no underestimating the importance of Freud's change of heart. He had made what is called *a paradigm shift*—a change in his basic view of what most affects the human mind emotionally and unconsciously, and how the mind operates. Paradigm shifts are often summed up in a few key words: For example, the statement that the sun rather than the earth is at the center of our universe. In principle, it is a matter of choosing from two competing core ideas or formulations. The view of the universe—mental, physical, or both—that emanates from a newly chosen basic proposition is very different in significant ways from its predecessor.

Many analysts would not accept these distinctions when it comes to psychoanalysis (Good, 2006). They would claim that Freud's pronouncement was more a shift in emphasis than a matter of choice—in this case between reality and fantasy—more like the nature-nurture controversy where both sides have valid points to make. Nevertheless, I intend to show that Freud's decision was in fact basically exclusionary, that as humans we are either affected *first and foremost* by the challenges presented to us by others and by changes physical world or in contrast, by our inner needs, errant or healthy, of which there are many. This means that we would, then, be in a different place and in possession of a different world view when it comes to the human mind if Freud had stayed with and broadened his first idea—that early life traumas are the main source of psychological suffering—than we are today based on the fantasy-centered theory which he favored and elaborated on. Indeed, as chaos theorists have shown, initial conditions—that is, first propositions—determine the fate and later history of a system, be it physical or psychological in nature.

The few analysts who, like myself, are convinced that in the matter of reality versus fantasy Freud made the wrong choice have an all but impossible task in trying to convince other analysts and the world at large that this is the case (Balmary, 1979). This problem arises not only because the Freudian position is so entrenched and has become part of our psychological folklore, but also, as I shall show, because it is biologically natural to think and see the world the way Freud eventually presented it (Langs, 2006, 2008). Trying to change a biologically driven, prejudiced viewpoint is a Herculean task.

Freud experienced a rush of insights on the heels of his proposition regarding the critical importance of the Oedipus complex. He expanded his thinking about the unconscious mind, filled out his grasp of the complex structure of dreams and their relationship to neuroses, created the first psychodynamic model of the mind (Freud, 1900); discovered and elaborated on the subject of infantile sexuality and articulated his libido theory (Freud, 1905c); and identified a series of basic clinical concepts like transference, repression, and resistance (Freud, 1899, 1912a, 1912b, 1913a, 1914a, 1914c, 1925, 1937a, 1940) on which his psychoanalytic technique was fashioned. In his wake, his followers and descendants have added countless other insights into the human mind and its development—far too many to be recounted here (Pine, 2003; Good, 2006; Rangell, 2006; Rosenbaum, 2009).

In this context, however, I must insert a note of caution. Useful findings are not evidence for the validity of a basic position. The erroneous view that the earth is the center of our universe was the basis for many valid astronomical insights and a great deal was known about the circulation of blood in the human body—some of it on the mark, much of it quite wrong—before Harvey developed the correct cardiac-centered theory of circulation. In principle, whenever a paradigm correction has been undertaken, knowledge of the field to which it pertains advances in countless directions that were not possible as long as essential, unrecognized misconceptions dominated the scene. So will it be, I believe, with Freudian-based psychoanalysis.

## SOME EARLY WARNING SIGNS

In the years of change, 1896 and 1897, Freud operated in the shadow of the death of his father, Jakob, which took place after an extended illness on October 23, 1896. Less than two months after his father's death, in a letter to Fliess (Freud, 1954, letter 52, December 6, 1896, pp. 173–181), Freud indicated that he was convinced that hysteria was caused by seductions by the father. Yet nearly a year later, as he approached the first anniversary of his father's death and purchased a headstone for the unveiling, in the letter that followed Freud's abandonment of his *neurotica,* he tells Fliess that through his self-analysis he has found that in his own case, his father played no active role (Freud, 1954, letter 70, October 3, 1897, pp. 218–220). He now claims that the originator of his neurosis was his earliest caretaker, an ugly, elderly but clever woman who engaged in seductive ministrations with him. In addition, he suggests that both seeing his mother nude on a train trip they took together when he was between two and two-and-a-half years old and the death of his brother Julius when Freud was eighteen months old played a role in his emotional problems. In this way, despite his statement that the death of a father is the most important event in a man's life (Freud, 1900, preface to the second edition, p. xxvi), he was exonerating his father in respect to any influence he had had on his neurosis.

The fact that Freud's rejection of the reality of early-life seductions was based in large part on the initiation of his self-analysis indicates that his new position had a strong personal aspect to it. Nevertheless, even as he was claiming success for his own analysis, Freud was expressing dissatisfaction with the results he was getting in analyzing his patients. This comment gives pause for thought as to the effectiveness and validity of his efforts at achieving personal insights. In addition, as I shall discuss in chapter 4, recent clinical studies from the vantage-point of the adaptive approach on which this book is based indicate that the approach to self-analysis used by Freud was doomed to lead to results that served his needs for defense and denial far more than true insight.

## THE FOUR REASONS

Freud offered four reasons for abandoning his seduction theory. None of them involved definitive clinical observations which spoke against his trauma-based theory (Balmary, 1979). In addition, Freud had previously repudiated two of these rationales in a series of papers written in 1896 (Freud, 1896a, 1896b, 1896c; Sulloway, 1979). They involved his arguments that fathers were implicated in neuroses far too often than seemed reasonable and that it was impossible to distinguish truth from unconscious fiction. The other two reasons he presented—that he wasn't getting the cures he had expected to get and that conscious resistances can't be overcome—also are highly suspect.

The absence of relevant clinical data and the weakness of his rationalizations for changing his opinion as to the veracity of the stories of harm that his patients told him suggest that there were significant hidden unconscious reasons for Freud's change of heart. Initial indications are that they had something to do with his relationship with his father and his father's death—a subject I shall explore in detail in the final two chapters of the book.

Many questions also arise in respect to the Oedipal-based solution to neuroses that Freud proposed. Why the Oedipus myth? There are dozens of other Greek myths brimming with issues that are fundamental to life on earth. What makes the Oedipus myth the most telling story of them all? And why Greek mythology and not the Bible? The Bible is replete with tales that deal with the basic challenges of life and death. And even if Freud was right and the Oedipal story and its allusions to incest and murder are fundamental to human psychology, why is it not a prominent theme in the Five Books of Moses, instead of being a part of the minor story of Lot and his daughters, with an occasional smattering in the later stories of the Kings and prophets? Indeed, the prohibition against incest is not even one of the ten commandments.

More questions come up when we turn to the contents of the Oedipal saga itself (Taylor, 1986). Freud insisted that the core wish and central conflict in the myth is the child's incestuous desire to sleep with his mother and do away with his rival, his father. But a look at the story shows that the exciting incident of the story arises when Oedipus is told that his supposed parents, the King and Queen of Corinth, are not his biological parents. Thus, information regarding his identity sets the story in motion; the search for one's biological parents has nothing to do with the incest issue. In addition, there are eight acts of violence in the story and only one act of incest, so why stress sex when the story itself emphasizes death and violence? Did Freud misread and misrepresent the basic message of the tale?

There are, then, enough manifest uncertainties surrounding Freud's shift in thinking to suspect that he had a strong unconscious need, much of it connected with the life and death of his father, to prompt him to needlessly flee reality and escape into the world of imagination and fantasies. To these indicators of unconscious influence, I would add five other considerations which cast doubts on the validity of Freud's change in position; each will be explored as the book unfolds:

First, there is a hidden premise basic to Freud's thinking to the effect that fantasy exerts more power over our lives than reality. At face value, this is a most dubious assumption.

Second, in the course of my many years as a psychoanalyst and psychotherapist working with patients suffering from all manner of emotional problems, I have never found Oedipal conflicts to play a significant unconscious role in their difficulties. Thus, even though I was trained as a classical Freudian psychoanalyst, I have not been able to clinically validate Freud's claim for the primacy of Oedipal issues in emotional life.

Third, in the course of developing an alternate theory of the mind, I was able to come up with an *unconsciously mediated* method by which the interventions of therapists and analysts can be shown to be valid or invalid. This method is based on the discovery that the emotion-processing mind possesses a deep unconscious wisdom system that is capable of evaluating the accuracy and healing powers of every major intervention made by a therapist. The system's evaluations are conveyed through encoded narratives like dreams and stories that arise in response to an intervention. When the analyst is on the mark, the system comes up with disguised stories of people who are wise, insightful, and helpful—imagery that is generated spontaneously in a manner that is beyond conscious control. In contrast, whenever a therapist is off the mark and has intervened incorrectly, the stories are about people who are blind, ignorant, unhelpful, and unwise (Langs, 2004, 2006).

On the basis of this standard, the types of interventions used by Freud and later-day Freudians do not tend to obtain validation. I know about this kind of refutation personally because I was trained to use these kinds of interpretations when I first began to work as a psychoanalyst and found that once I had discovered this form of unconscious confirmation, my patients consistently refuted my Freudian-based efforts at intervening. This was a major reason that I began to seek a revised and more accurate understanding of their clinical material; I needed to find a psychoanalytic theory that enabled me to intervene in more effective, validated ways.

All in all then, based on personal clinical experience as well as observations of the work of supervisees and the case material found in the psychoanalytic literature, I have been unable to validate interventions based on the various approaches to psychoanalysis that are based on Freud's shift from reality to fantasy. I have instead found strong clinical reasons to question his change in position and have experienced a repetitive, encoded call to return to his reality-based theory because it alone, suitably modified and updated, has enabled me to generate unconsciously validated interventions.

This takes me to the fourth cause for doubt, namely that there is an enormous amount of support, manifest and encoded, for the theory that seduction, expanded to include all manner of traumatic events, is the prime mover of emotional life.

Fifth and last, most importantly, Freud himself has produced a huge number of encoded narratives that speak against the validity of his change in position and in addition, tell us about the likely unconscious reasons he did so. This means that even though Freud consciously elaborated and defended the validity of his shift in focus to human fantasy life, he unconsciously told us that this shift was an error driven by the traumas of his early life.

## SUMMING UP

Summing up, in the fall of 1897 Freud changed his basic view of the human mind as a reality-centered entity to one that is fantasy-centered. In so doing he laid the foundation for the future study of the psychodynamics of emotional life. He made what is called a *paradigm shift,* a change in the foundational position of dynamic psychology. It was a shift in belief on a par with the shift from an earth-centered to heliocentric view of our universe. And it has had a profound effect on each and every one of us, individually and collectively.

It is well to appreciate, however, that paradigms and paradigm shifts are created and accepted by human minds. This means that their features are shaped by both observation and mental inclinations. They therefore are affected by *archetypes,* universal tendencies to think and behave in particular ways—archetypes that are especially influential in shaping and sustaining qualitative theories like psychoanalysis. Although Freud viewed the Oedipus complex as an archetype, he did not by and large think about human psychology in these terms, nor did he study his revised way of thinking about the human mind as a newly formed paradigm. Had he done so, he might have garnered some unexpected insights into what he had done—and why he had done it. With this in mind, let's look now at the psychology behind paradigms, paradigm shifts, and archetypes.

*Chapter 2*

# Paradigms and Archetypes

In addition to the vagaries of his clinical data, two fundamental psychological forces of nature played a significant role in Freud's revision of his overarching view of the sources of neuroses: The need to create paradigms in order to organize our thinking about basic aspects of animate and inanimate nature and the influence on these creations of evolved or in-built psychological archetypes or universal natural inclinations. An exploration of each of these entities sheds considerable light on the choices Freud made and their underlying causes.

## PARADIGMS

A *paradigm* is a basic framework that defines a scientific discipline within which theories, laws, and generalizations are formulated and supportive experiments are performed. Broadly speaking, then, a paradigm is a philosophical or theoretical framework of any kind and thus, although subject to debate in some quarters (Kuhn, 1962), the term can applied to the basic framework of psychoanalytic theory and thinking.

Several features of paradigms deserve our attention. One is that they dictate and direct, and thereby restrict, the kind of thinking and research that transpires in the fields to which they apply. Another is that they tend to resist being overturned: the broad range of scientists who accept and defend a given paradigm are disinclined to accept or seek viable alternatives even when there is data that strongly suggests that there are basic flaws in their current position. This is an especially daunting problem in qualitative sciences like psychoanalysis because it is virtually impossible to come up with a definitive measurement failure that demands a reconsideration of existing propositions.

*Paradigm shifts* are, then, cataclysmic, revolutionary changes in basic beliefs and theories. They change the direction of thinking about the world at large and in respect to the individual subject involved, and they redirect research and conceptualizing. These shifts in fundamental viewpoints usually take place through the efforts of a single scientist or thinker, and a general acceptance of the new way of thinking usually is slow to take hold. Max Planck, who was one of the engineers of the paradigm shift from the deterministic physics of Newton, with its view of matter as continuous, to quantum physics with its indeterminism, notion of quanta, and thus, the discontinuity of matter, pointed out that the old guard had to die off before the new physics took hold. As we shall see, in addition to its lack of quantitative data and testable predictions, there are a number of factors in both the psychological foundation and social structure of the psychoanalytic movement that make a transition to a new theory and world view especially difficult to achieve even in the face of mounting impressionistic evidence that a change in basic perspectives is in order.

Overall, then, there is an evident archetypal human need driven by powerful unconscious forces to cling to established viewpoints and especially to first paradigms—for example, that the earth is the center of the universe, deterministic Newtonian physics, and the like. Strikingly, this observation means that in shifting from a trauma-centered to mind-centered psychological theory, Freud was defying the need-for-constancy archetype. On the other hand, given that Freud's second paradigm was the first elaborated basic theory of psychoanalysis, after his first defiant venture, both he and his followers conformed to the change-resistant archetypal pattern—he became, and his heirs are, extremely change-resistant. As we shall see, Freud's second paradigm shares features with natural first paradigms that makes this conformity quite understandable.

## ARCHETYPES

An archetype is an eternal, ever-lasting ideal form (Plato), a universal human trait or relatively fixed behavioral or psychological tendency. The concept was championed by Carl Jung (1968, 1972) who discovered the existence of archetypes in his patients as well as in mythical tales. Jung tended to use the term to describe the shared features of the human psyche and personality types. He wrote of five basic archetypes that make up the human personality: The self, shadow, anima, animus, and persona. And he also described behavioral archetypes such as the child, hero, great mother, wise old man, and trickster or fox. Archetypes for Jung were, then, innate universal human prototypes which he linked to his idea that part of the psyche takes form as an inherited collective unconscious component (Jung, 1972).

More recently, studies undertaken from the adaptive approach, which is grounded in a theory that is akin to Freud's original trauma-based conceptualization of neuroses, have extended the concept of archetypes to allude to universal and thus genetically acquired, specific patterns of thinking, behaving, and coping (Langs, 1996, 2006). Most of these newly identified archetypes operate outside of awareness—*unconsciously*—so their existence and influence are not palpable consciously. In general, they are revealed through seemingly inexplicable behaviors and the encoded, double-meaning, narrative unconscious messages emitted by the deep unconscious part of the mind.

Many of these archetypes involve the means by which humans tend to cope with death and the three forms of death anxiety it evokes—predatory, predator, and existential (see chapter 4). They are unconsciously driven patterns of behavior and thinking which greatly effect how we deal with the most basic challenges in life. They tend to be activated in response to death-related traumas and their presence and ramifications can be found in early writings like the Bible and Greek mythology as well as in patients seen today in psychoanalysis and psychotherapy—they are timeless universal responses to traumatic events (Langs, 2008).

Indications are that these archetypes are a prime factor in the development of paradigms and paradigm shifts. Because death-related traumas are all but inevitable in a given lifetime, it is highly likely that Freud suffered from such incidents and that they affected the development of his two theories of the mind and his decision to settle on the fantasy-based paradigm. Given that his paradigm shift was based on belief rather than clinical data, we should expect that a combination of hidden personal factors and unconsciously driven archetypes played a significant role in his change of viewpoint. It therefore behooves us to turn now to a study of the human archetypes that tend to influence the development of both physical and biological paradigms of nature. As we shall see, there are some striking consistencies in this regard and they will help us to better understand Freud's fateful selection of a settled paradigm for psychoanalysis.

## THREE BLOWS TO HUMAN NARCISSISM

Not surprisingly, the psychological approach to investigating the creation and modification of paradigms is strongly affected by the psychoanalytic paradigm to which a researcher is committed. On the one hand, adherents to Freud's second, inner-directed paradigm will look to needs for incestuous Oedipal triumphs, nurturance, narcissistic supplies, relatedness, and the like for the deeper sources of a preferred paradigm. But on the other hand, adherents to

Freud's first, reality-centered paradigm—suitably expanded and updated—will look to efforts to cope with personal life traumas and their death-related meanings as the driving forces behind such decisions. In this context, in settling on a final paradigm for psychoanalysis, it can be said that unconsciously Freud was choosing between sex and death—and he chose sex.

Freud had little to say directly about paradigms and paradigm shifts. He did however contribute to our understanding of these phenomena when, in 1917, he turned to the history of psychoanalysis and wrote about the traumatic effects of certain paradigms and their influence on human narcissism. His comments were part of an attempt to offer an historical perspective on the rejection in some quarters of psychoanalytic thinking. In so doing, he brought up three of the most important paradigm shifts in the history of science—those engineered by Copernicus, Darwin, and himself:

> In the course of centuries the *naïve* self-love of men has had to submit to two major blows at the hands of science. The first was when they learnt that our earth was not the center of the universe but only a tiny fragment of a cosmic system of scarcely imaginable vastness. This is associated in our minds with the name of Copernicus, though something similar had already been asserted by Alexandrian science. The second blow fell when biological research destroyed man's supposedly privileged place in creation and proved his descent from the animal kingdom and his ineradicable animal nature. This reevaluation has been accomplished in our own days by Darwin, Wallace and their predecessors, though not without the most violent contemporary opposition. But human megalomania will have suffered its third and most wounding blow from the psychological research of the present time which seeks to prove to the ego that it is not even master in its own house, but must content itself with scanty information of what is going on unconsciously in its mind. (Freud, 1917, pp. 284–285)

Freud was quite on the mark in claiming that he had introduced a monumentally important paradigm pertaining to our view of the human mind. Historically, he can be thought of as having made three unprecedented ventures into defining the basic features of the human psyche and its psychology. The first paradigm he forged was a shift from a dynamic psychology centered on the contents of the conscious mind to one that gave primacy to the contents of the unconscious mind. This psychology, which Freud eventually named *psychoanalysis* when he announced his need-centered theory, had many precedents, as the crystallization of a paradigm often does. Previous writers had not, however, synthesized their findings and ideas into a paradigmatic world view (Ellenberger, 1970).

Freud struggled throughout the 1890s to develop his understanding of the unconscious mind into a paradigmatic position and he did so in limited fashion when he established his seduction theory of neurosogenesis. But it was only after he had settled on his fantasy-centered theory of neuroses and the human mind that he lighted on what was to become his basic paradigm of psychoanalysis. On that basis, he was able to undertake an extensive investigation of the operations of the unconscious mind as it dealt with forbidden sexual and other potentially disruptive inner needs, among them narcissistic needs connected with the maintenance of a sound level of self-worth and self-esteem. The effects of this research and the use of the paradigm on which it was based can be seen in Freud's view of the effects of the three paradigm shifts to which he alluded in 1917. His understanding was based on the theory that satisfying healthy inner needs are paramount in emotional life and that damage to the paths to their satisfaction can cause emotional harm and suffering. There is evident validity to this insight, but it appears to be superficial and insufficient so let's dig deeper.

## THE FOURTH BLOW

Had he stayed with his initial reality-centered paradigm, Freud would have delivered one more psychoanalytically founded blow to humankind. The third blow would still have been based on the realization that the conscious mind is not master in its own house—that this dominance falls to the unconscious mind. But he then would have added a fourth and crushing additional blow to humankind's hubris, namely, that many of the most critical determinants of the course of our lives life are entirely beyond our control—that from the moment of conception, our lives are driven by coincidental natural events and other individuals who happen to cross our paths. Focusing first and foremost on the ramifications of traumatic incidents would have led Freud to eventually realize that accidents of fate play an overriding role in our lives. He would have seen that such matters as where, when, and to whom a person is born, natural disturbances and disasters, the actions of others, social and economic conditions, and the like almost always matter more than the choices we make on our own.

This realization is clearly manifested in Freud's own choice of the archetypal narrative he believed to best characterize the basic challenges of human emotional life—the myth of Oedipus (Taylor, 1986; Freud, 1900, 1917, 1924, 1954, letter 71, October 15, 1897, p. 221; see also Freud, 1910a and chapter 8). Well before his conception, Oedipus is fated by the gods to murder his father and sleep with his mother—he has no choice but to do so. Indeed, there are no indications that Oedipus is being driven by a conscious or unconscious wish to sleep with his mother and murder his rivalrous father. Instead, the path taken by his tragic story is entered because of doubts cast by a friend as to who his biological parents were, that is, the identity of the couple who determined his lifeline both before and soon after he was born. Furthermore, as Oedipus moves into adulthood, he is far more reactive than proactive, responding to an assault by a party led by a king who, unknown to Oedipus, turns out to be his father; meeting the challenge to his life posed by the Sphinx; and accepting the reward for this victory set by Jocasta's brother, Creon, which is to marry the Queen of Thebes, whom he later discovers to be his mother. The revelation of this hidden truth then causes her to commit suicide which prompts Oedipus to blind himself—grim incidents whose causes were well beyond his control.

Even though there are moments when Oedipus draws on his own strength and wisdom to take his future into his own hands, the myth bears witness to how seldom this is the overriding factor in a human life and how often a person lacks the information and power to determine his or her own fate. Indeed, the only inner need that drives the Oedipal story is the drive to discover the truth about his origins—and this is necessary because of the fate assigned to him before he was born and the death-related trauma—an attempt to murder him—that he suffered at the hands of his father soon after his birth.

Our relative helplessness in the face of external forces haunts us from the cradle to the inevitability of the grave. This latter blow, which is an assault on the human hope for immortality, is without question the most daunting of them all. And it is the blow that Freud avoided dealing with by shifting paradigms. Despite acknowledging the hidden power of unconscious thoughts and wishes, his second paradigm fails to deal in any substantial manner with the universal trauma of the inevitability of personal death. In its place, the paradigm takes on a hopeful tone by promising to provide us with the means by which we can access our conflicted inner needs and successfully ameliorate their detrimental effects on our lives. In contrast, there is very little that we can do to change most of the truly fateful external events that impact on us and so greatly determine the path taken by our lives to their very end.

We are, then, victims of fate, nature, and the evolved design of the human mind. While we are not entirely helpless against reality's inputs into our lives—for example, we can improve our chances of personal survival, lessen the frequency of natural disasters, use valid forms of psychotherapy to lessen the effects of our early life traumas and our guilt-ridden needs for self-harm, and engage in similar kinds of activities that enable us to wrest a small measure of control over our destinies. But the inevitability of personal demise casts a dark shadow over these momentary triumphs for in the end, nature and not our personal wishes holds sway.

This grim picture of the realities of life on earth presents one reason why the trauma theory of neuroses and emotional life is difficult to embrace and remain committed to. There is an enormous amount of human helplessness realistically reflected in the theory and on the whole the best we can do is lessen the impact of this helplessness on our lives and come to terms with the unbearable truths of our personal and collective limitations and of life itself. The fantasy- and need-based second paradigm essentially ignores these daunting truths and does not attempt to address them in any substantial manner. This avoidance and denial, and the failure to deal with these inevitable issues, may bring a measure of temporary relief, but it has caused much suffering and grief as well.

Paradoxically, then, adherence to Freud's second paradigm has served to deny the stark limitations that accrue to our controlling our fates, but it also has, by by-passing these very limitations, added to the helplessness bathed in denial and ignorance we suffer in the face of trauma. But we can see why Freud turned away from reality when he was on the brink of creating the field he was to call psychoanalysis—and why so many have followed him down the path he chose and why so few have questioned his second paradigm or appreciated his first. Indeed, there is a parallel between the human need to think of the earth as the center of the physical universe and the need to think of our own inner needs as the center of our emotional universe: Both beliefs are erroneous and both serve human narcissism but even more so, each in its own way, serves the human need to deny death.

We begin to suspect—and shall soon see—that turning away from reality and dwelling on inner mental needs is a reflection of a basic, death-denying human archetype, one that unconsciously influenced Freud's paradigm shift. But as noted earlier, this also means that Freud went against archetype in formulating his first paradigm of neuroses—only to conform to archetype in fashioning his second theory of the mind. Let's delve further into this subject of paradigms and the psychological archetypes that affect their formulation and adoption in order to understand why Freud carried out this remarkable, far reaching flip flop.

## PARADIGM SHIFTS AND EXISTENTIAL DEATH ANXIETY

Observers and theoreticians using Freud's second paradigm have had little to say about the underlying psychological factors and archetypes that affect the creation and modification of paradigms. On the other hand, those working with a modified version of Freud's first paradigm, which stresses the critical role of death and death anxiety in the psychology of human endeavors, have developed a set of viable ideas about the nature of the unconscious sources of paradigmatic thinking. I begin my study of this phenomenon with the two paradigm shifts Freud alluded to in his story of the narcissistic blows to humankind.

## The Center of the Universe

The first paradigm shift mentioned by Freud is the Copernican revolution which dealt with the position of the earth, and thus our personal position, in the universe. It entailed a radical departure from the original Ptolemaic view that the earth was the center of the universe, and it afforded this honor to the sun.

As is characteristic of the history of paradigms, the erroneous Ptolemaic position had prevailed for some 1400 years before it was rescinded. Furthermore, the general acceptance of the revised paradigm needed about another 100 years to effect—much of it through the observations and advocacy of Galileo (Sobel, 2000) and Kepler (Gilder and Gilder, 2004). This time lag arose largely because the new paradigm was fiercely opposed by the Catholic church: Orthodoxy defending a flawed and erroneous basic position also is archetypal for initial paradigms of nature, and this natural tendency frequently plays a major role in the opposition met by those who offer well documented reasons for making a paradigm shift.

Freud (1917) did not comment on this paradigm shift; he simply viewed the new paradigm through the lens of his fantasy-centered theory. As noted, he suggested that the new paradigm entailed a loss of importance for the earth and thus was a narcissistic blow to humankind—our need for the narcissistic gratifications and support that enhance our self-esteem and self-worth were dealt a serious blow. We became far less important than we thought we were in light of the prior Ptolemaic view of the universe. This is a prime example of how a paradigm pertaining to natural phenomena affects our view of ourselves and our place in the world at large—much of human psychology is determined by our view of our place in the universe and in nature.

## Galileo's Astounding Insight

Writing in the 1600s, Galileo also commented on the psychological impact of the Copernican revision and, most remarkably, on the underlying psychology behind the adherence to the first, Ptolemaic view which was prevalent at the time (Sobel, 2000). As a reflection of his genius, he intuitively chose a perspective that was comparable to Freud's first, trauma-centered paradigm of psychoanalysis in order to explain the basic unconscious source of the earth-centered position and the broad opposition to the heliocentric view.

The back story is this: For centuries, astronomers, the Catholic church, and people in general believed, as first argued by both Aristotle and Ptolemy, that the earth was the center of the universe. Inherent to this contention was the further belief that while the earth moves and is changeable, the planets are fixed and immutable—that they are embedded in unchangeable, invisible, material spheres set at fixed distances from the earth. Their fixity was seen as a reflection of their ever-lasting qualities which provided humans with a symbol of eternal life and thus of God and their own immortality.

In the course of defending the Copernican viewpoint and criticizing the Aristotelean-Ptolemaic position, Galileo, speaking through his fictional character, Sagredo, commented:

> The deeper I go in considering the vanities of popular reasoning, the lighter and more foolish I find them.... Those who so greatly exalt incorruptibility, inalterability, etc. are reduced to talking this way, I believe, by their great desire to go on living, and by the terror they have of death. These individuals do not reflect that if men were immortal, they themselves would never have come into the world. Such men really deserve to encounter a Medusa's head which would transmute them into statues of jasper or of diamond, and thus make them more perfect than they are. (Sobel, 2000, pp. 148–149)

Galileo appears to have been one of the first advocates of Freud's first paradigm of psychoanalysis! In so doing, he seems to have probed more deeply than Freud into the nature of the anxieties that unconsciously lead to false beliefs, errant paradigms, and by implication, to human neuroses. In particular, he appreciated that the prospect and fear of death—that is, the recognition of human mortality—is far more critical in human life and its emotional dysfunctions than inner mental needs which play a secondary role to, and are affected by, the realities of personal death.

Inherent to Galileo's profound insight is the realization that the first paradigmatic belief system regarding the solar system was unconsciously fashioned to support the belief that humans live forever—the idea that the immortality of the universe makes human immortality an actuality and real prospect. The propositions developed by Aristotle and Ptolemy were unconsciously driven by the need to deny the inevitability of death and to alleviate the existential death anxiety that this prospect—this certainty—evokes in everyone. Their view of the structure of the universe was, then, unknowingly fashioned as a physically grounded, cosmic denial-of-death system.

Given that Freud's wish-centered, second paradigm of psychoanalysis precludes the realization that death and its attendant anxieties are the prime movers of human neuroses, the Aristotelean-Ptolemaic position can be seen to be akin to Freud's second theory of psychoanalysis: Both paradigms serve the unconscious denial of human mortality! In contrast, the Copernican-Galilean paradigm, which eventually replaced the Aristotelean-Ptolemaic denial-of-death system, is consonant with Freud's initial, trauma-centered theory of emotional life and the emotion-related mind. Both of these latter paradigms are without a means of supporting the denial of the finality of personal death, leaving us as humans with the utter necessity of finding other, constructive ways to deal with this most disturbing prospect.

Notice too that the two physical paradigms are incompatible: Either the earth or the sun is the center of the universe; both cannot be so placed. And either the heavens are as changeable as the earth and thus neither immutable nor ever-lasting or the heavens are fixed and eternal. In addition, as noted, while the first system affords indirect support for human immortality, the second system does not; no system can both support and not support this belief. As I shall show, these archetypal insights have a bearing on the nature of Freud's two theories of psychoanalysis which, although many analysts contend that they blend into each other, actually are far more competitive and mutually exclusive than complementary.

It is, then, not surprising that the Catholic church fiercely supported the Ptolemaic position. The church, was—and still is—a bastion of death-denying religious beliefs. It therefore punished those who, like Galileo and Kepler, cited evidence and made claims that challenged the church's denial-based position. Adherents to death-denying paradigms tend to be quite punitive towards those who challenge their position and as we shall see, this archetypal trend is evident in psychoanalysis to this very day.

## Kepler and Another Paradigmatic Battle

In addition to properly locating the center of the universe, there was another astronomical battle that pitted Johannes Kepler against the main body of scientists and the Catholic church during his lifetime. In this case, the conflict revolved around the nature of the paths taken by the planets as they move across the sky. The issue was this:

Kepler had made exquisite use of the careful measurements of sequential planetary positions carried out by Ticho Brahe and on that basis, he concluded that the planets did not move in circles as was the common belief, but in ellipses (Gilder and Gilder, 2004). The first paradigm here, which postulated circular motion, was another physical belief that shored up the human wish for eternal life because it supported the belief that God had created the universe in a perfect manner. Circular motion was an ideal that had been taken as proof that God existed and that humans could be immortal and attain eternal life in heaven. In contrast, elliptical motion was thought of as a non-ideal form of movement and its empirical discovery undermined the denial-of-death system created by the Catholic church—and other religions as well.

On both counts, then, the church supported first paradigms that spoke for human immortality and thus the denial of death, and it opposed second paradigms that failed to support the existence of God and thus, the belief in ever-lasting human existence. Humankind in general was in agreement with the thinking of the Catholic church on these matters. This appears then to be an archetypal response: A preference for paradigms that support the denial of death and the rejection of those paradigms that do not do so.

In this regard, as configured at present, psychoanalysis implicitly stands with the Catholic church: It is committed to Freud's second paradigm which inherently ignores and thus denies the critical role that human mortality and other forms of death anxiety play in human life. One of the clearest statements of this denial appears in *The Interpretation of Dreams* (Freud, 1900) where Freud alludes to the timelessness and inextinguishability of unconscious instinctual drive inner needs. This property applies to other human need systems as well and it gives an aura of immortality to the second paradigm as it speaks for psychobiological needs that last forever, so to speak.

In this connection, it is well to be reminded that the sequential position of Freud's second paradigm is an aberration in that the theory is aligned with what usually are first paradigms. Freud seems to have been on the verge of developing a major counter-archetypal trauma-centered paradigm when he fell into line with the paradigm-forming archetype by forging his second theory of the mind. Once set, adherents to this theory, from its founder down the line, have behaved in ways that are typical of those who support a death-denying paradigm. Indeed, a return to Freud's first paradigm would eliminate these denial mechanisms and lead to an inevitable confrontation with death and death anxieties, especially as they operate psychologically and on the level of unconscious experience.

The persecution and excommunication of those who opposed the church's death-denying viewpoint also has its parallel in the history of psychoanalysis. The most notable example of this trend is seen in the way that Freud and his followers condemned and excommunicated Ferenczi for trying to reinstate the first Freudian paradigm with a strong emphasis on the (death-related) violence done by seducers of young children to their victims (Masson, 1984; Good, 2006). Whereas other factors, such as the outright seductiveness of the techniques of psychoanalysis advocated by Ferenczi, played a role in this repudiation, his outspoken support for the trauma theory of neuroses appears to have been the main reason for the exclusionary treatment he received. Carl Abraham, an early follower of Freud, who also advocated aspects of the trauma theory, was quickly repudiated by Freud and just as quickly retreated from this position (Masson, 1984).

The adaptive approach is a clinically derived, trauma-centered theory without evident dubious features; it adheres entirely to basic psychoanalytic principles. Nevertheless, the approach also has met with a similar kind of unexamined, outright refutation (see chapter 3). It appears, then, that those who create death-denying paradigms are welcomed by their fellow scientists and the population at large, while those who discover valid reasons to rescind a flawed or erroneous death-denying paradigm find themselves rejected and persecuted on all sides—a response that tends to last for centuries until the truth of the death-related paradigm finally wins out. With a qualitative science like psychoanalysis that is focused on the unmeasured vagaries of human psychology this waiting period may be far longer than usual.

The basic human archetype that is involved in these scenarios involves the evolved default position of the conscious system of the emotion-processing mind (Langs, 1996, 2004, 2006). This system of the mind is naturally inclined to adopt mechanisms and beliefs that support the denial of death and thus inherently favors paradigms, be they of the material or mental world, that indirectly or explicitly supports this need. As I have already indicated, for a brief five years or so, Freud was an exception to this archetypal rule. But then, evidently goaded by fate, the death of his father, and unconscious memories of early death-related traumas, he succumbed to hidden, unconscious pressures the prompted him to fall in line with his archetypal needs and did so. Before discussing the likely reasons for his original theory and its abandonment, let's look at several more choices humans have made in creating natural paradigms to see if we are in fact dealing with an archetypal human propensity.

## God and the Origins of Species

Paradigms related to the origins and adaptive capacities of the species that populate the earth today and in past eras are closely tied to paradigms pertaining to religious beliefs and the question of the existence of a deity. As for religion, there has been a basic but partial paradigm shift from a first paradigm that fostered an all but unanimous belief in the existence of God to a second paradigm in which God is seen by many individuals as a non-existent, imaginary figure. Each of these paradigms—one religious, the other secular—sponsors a world view of creation. Believers are convinced that God created the universe and the species on our planet in one fell swoop, while non-believers are committed to the theory of evolution which Freud alluded to in his 1917 comments.

### The First Paradigm of Creation

For thousands of years prior to the intervention of Darwin and Wallace, most biologists and people in general, religious and otherwise, accepted the basic thesis that God had created the universe in seven days some ten thousand years ago and that he placed living beings on the earth in eternal forms that are immutable—that is, forms that have existed unchanged since creation and thus are ever-lasting. This is the creationist paradigm (Scott, 2005) and it is a biological counterpart to the belief in the immutability and fixity of the stars and planets in the physical universe. It is, then, another first paradigm inherently designed to support a death-denying aura of human immortality.

A more recent form of this type of thinking which supports the human belief in God and eternal life is the theory of intelligent design (Scott, 2005). This version of the first biological paradigm is based on the belief that humans and other living beings are so complex and made of such intricate organ systems that they cannot have arisen as the result of a gradual evolutionary process, but must have been set in place in one fell swoop by God Himself. All of the versions of this paradigm—some existed for ages before Darwin and Wallace argued otherwise, others are counter-reactions to their ideas and to the second paradigm of creation which they both advocated—serve unconsciously to alleviate humankind's existential death anxieties through the denial of death via the belief in the existence of God. This belief system is the age-old, death-denying default position of the human mind—a first paradigm that deals with questions pertaining to the purpose and nature of human existence and issues pertaining to the permanency or non-permanency of a human being.

Variations of this first religious paradigm existed unchallenged for centuries. The second paradigm, which is atheism, is a world view that eliminates the denial defense inherent to the belief in God and speaks for human mortality. While theism has existed since the origins of civilization, atheism as a common belief system and paradigm first took hold in the Western world in late eighteenth-century Europe. To this day, only a minority of humans are atheists, some are agnostics, and the overwhelming majority are theists. So here too the paradigm that supports the denial of death came first and remains the archetypal religious belief system for most of humankind. The religious paradigm is, of course, incompatible with atheism, so once more a choice must be made between these two positions.

There is, however, a contrast to be made between theories pertaining to the location of the center of the universe and those that deal with the existence of God. The former issue is subject to resolution through measurement, the generation of quantitative data, and prediction, while the latter is not. There is no quantitative measure that could resolve the question of the validity of the God proposition—belief or non-belief are matters of faith rather than measurement. Thus the arguments for and against the two competing paradigms—that is, between a world view that includes or does not include a death-denying belief in the existence of God—engender debates that go on interminably.

This too should serve as fair warning to psychoanalysts regarding their preferences for one or the other paradigm of the human mind because Freud based his paradigm shift on a matter of belief, that is, on his no longer having faith in the reality of the stories of seduction that were being told to him by his patients. In making this decision, he was unwittingly conforming to the archetype that is expressed through a preference for death-denying psychological paradigms over those that accept the realities of death and death-related traumas. Even though Freud and his followers have garnered clinical support for their position, we should make note again that the Ptolemaic paradigm enabled scientists, through certain mathematical manipulations, to correctly predict the movements of the planets. So given that the support for Freud's second paradigm is entirely impressionistic and correlational in nature, none of these findings constitute definitive proof of the validity of the inner-mental theory that Freud settled on for the foundation of psychoanalytic thinking.

## *The Second Paradigm of Creation*

Despite the enormous amount of supportive evidence garnered by the followers of Darwin and Wallace (Langs, 1996; Clodd, 2005)—the theory of evolution is the most successful theory in the history of biology and the foundation of many developments in its own and other sciences—half the population of the United States does not believe that the theory of evolution is a valid or viable paradigm. Most of these individuals believe in the first paradigm of nature, that is, that God created the species populating the earth today and that they are virtually identical to the species God created ten thousand years ago.

Scientifically, evolutionary theory, with its theses of natural selection (Darwin) and survival of the fittest (Wallace), is the most fundamental paradigm within the field of biology. Not only does the denial of death play no meaningful role in this paradigm of nature, death in the form of the extinction of species is a central concept—more than ninety percent of all past living species have become extinct over the ages. The threat of death is a central proposition of this paradigm and evolving the means of defeating death and surviving from one moment and generation to the next is its central challenge. The theory of evolution is then intensely death-centered, much as the Freud's first trauma-centered paradigm would have been had he pursued it. As we shall see, this thesis is borne out by the fact that the reality-focused, independently developed adaptive approach, which is akin to Freud's first paradigm, is an intensely death-centered theory in its own right.

Adherents to the second paradigm of biology postulate that there are two basic mechanisms through which the evolution of species takes place; both play a role when their survival is threatened. The first mechanism, which was the main focus of Darwin's thinking, involves competition for survival between neighboring species. This process began eons ago when our planet became over-populated and organisms had to compete for living space and nutriments (de Duve, 1995). This competition took shape as an arms race in which one species became the predator and another species its prey. By means of its existing natural abilities or by virtue of favorable mutations, the predator developed the ability to destroy its prey. But in response, largely through favorable mutations of its own, the prey tended to develop fresh defenses that rendered it capable of fending off the threatening predator, thereby enabling it to survive and reproduce.

In principle, this kind of arms race tends to escalate as one generation passes on to the next and in general, the predator is favored in one epoch and the prey in the next—unless the prey becomes extinct. This is clearly a life and death scenario with no guarantee of survival in which chance plays a prominent role and there is no palpable support for a belief in a God-given purposefulness to these struggles. It speaks loudly against eternal life for living species including the human observers of these fateful rivalries.

The second mechanism of evolutionary change, which was championed by Wallace, involves the emergence of adverse environmental changes that present threats to the survival of the living beings confronted with such unstable living conditions. In these situations, those species that have the natural resources to survive the new threat or who experience spontaneous mutations that enable them to do so, will live on; those of lesser capabilities to deal with the new dangers will die off. Here too matters of chance, as compared to a God-given purpose, are notable factors.

In both versions of this second biological paradigm, adaptation to external circumstances—be it to the threat from competitors, those bent on causing harm, or from natural disasters—is the basic function of all living beings including humans. Because humans are explicitly aware consciously of death, these threats to survival involve not only death itself but also various forms of anticipatory and reactive death anxiety. Added to the complexity of this situation is the fact that humans not only experience dangers consciously, but also do so unconsciously (see chapter 4).

Despite the overwhelming physical and predictive evidence for the evolutionary paradigm and considerable evidence to the contrary regarding the creationist paradigm, the battle between these two competing theories—actually the evolutionary position is a scientific theory, while the creationism position is a belief system lacking in scientific support—is some one hundred seventy years old. A handful of scientists have tried to unite the two paradigms by accepting the basic ideas of evolutionary theory and appending to them a belief in the existence of God. These efforts have not been convincing and the view that these two theories are mutually exclusive prevails. Here too we are reminded of the situation regarding the two paradigms of psychoanalysis: Some analysts have tried to combine the fantasy theory with the trauma theory, but they too have been unsuccessful because it can be shown that each of these paradigms leads to a distinctive set of principles and constellation of ideas that largely fall at opposite poles (see chapter 4).

The duration of the God/creationism versus evolution debate in the face of overwhelming indications as to the more valid position presents us with striking evidence that unmastered, largely unconscious death anxieties have enormous power to distort human common sense and rational reasoning. This situation also shows the extreme measures and beliefs that humans will resort to in trying to cope, however irrationally, with their evident mortality and the degree to which they seek and endorse almost any thesis that supports their need to deny death. Relevant here is a recent book entitled *50 Jewish Messiahs* (Rabow, 2003) which describes fifty individuals who, after the death of Jesus, claimed to have Messianic gifts and assignments, and who attracted intensely devoted followers who gave up their worldly goods and even their lives for these individuals despite the transparent folly of their claims. Each of these purported Messiahs promised their faithful eternal life and of course, none of them was able to fulfill their promises. Most of their stories are so patently absurd as to defy all sensibility. Were it not known adaptively that the prospect of death and the three forms of death anxiety it evokes drives humans insane, these most absurd scenarios would defy explanation. Here too we as psychoanalysts are advised to examine carefully any death denying paradigm Freud or anyone else has offered us—we are naturally inclined to believe in any false system that enables us, consciously and especially unconsciously, to defend against the inevitability of death.

We can see then that it is extremely difficult for humans to modify or give up any paradigm that supports their denial-based defenses, whatever their cost in loss of knowledge, misleading ideas, and maladaptive behaviors—and possibly the ultimate destruction of life on this planet. Catholicism and other religions speak for the broader human need to believe in an individual's immortality, a belief for which countless humans have given their lives in the patently false belief that doing so is proof of this contention. Indeed, the massive violence that believers in God have foisted on non-believers is an extreme example of the intolerance for opposition by those who adhere to a death-denying paradigm of nature (Langs, 2008). This too is an archetypal phenomenon that exists within psychoanalysis as well (see chapters 3 and 4). Once Freud had shifted to a death-denying paradigm of emotional life and the emotion-related mind, the resistance to returning to his trauma-centered paradigm in which the denial of death is no longer an explicit or implied feature has been as intense as that seen with the Catholic church and creationists.

Evolutionary theory, with its focus on adaptation to environmental conditions and to the threats posed by other living beings, is, as noted, the fundamental, overarching subtheory within all of biology. Freud's second paradigm takes exception to this theory and insists that adapting to dysfunctional inner needs rather than external, environmental threats are of paramount importance in human emotional life. Neither Freud nor anyone else has offered a justification for this position which runs counter to the most basic archetype pertaining to the very existence of living entities. Indeed, in this light, the second paradigm created by Freud and in vogue in some form to this very day seems to be quite wrongheaded and misleading. It suggests that here too the archetypal human need to deny death has overpowered human reasoning—a thesis for which we shall soon find ample support.

## Some Other Paradigm Shifts

The archetypal pattern is, then, for denial-based defenses against existential death anxiety to be the driving force for the first version of most scientific and religious paradigms in the animate and inanimate realms. In situations where the collection and working over of new data indicates that a first paradigm is significantly flawed—as often is the case—one requisite for the development of a new and more viable paradigm lies with the ability of practicing scientists to find the wherewithal to give up the denial-of-death defenses that are an inherent feature of the first paradigm—but not the second. This step, which is yet to be accomplished in religion or psychoanalysis, may take centuries to accomplish. By and large it takes the emergence of a revolutionary scientist-thinker and a set of overwhelming findings which contradict a flawed first paradigm, and decades of processing of these findings, to engineer this kind of called-for paradigmatic change. The absence of such data in psychoanalysis has made—and is making—this shift extremely difficult to achieve.

These archetypal patterns are seen again in several other first paradigms and paradigm shifts that Freud did not bring up. The paradigm shift that was involved in Newton's discovery of the laws of motion and gravity is one example (Gleick, 2004). Strikingly, the subtext here is very much like that which underlay the issue of the location of the center of the universe. The prevailing paradigm before Newton's revolutionary insights entailed the belief that the earth was a part of the solar system that stood apart from the stars and planets which are set above in the skies, and that the changeable laws that prevailed on earth are different from the eternal laws that prevailed in the immutable heavens. Newton's key insight was that to the contrary, identical laws operate in both the skies above and the land below. As such, his new, second paradigm, which unified the two domains—heaven and earth—was another blow to an existing paradigm, another change in world view that deprived humans of support for their need to deny the finality of death. Gone was a paradigm that supported this denial by implicitly sustaining the belief that while the laws pertaining to the inevitability of death prevail on earth, they do not apply to the heavens where the law of immortal life holds sway. As a result, here too death anxiety was lain bare and needed to be dealt with in some way other than through denial and obliteration.

Newtonian physics was strictly deterministic as was his theory of the nature of matter, so despite his unifying the heavens and earth, his theory offered a modicum of support for the human need for denial in that it implied the existence of a perfectly lawful and therefore God-given universe. But given that physics is a quantitative science, measurements arose that were not in keeping with the Newtonian position. The main phenomenon in question, called black-body radiation, could not be accounted for through equations based on Newtonian principles and in addition, certain features of gravity also did not fall into line with expectations.

Matters were set straight when Planck developed a viable set of explanatory equations that were based on the idea that matter was not continuous as proposed by Newton, but instead came in packets of energy and mass called quanta (Isaacson, 2007). This new paradigm of nature spoke against a simply ordered, God-given universe in which immortal life was possible. On its heels came Einstein's theory of relativity, which spoke against fixed spatial quadrants and ordered motion, and quantum physics in which the order of subatomic nature was no longer seen as rule-bound and regular, but as a matter of probabilities and chance. In each of these cases, the new paradigm entailed a loss of implicit support for the denial of death and in each case, the initial opposition was fierce. This state of affairs is captured by Planck's aforementioned statement that the physicists of the time never accepted quantum physics; they had to die off before the new paradigm took hold—this in the face of massive supportive quantitative findings.

For his part, after he made his contribution to the new physics, Einstein tried to repudiate its findings and its probabilistic world view. He insisted that God does not play dice with the universe. His change of heart is reminiscent of Freud's change of heart in that both men had first forged or contributed to a paradigm that eschewed the denial of death and implicitly called for an accounting of death and death anxiety. Subsequently, both men refused to accept the findings that they and others had generated which supported their initial mortality-questioning viewpoint.

It is at this juncture, however, that Freud and Einstein part ways. Freud was dealing with a qualitative science in which clearly defined measures were non-existent (see however, Langs, Badalamenti, and Thomson 1996), so he was able to easily shift positions. On the other hand, Einstein was dealing with a quantitative science and as a result, he could not return to a death-denying deterministic physics without supportive measured findings. It took some time, but eventually an experiment was crafted to test his deterministic predictions against those made on the basis quantum physics—it involved non-local subatomic influence or action across huge distances. The results, which were definitive, went against Einstein's position (Isaacson, 2007). So even though he continued to press for an alternative to quantum physics, Einstein no longer held a tenable position and there was no groundswell of physicists to rally to his side as there were with Freud whose ideas were never put to the quantitative test. Quantification makes a great deal of difference in deciding between competing paradigms and in being compelled to give up false or incomplete theories; psychoanalysis is all the poorer because it lacks such measures.

That said, we may make note of one last similarity between Freud and Einstein. When his father died, Freud responded by reasserting his trauma theory of neuroses; then, at the time of the anniversary of his father's death, he repudiated that position. For his part, Einstein published three highly original papers pertaining to atomic theory, relativity, and quantum physics in 1905. Around the time that he began work on these papers, his illegitimate daughter, Lieserl, died. So death and unconscious death anxiety appears to have driven his creativity, much as it evidently did with Freud. I have not been able to pinpoint the personal events in Einstein's life that motivated him to repudiate his contribution to quantum physics largely because Freud's prevailing second paradigm of psychoanalysis does not recognize the powerful role that death and death anxieties play in human life. As a result, historians seldom pursue and record many of the most crucial traumatic events in the lives of our most creative—and in some case, most destructive—leaders.

Finally, these realizations also recall the fact that Newton's sudden insight into gravity and the universality of the laws of the universe occurred to him at a time when he was at leisure because his area was beset with the plague. He too undoubtedly was suffering consciously and unconsciously from both existential and predatory death anxieties and it can be conjectured that the intensification of these anxieties played a role in his breakthrough. His para-doxical response to the intensification of these anxieties, as seen in fashioning a theory that no longer supported the denial of death, stands in contrast to Freud's reaction to the anniversary of the death of his father. Freud's reaction went in the opposite direction: He gave up a potentially death-related para-digm of emotional life to one that was constructed in a manner that implicitly supported the denial of death. Let's look at this matter a little more closely.

## FREUD'S SHIFT FROM COUNTER-ARCHETYPE
## TO CONFORMITY

Freud's paradigmatic positions ran counter to the more usual, archetypal sequence which involves a first theory that supports the denial of death and a second theory that no longer does so. The scientists who made this shift—Copernicus, Galileo, Newton, Darwin, and Einstein—did so by defying their own nature, their natural need to deny death implicitly or explicitly. In their cases, given that the rest of the population was fixated on and strongly invested in such denial, their second paradigms were quite unpopular and took many years to become established as validated scientific "facts" for however long they will prevail as such—that is, until another paradigm shift, if called for, takes place.

In contrast, Freud's paradigm shift went from a potential openness to death-related issues to a closed-minded denial of death. As a result—and here's the rub—despite his own despair over the adverse effects of this development on his career, his second position received slow but increasingly large support from psychologists and the population at large. This happened because he went from defying a crucial archetype to conforming—and in these matters, humans archetypically prefer death-denying theories.

There appears to be at least two reasons why Freud initially ran counter to archetype—one was general and the other personal. The general reason is suggested by an analogy with the paradigms developed regarding the geography of the earth. The first paradigm saw the earth as flat and formulated a related danger of falling off its edges. This clearly was a death-related paradigm which was changed only after fearless explorers like Magellan actually circumnavigated the earth and found it to be a globe. In this case the existing initial data spoke overwhelmingly for a flat earth and there was no data to the contrary. The paradigm shift arose only after such data appeared.

Similarly, Freud's own clinical observations and the reports he obtained from his colleagues and the French psychiatrists he visited in Paris spoke overwhelmingly for the central role of early trauma in the development of neuroses (Balmary, 1979; Masson, 1984). Even so, his emphasis on seduction—that is, on sexually based early traumas—suggests a need on his part to avoid formulations in which assault, violence, and death played a pivotal role. We may take this as a sign of unresolved death anxieties and mark it for further study later in the book.

As a committed empiricist, then, Freud forged an initial paradigm of emotional life that was trauma-centered. It was, then, the massive amount of trauma-related clinical data that Freud collected that prompted him to theorize against his own archetypal inclinations.

As for personal reasons for defying his archetypal tendencies, the most likely conjecture is that Freud adopted his first viewpoint because he had a smattering of conscious and a strong set of unconscious reasons to suspect or know that his father and others had subjected him to early-life traumas, seductive and otherwise. The actual level of awareness at which Freud experienced these incidents is unknown, but this hypothesis is suggested by his initial conviction that seductions by fathers, including his own, played a role in neurosogenesis (Freud, 1954, letter 52, December 6, 1896, p. 180; letter 60, April 28, 1897, p. 195; Sulloway, 1979; Masson, 1984). Whatever Freud knew consciously and unconsciously, it facilitated the development of his first paradigm of neuroses (Freud, 1896a, 1896b, 1896c, 1898a), and this knowledge and his commitment to the truth were strong enough as unconscious motivators, yet in a sufficiently tolerable state, to enable him to articulate his first reality-centered theory.

A year later, however, at the time of his father's unveiling and after efforts at self-analysis of which we know very little in the way of specifics, Freud denied the role of fathers as seducers in neurosogenesis—personally and collectively (Freud, 1954, letter 69, September 21, 1897, pp. 215-216; letter 70, October 3, 1897, p. 219). More broadly he gave up his pursuit of his patients' and his own early traumas and focused instead on guilt-ridden incestuous fantasies. It seems likely that Freud was approaching a less disguised or partially conscious awareness of the truths of his early-life traumas—horrible as they must have been—and that this situation unconsciously drove him to abandon their pursuit. Gone was the centrality of external traumas in the vicissitudes of his own emotional life and that of others; in its place, he and his followers entered a world of make believe and fantasy. There are reasons to believe that at the time Freud was in an acute crisis state and that, as I shall try to show later, he actually saved his life by making this paradigm shift (see chapters 7 and 8).

That Freud knew on some level that he had copped out is suggested in his pivotal letter of disbelief written to Fliess (Freud, 1954, letter 69, September 21, 1897, pp. 215–218); it was expressed through an allusion to the Biblical Rebecca taking off her gown because she no longer was a bride. On one level, mostly unconsciously, Freud seemed to know that he had retreated from the truth and no longer deserved the fame and riches of a great man of discovery—that he no longer deserved to stand privileged next to Copernicus and the others who had defied their personal and universal archetypes to establish more valid paradigms of nature. What Freud could not have known is that he had given up a heroic contra-archetypical position only to succumb to his nature in a way that took him on a journey marred with blindness and false premises. Even without identifying the early traumas that must have fueled his decision, we are entitled to see this as yet one more example of how fate sets the course of a human life—and because the life belonged to Sigmund Freud, fate also helped to establish a flawed operative paradigm of psychodynamic human psychology that has prevailed for many years after its inception.

## Chapter 3

# A Tale of Two Paradigms

On the face of it, the historical situation can be described in simple terms: Freud initially believed that actual sexual seductions in early childhood were a precondition for the formation of a psychoneurosis in later years. But then, for reasons that seem to have been quite ambiguous, he became convinced that most if not all of the stories of early seductions his patients told him were untrue, that they were fantasies stirred up in adulthood by current events and transposed back into earlier years. And while he did not entirely set aside the consideration of actual traumas in exploring neuroses, Freud's main emphasis thereafter was on the role played by inner mental fantasies and wishes—especially those that were experienced unconsciously—in these dysfunctional syndromes.

A closer look at the situation, however, indicates that this summary does not do justice to this critical moment in the history of psychoanalysis and does little to enhance our understanding of the human mind and human life. In an effort to clarify the situation, we need to raise and answer the critical question as to whether this shift in focus was a justified advance in Freud's psychoanalytic thinking or an essentially erroneous move—a symptomatic act that has taken psychoanalysis on a long detour away from the greater truths of emotional life (Balmary, 1979). Then too there is the related question as to whether there is validity to each of Freud's positions, and if so, how they rank in importance. Or do aspects of one paradigm contradict and invalidate their counterparts in the other theory? More importantly, we also need to ask just how critical this shift in thinking was at the time and how important it is at present. If this is a simply matter of the ever-present conundrum of nature versus nurture—instinctual drives and other biological needs versus environmental pressures, that is, fantasy versus trauma—then the change of heart would be of only minor importance and of little consequence. But on the other hand, as I have been suggesting, if Freud was making a basic paradigm shift, his decision would have had (and indeed has had) lasting major consequences.

Another noteworthy point is the realization that if Freud's shift in focus was an advance in his psychoanalytic thinking, there would be little reason to delve into his personal life searching for hidden secrets. But on the other hand, if indications are that Freud had gone astray, we would be strongly motivated to search his life and mind for clues to why he veered off the more promising path—and as a corollary, we would then be compelled to ask why so many psychoanalysts and others have uncritically followed him on his errant journey. And while we would then be quite certain that unconscious forces were at play, the particular direction our search would take us would depend on which paradigm—Freud's first or second theory—we see as most cogent for emotional life and most likely to direct us towards sound answers to the questions I am raising.

## FREUD'S FIRST PARADIGM

It is widely agreed that in 1897, a year after the death of his father, Freud decided on a dramatic change of course for his newly emerging dynamic form of psychology which he came to call psychoanalysis. Having argued convincingly for the power of repressed, unconscious memories, Freud's first theory of neurosogenesis was centered on the clinically grounded idea that actual events and certain kinds of traumatic realities, all of them involving sexuality, played a fundamental role in emotional disorders. In the face of many uncertainties but shored up by clinical observations, it took Freud some ten years to develop this basic proposition which he first announced to the world in 1895 and penned in 1896 (Freud, 1896a, 1896b, 1896c; Balmary, 1979). This thesis was the basis for his first psychodynamic paradigm.

In the mid-1880s Freud went to Paris to observe Charcot's work with hypnosis and post-hypnotic suggestion and he spent time meeting with and studying the work and writings of several other French psychiatrists (Masson, 1984). By and large, they placed great stress on the frequency with which adults sexually violated young children and the extent to which violence accompanied these sexual exploitations. They believed that these traumas—along with many other factors such as inherited dispositions—contributed in some way to the development of neuroses when these children became adults, but they were unable to define the exact nature of the connection between the past and present.

On the basis of these reports and his own clinical work with patients, Freud began to develop the idea that emotion-related symptoms, which were broadly viewed by others as meaningless, physically based, hereditary aberrations, actually do have meaning—much of it expressed outside of conscious awareness. As a result, he initiated a series of clinical investigations into what lay behind his patient's symptoms. Based on repeated reports from his patients, he proposed that sexual seductions by caretakers and others in the early years of his patients' lives were the root cause of these ills (Freud, 1896a, 1896b, 1896c, 1898a). Using the hypnotic technique of tracing particular symptoms to their origins—a procedure invented by his mentor, Josef Breuer (Breuer and Freud, 1893–1895)—Freud found that relief often transpired when a previously unconscious memory broke through the barrier of repression that had sealed it off from awareness and entered the patient's conscious thoughts.

Freud (1898a) proposed two types of emotional syndromes: *The actual neuroses* which are caused by disruptive sexual practices like masturbation and *coitus interruptus,* and *the psychoneuroses* which were the result of early childhood seductions by perverse adult caretakers. In this context, he started to explore the role of repression and the return of repressed memories in the development of neuroses—hysterics were said to suffer from (unconscious) reminiscences (Breuer and Freud, 1893–1895). He also looked into the nature of his patients' resistances to recalling these traumas. In this context, he postulated the existence what he called *transferences*—his patients' inappropriate reactions to him as their therapist which were displaced or transferred from experiences in their early lives with family members (Breuer and Freud, 1893–1895).

All in all, then, Freud's early clinical observations had taken him down a most interesting and original path of investigation (Sulloway, 1979). He recognized the need to explore his patients' material, especially their dreams, in light of their early traumatic, sexual experiences and the sexual conflicts that these incidents had created—and were creating—in them. He thereby adopted a dual orientation in which both the patient and others, reality and inner mental responses, played a role (Balmary, 1979; Good, 2006). The causes of neuroses were real; the mind was damaged by hurtful realities that left unconscious traces behind them. And these traces were reactivated by incidents that overwhelmed the ego and thereby caused mental dysfunctions. Symptoms were not meaningless entities, nor were they matters of unbridled imagination; they were mentally based responses to harm from others.

Freud's multiple causation approach called for the investigation of at least three factors in neuroses: The role of the other, including the identity of, and relationship with, the sexually perverted person who had abused the child; the nature of the trauma and of the harm it had caused, including the particular effects it was now having on the patient; and the status of the mind of the patient—his or her predispositions and current mental state. He had fashioned a remarkably comprehensive theory that pointed to the need to investigate every possible aspect of an emotional problem; the potential for discovery was limitless. Importantly, his researches consistently began with and focused on the quest for the repressed trauma that was at the root of a given patient's neurosis.

Freud's seduction theory was an adaptation-oriented theory. It saw the formation of neuroses as being initiated by an early sexual trauma—an external event—which left residuals of unconscious memories in their wake, and which were re-aroused when a later-day trauma—another external event—befell the patient-victim. We may speculate, as have others (Good, 2006), that his call for the study of actual seductions eventually would have led Freud to broaden his view of the nature of these pathogenic realities. In time, then, he might well have found clinically that sexual traumas tend to be assaultive and this would have prompted him to consider the role played in emotional life by nonsexual traumas such as physical attacks, bodily and psychological harm, and natural disasters. With attentive listening to patients, and with the necessary help of a measure of personal insight derived from a well-rounded effort at self-analysis based on these adaptation-oriented findings, he probably would have come to realize that coping with the threat and inevitability of death and the death anxieties that this evokes are a major factor in human emotional disorders. The basic thesis of these extensions of Freud's first paradigm would have been to the effect that the most crucial factors in emotional life lie with how a person adapts mentally and physically to what evolutionists call *environmental disasters*—interpersonal and natural in nature. The investigation of the mind in light of how it copes with these traumas would have been the starting point his new psychoanalysis.

In giving up this first paradigm, Freud set a course in which none of this would happen as mainstream psychoanalysis developed—and none of it has. Indications are that this development has all the earmarks of a great blow to our in-depth understanding of the human mind and of the human condition as well.

## FREUD'S SECOND PARADIGM

The seeds of Freud's turning away from his first paradigm of neurosogenesis to his second theory of emotional life can be found in his mind-centered *Project for a Scientific Psychology* (Freud, 1895). Indeed, from the very beginning of his investigations, Freud vacillated on the question of which had primacy in emotional life: reality or fantasy. But by 1897, he began to doubt the truth-value or factuality of the sexual transgressions that his patients had described to him. He felt at sea for a while, but eventually gained what he experienced as clarity with a new formulation—his patients were describing their fantasies to him rather than actual traumas. Inner mental, biologically driven wishes had taken center stage in the story of emotional ills.

There are two primary markers of Freud's change of heart. The first seems to have developed quite unconsciously, while the second entailed the conscious articulation of the change—essentially his announcement that he no longer believed in the reality of the traumas his patients reported to him; he became convinced that they were coming from his patients' imaginations. He then gave the reasons for his change in viewpoint.

As background, six weeks after the death of his father (Freud, 1954, letter 52, December 6, 1896, pp. 173–181), Freud changed his position regarding the identity of the individuals who seduced hysterics in their childhood. The shift was from his previous impression that as a rule, they were siblings or caretakers like nursemaids to his fresh conviction that this role fell exclusively to fathers. We do not know if this proposition came from a re-evaluation of his clinical material or from observing a series of new patients. It also might have been driven primarily by trauma-related, inner unconscious needs far more than clinical observations—a view strongly advocated by Balmary (1979).

There is some striking support for this particular conjecture. Indeed, the personal investment that Freud had regarding his view of father, and his own father in particular, was dramatically conveyed in a letter that was omitted from the 1954 collection of letters (Freud, 1954), but included in Masson's 1985 presentation. In a letter dated February 11, 1897, Freud wrote the following to Fleiss:

> Unfortunately, my own father was one of these perverts and is responsible for the hysteria of my brother (all of whose symptoms are identifications) and those of several younger sisters. The frequency of this circumstance often makes me wonder. In any case, I shall bring a lot of strange material with me to Prague (Masson, 1895, pp. 230–231).

Given that Freud mentions younger sisters but does not indicate that he is referring to a younger brother, we may speculate that he is alluding to Phillip who has been described as far more neurotic than his sibling, Emmanuel. In any case, Freud's view of his father as a pervert and thus as a seducer of young children is blatantly stated, as is Freud's allusion to the troublesome frequency that this is, in general, the case. A few months later, he repudiates this general impression (Freud, 1954, letter 69, September 21, 1897, pp. 215–216) and soon after that, following a try at self-analysis, he does so regarding his father vis-à-vis himself (Freud, 1954, letter 70, October 3, 1897, p. 219).

In any case, less than a year later, Freud gave up his belief that early child-hood seductions always play a pivotal role in adult hysteria (Freud, 1954, letter 69, September 21, 1897, pp. 215–218). For a brief period of time, he drew a blank and had no viable idea as to the identity of the crucial etiologi-cal factors in these ills. He was inclined to afford hereditary dispositions this role, but it is evident that this idea did not satisfy his need for closure. He continued to explore the matter without realizing consciously that he was seeking an answer to neurosogenesis that would lead to the creation of a last-ing paradigmatic foundation on which the future psychoanalytic thinking and practice would be built. Although his focus was narrow, he nevertheless also was in the process of determining how humankind would view of the human mind and emotional life; the psychoanalysis he was about to create would offer the only comprehensive theory of the emotion-related mind available to human psychology. All of the other current and future psychodynamic theories, including those generated by dissidents like Adler and Jung, would be built on the foundation of his final choice of paradigm. With so much at stake and the main influences coming, it would seem, largely from trauma-related unconscious issues rather than clinical observation, it is well for us to be reminded of the third and fourth blows to human narcissism previously discussed, namely, that much in life, mentally and in reality, is beyond our personal control. Although Freud was a genius, his early life traumas appear to have been playing a powerfully disruptive role in his emerging position regarding the basics of human psychology—and with that, the future of its explorations and insights.

In less than four weeks after renouncing his seduction theory and turning his attention to the mind and its fantasies, Freud, who was now engaged in a personal effort at self-analysis, came to the conclusion that repressed needs and biologically driven fantasies are the key factors in human emotional life—in essence, that forbidden wishes of a sexual and aggressive nature are at the heart of neuroses (Freud, 1954, Letter 71, October 15, 1897, p. 223). These forces, he contended, were epitomized in the myth of Oedipus and the constellation of needs that it portrays he soon termed *the Oedipus complex.* As he continued to write, Freud established the claim that this complex and the vicissitudes of infantile sexuality were the universal driv-ing forces behind neurotic disturbances and emotional life in general (Freud, 1900, 1914b, 1917, 1924, 1940). His fantasy-centered theory of neuroses had come into being and it determined the main locus of his psychoanalytic investigations—a situation that has prevailed for more than a century since its invocation.

While his new paradigm did not entail a total rejection of his sexual-trauma theory, it did relegate such traumas to the periphery of his thinking and formulating—and thereby of the thinking and formulating of the analysts and others who would come after him. He no longer organized his propositions around environmental moments of harm and damage, human and otherwise, and the need to cope with them consciously and unconsciously. The consequences of this shift in focus is captured by one of Freud's own commentaries:

> I am well aware that it is one thing to give utterance to an idea once or twice in the form of a passing apercu, and quite another to mean it seriously—to take it literally and pursue it in the face of every contradictory detail, and to win it a place among accepted truths. It is the difference between a casual affair and a legal marriage with all of its duties and difficulties. (Freud, 1914b, p. 15)

Freud most certainly had divorced himself from his trauma theory of neuroses and took as his bride—to use his own metaphor—the alluring images that prevail in the world of fantasy.

The essence of Freud's second theory of the mind lies with the proposition that the root cause of emotional disturbances lies with forbidden and conflicted, biologically driven inner mental needs, fantasies, and wishes. The beam of light cast by Freud in exploring emotional life and the analytic process moved away from its primary focus on reality to a basic focus on the inner mind, especially the unconscious mind and unconscious mental contents. Put another way, *the basic conflicts* in emotional life were no longer seen as mainly occurring between the patient and outside figures in his of her life, but as *taking place between the different agencies of the mind.* Reality was no longer seen as the first cause of damage to the human psyche; inner mental conflicts were the culprits. Reality was evocative but not directly harmful; it activates internal conflicts and other psychological issues and does its damage through how it affects the mind—effects that are influenced by a person's current needs, past history, and how he or she personally interprets a given incident (Good, 2006).

The prototypical conflict was, as noted, captured in the myth of Oedipus which Freud saw essentially as the expression of the boy's universal love for, and wish to cohabit with, his mother and his corresponding wish to do away with his rival for her—his father. A similar set of wishes and conflicts, called the Electra complex, were also formulated for young girls. Within the mind, the conscience protests against the expression of these repressed, forbidden incestuous and murderous wishes and it creates pressures to generate a suitably disguised compromise-formation that expresses both the wish and the defense against its expression. Emotional symptoms are one of the main results of this compromise formation (Freud, 1900).

## THE PIVOTAL LETTER TO FLIESS

Freud announced his paradigm shift in a well known letter to his colleague, Fleiss (Freud, 1954, Letter 69, September 21, 1897, pp. 215–218). Early in the letter he announces that he no longer believes his *neurotica,* by which he means the stories of seduction with which his patients were regaling him and thus his seduction theory of neuroses. He then offers four clusters of reasons for his decision, all of them both interesting and suspect—sufficiently so that, as I have been suggesting, they strongly suggest that unconscious forces are at work.

The first set of reasons involves Freud's disappointment regarding his attempts to bring his analyses to real conclusions; the running away of patients who for a time seemed to be favorably inclined towards their treatment; the lack of complete success which he had counted on; and the possibility of explaining his partial successes in other, familiar ways—that is, through the power of suggestions.

Coming from someone who kept revising his impressions as to the key sources of neuroses and only recently had come upon new ways to understand and treat emotional ills, this group of reasons seems to be insubstantial and based on short-sighted, unrealistic expectations. Freud essentially was doing therapy in a new way and he had few if any colleagues who could help him to investigate and improve his therapeutic techniques. Disappointments of the kind Freud was experiencing were inevitable, so this group of reasons for abandoning his seduction hypothesis seem to entail conscious rationalizations for a decision that has been unconsciously rather than logically driven.

The second group of reasons for abandoning his *neurotica* was Freud's astonishment that in every case he studied blame was laid on perverse acts of the father; that the frequency of hysteria was unexpectedly high; that in every case the same thing applied; and that it was hardly credible that perverted acts against children were so general.

To offer an analogy, this is like rejecting the contention that every case of staphylococcus infection is caused by a staphylococcus organism. Consistency does not imply impossibility and disbeliefs that contradict clinical findings need to be re-examined rather than used as a basis for revising one's thinking. Here too we have cause for suspicion and a further indication that some other factor of which Freud was unaware was causing him to change his viewpoint. (Sulloway, 1979).

The third reason for Freud's decision lay with his belief that there is "no indication of reality" in the unconscious, making it impossible to distinguish between truth and emotionally charged fiction. Freud was arguing here that it was not possible to distinguish a fantasy from a reality, a conundrum that plagues second paradigm analysts to this day—though not however first paradigm analysts (see chapter 4). Based on this premise, which could reflect a problem in Freud's therapeutic acumen rather than an irresolvable distinction, Freud put himself in a position where he could have argued for a combination of fantasy and reality in neurosogenesis—the essence of present-day mainline thinking. Alternatively, he could have made a basic choice: To go forward based largely on the idea that realities are the essence of the problem and that they are denied or obliterated by being given the guise of fantasies—a formulation that would have enabled him to sustain his trauma-centered theory. Or he could have suggested that fantasies are built from biological drives and the like rather than on the basis of actual incidents (or minimally stimulated in this manner), and then claim that fantasy is the critical phenomenon in emotional life. In his letter to Fliess, Freud was moving towards the latter position but he offered no sound reason for doing so. Finally, it can be argued that difficulties in distinguishing memories that are based on real events from those that are based on imaginary wishes do not constitute a reason to abandon a reality-based hypothesis pertaining to the development of neuroses. Instead, it calls for the development of methods to establish whether a recollection, conscious or unconscious as recalled via encoded imagery, is veridical or fantasied—and then deciding whether reality or fantasy is the more critical factor in emotional ills.

The fourth pair of reasons for Freud's change of heart was his finding that even in the most deep-reaching psychoses, unconscious memories do not break through—that is, that the secrets of infantile experiences were not revealed even in the most confused states of delirium. Freud also indicated that when one sees that the unconscious never overcomes the resistance of the conscious, one must abandon the expectation that in treatment the reverse process will take place to the extent that the conscious will fully dominate the unconscious.

This is a most intriguing but similarly unconvincing argument. Freud is indicating that significant unconscious memories of traumatic incidents do not break through whole cloth into awareness—that they are obliterated by conscious defenses. He then gives up all hope of modifying these conscious defenses, but he does not refute the possibility that nevertheless, repressed memories of actual traumas are playing a role in neurosogenesis. Nor does he allow for, as he will three years later (Freud, 1900), disguised expressions of these unconscious memories. This problem therefore does not justify the abandonment of the study of traumatic experiences and the search for the means by which they could, with the help of the analyst, attain conscious realization by a patient.

Freud could have viewed this particular insight as a call for a deeper study of the nature of traumas and the manner in which they are stored in the unconscious part of the mind and then disguised in both symptoms and dreams. But he directed his attention to these latter issues only after he had shifted to exploring unconscious fantasies. He could not deign to do this in connection with reality and actual seductions, that is, the idea of *encoded unconscious perceptions* and disguised representations of actual early-life and later-day traumas was not one that he was prepared to entertain. As early as 1895, he had found the key to the encoding process that created disguised manifest dreams and thus to the means by which, reversing the process, their disguised messages and meanings could be decoded (Freud, 1900). He was prepared to apply this knowledge to disturbing fantasies, but not to disturbing realities. In its modern-day version, the adaptive approach, which is akin to Freud's first paradigm, replaces the primacy afforded by his second paradigm to encoded unconscious fantasies with the primacy of encoded unconscious traumatic realities.

All in all, Freud's conscious reasons for abandoning his seduction hypothesis are quite unconvincing. They do not in the least justify his shift in thinking and suggest that forces of which he was unaware had a far greater influence on his decision than anything he had observed clinically or thought through rationally. Indeed, in the next chapter I shall offer evidence that that not only was his shift in paradigm unconsciously driven and uncalled for, it also was a move that was far more deleterious to analytic thinking than it was helpful.

## FREUD'S LAST CHANCES

Freud had several generally unrecognized opportunities to redress his flight from reality and to thereby reverse or modify his flawed inner mental paradigm of emotional life and the model of the mind that he fashioned to support it. The first occurred in 1912 when he contemplated the means by which the analyst listens to his or her patients' free associations. In the passage I quoted in the introduction to this book (Freud, 1912b), he suggested that the analyst turn his unconscious mind towards the patient's unconscious to receive the patient's messages. Instead of being abandoned as an isolated, albeit remarkable but undeveloped insight, this line of thought could have led Freud to explore the patient's and analyst's unconscious experiences of the actual inputs from each other and could have prompted him to explicitly recognize and introduce the concept of *unconscious perceptions* into psychoanalysis. This critical faculty is the basic way that many aspects of traumatic events are experienced. Indeed, the realization that entire traumatic experiences and many of the most disturbing meanings of consciously recalled traumas are perceived and processed unconsciously is critical to developing a full appreciation of the role of traumas in human life.

A related opportunity for revision came about even more specifically in 1915 when Freud added a footnote to his dream book (Freud, 1900) that acknowledged the work of Poetzl (1917) who had presented convincing evidence that humans have a striking capacity for subliminal—that is, unconscious—perception. But Freud merely acknowledged Poetzl's work and did not pursue any of its potential ramifications. Evidently Freud was unable to avoid repetitive brushes with the unconscious experience of emotionally charged realities, but he dealt with them largely by turning away from the subject as quickly as possible. To this day second paradigm psychoanalysts treat subliminal forms of perception as laboratory curiosities rather than as a major adaptive capacity of the deep unconscious mind.

Another notable opportunity to reconsider the role of reality in emotional life arose when Freud chose to study the writings of the hospitalized, psychotic Judge, Daniel Schreber (Freud, 1911) in an effort to explore the psychological factors in the development of paranoid schizophrenia. There was abundant available material in these writings that indicated that Schreber's delusions were constructed on the basis of the violently punitive disciplinary actions of his father, but Freud did not pay careful attention to this fact (Lothane, 1992). Even so, he did point out that there always is a kernel of truth in a delusion—that is, that there is a realistic core within this form of madness. Here too Freud did not allow this information to take him back to and reexamine his trauma theory of emotional ills. Even though it has become clear to later-day analysts that traumatic realities play a significant role in psychoses (Searles, 1979; Langs and Searles, 1980; Shengold, 2000; Good, 2006), this insight has not served as the basis for a call for a complete or partial revision of the prevailing Freudian inner-mental theory of emotional ills.

## SOME FINAL PERSPECTIVES

Psychological theories that are forged by conscious minds without the help of deep unconscious wisdom—that is, the use of trigger decoding—tend to reflect the archetypal needs and rules of operation of the conscious system of the emotion-processing mind (Langs, 2004, 2006). As we shall see in the next chapter, adaptive studies have shown that among these rules there is an overwhelming, unconsciously driven, universal conscious effort to deny death at all cost. There is as well a related need to deal with the existential death anxieties inherent to psychotherapeutic endeavors through denial-based behaviors and beliefs that implicitly and explicitly refute the inevitability and finality of death for all humans. These tendencies are evolved biological givens, archetypes that are affected—but not modified—to a limited extent by a given person's history of nurturance and, more importantly, of death-related traumas. This is a major psychological reason why almost all of the consciously forged first paradigms alluded to in the previous chapter inherently supported the human need to deny death and why the paradigm shifts that came later and did not support this denial were met with such resistance.

Much the same has happened and is happening today in psychoanalysis: Freud's second paradigm, which is grounded in the denial of death, appears to be unassailable and those who advocate his first paradigm are either ignored or excommunicated—or both. To appreciate the dire consequences of this situation, I turn now to a comparison between the present versions of each of these two competing paradigms—the loosely affiliated forms of classical psychoanalysis that are heir to Freud's second paradigm and the adaptive approach which, although independently derived, can be thought of as a descendant of his first theory of neuroses.

*Chapter 4*

# The Descendants of Freud's
# Two Paradigms

Some of the clearest evidence that Freud developed two distinctive paradigms of psychoanalysis can be found by examining the off-shoots and later-day versions of each of his theories. Doing so reveals that, despite evidence that Freud never entirely stopped considering the role of reality in emotional life, there are sharp, irreconcilable differences between these two theories. Each paradigm maps distinctive domains of human experience and sponsors very different world views when it comes to the human psyche and emotional life. In terms elaborated by Rorty (1989), each describes the emotion-related world with its own set of word definitions, vocabulary, and language and conversations across theories are difficult if not impossible.

In the present chapter, I shall attempt to characterize the current versions of each paradigm. In so doing, I shall keep in mind the need to provide a definitive answer to the question that overhangs this book: Was Freud's paradigm shift primarily a step forward or a step backward for psychoanalysis? That is, in the face of ample evidence that his shift to an inner-mental focus brought countless insights into emotional life and the psychoanalytic process, was—and is—his new approach to the mind laced with significant blind spots and errors? If the answer to this question is in the affirmative, it would, as I said, indicate that there were unconsciously driven, neurotic aspects to Freud's shift in emphasis from reality to fantasy. Such a conclusion would, of course, constitute a call for a thorough search for the trauma-driven, psychological sources of his flight from critical aspects of reality.

Simply listing the key features of each approach has only limited value. As I shall show, doing so would merely reveal a series of marked differences in the methodology and understanding of each paradigm, but would tell us little about the extent of the limitations and misconceptions of each position.

In order to delve more deeply into the features these theories, then, I shall make use of another way of assessing each paradigm. That is, I shall turn to a comparative study of each theory, using its opposite as a standard that will enable me to identify previously unrecognized features and missing elements inherent to each approach. That said, however, I must say in advance of presenting the results of this effort that the second paradigm has few if any fresh perspectives to offer regarding Freud's first theory of the mind, while paradoxically, the first paradigm has many reasons to take issue with Freud's second version of psychoanalytic theory.

Oddly enough, this observation supports the claim that the first paradigm of psychoanalysis actually is superior and superordinate to the second paradigm despite the fact that the second theory replaced the first theory and became the standard-bearer of psychoanalytic thinking over the first hundred or so years of its existence. The archetypal rule indicates that replacement theories are built from discovered flaws in an original theory, corrects these flaws, and offers a set of principles that extensively critique and replace the previous way of thinking. Freud's second paradigm has none of these features. It was based on belief and did not include an incisive rejection of first-paradigm thinking. These realizations tend to support the thesis offered in the previous chapter that Freud's paradigm selections went against his natural archetypes.

Being able to use the features of the first paradigm as a measuring rod for the second version of psychoanalysis is especially fortuitous. In the absence of an independent standard, qualitative theories tend to become self-fulfilling closed systems and their inevitable problems and misconceptions are virtually undetectable by their adherents. All that can be done is to compare the paradigm's competing subtheories—in this case, object relations, self-psychological, classical drive theory, interpersonal, and intersubjective—with each other, but the problem is that each of these approaches is committed to the same basic, inner mental, psychic reality foundation of the second paradigm. Not surprisingly then the outcome of these efforts has been the recognition that each of these approaches appear to be based on a seemingly sound line of thought and each deserves to be incorporated into a grand synthesis of modern-day, psychoanalytic thinking (Pine, 2003; Rangell, 2006; Rosenbaum, 2009). Nevertheless, as soon as we take the first paradigm's adaptation-oriented approach as our standard for the second paradigm, flaws in this seemingly logical conclusion begin to emerge (see below).

The revelatory powers of a comparative study of competing systems was seen when the adaptive approach recognized that the emotion-processing mind is a two-system entity with a conscious and deep unconscious system, each operating with relative independence from the other (Langs, 2004, 2006). The prevailing view before these two systems were subjected to a comparative study of their adaptive capacities and operations was a relatively naïve one. Investigators simply recognized that the conscious system tries to adapt to incoming traumas as best it can—effectively or, if impaired, ineffectively, and that the deep unconscious system also responds to these traumas as best it can, doing so with somewhat greater effectiveness.

But then by comparing (manifest) conscious and (encoded) deep unconscious responses to the same traumatic triggering event, many entirely new findings emerged. For example, it became clear that deep unconscious adaptive wisdom is far more perceptive, incisive, and effective than conscious adaptive wisdom. In addition, quite surprisingly, it turned out that the conscious system is basically designed for defense and denial when it come to traumatic incidents and the death anxieties that they evoke. Many of the death-related meanings of these events are blocked from conscious awareness, even as they are perceived and processed deep unconsciously. The results of this conscious obliterating stance include serious impairments in conscious system thinking and coping, and many types of misconceptions and errors in adapting to incoming stimuli. This arises because the denial of reality and the obliteration of available information overrides and interferes with accurately perceiving and properly solving many of the emotionally charged issues that it faces.

With this in mind, I turn now to the features of the two basic paradigms of psychoanalysis.

## ELABORATIONS OF FREUD'S SECOND PARADIGM

Psychoanalysis, as it is generally structured and practiced today, is an elaboration of Freud's fantasy-focused, inner biological need paradigm. Freud himself accounts for several critical developments of this approach. Quite soon after giving up his *neurotica,* he identified the Oedipus complex as the essential instinctually driven, unconscious source of neuroses (Freud, 1954, letter 71, October 15, 1897, pp. 221–115). His drive-centered theory then led to an elaborate study of infantile sexuality (Freud, 1905c), while his focus on unconscious fantasies and wishes prompted him to solidify his ideas about the structure and meanings of dreams (Freud, 1900). He also used his new paradigm as a basis for examining the analytic situation, including the phenomenon of transference, which he defined as the patient's fantasy-based distorted view of, and inappropriate reactions to, the analyst based on unconscious needs and memories derived from experiences with early-life figures (Breuer and Freud, 1893–1895; Freud, 1912a). A review of his clinical writings, of which his notes on the case of the Rat-man are most exemplary (Freud, 1909c), indicates however that Freud invoked the concept of transference in the actual clinical situation only when his patients spoke directly about himself and his family; the unconscious aspect of these transferences lay with their purported, implied sources in the past relationships of the patient.

Freud also investigated aspects of the ground rules of analysis and wrote of the need—in general and with exceptions—for a secured frame (Freud, 1912b, 1913a). In exploring the difficulties in the path of a successful analysis, he elaborated on the concepts of resistances and the repetition compulsion (Freud, 1912a, 1914a, 1914c), and he described such techniques as interpretations and the reconstructions of significant past traumas (1914c, 1937b, 1940). He also introduced but did not develop the concept of counter-transferences within the analyst as a limitation to the process of cure and suggested that analysts have a need for personal analysis in order to limit the frequency and effects of this interfering factor (Freud, 1910b, 1914b). As later-day analysts shifted from the view of the analyst as a relatively detached observer of the patient and his or her material to that of a participant-observer, the analyst's counter-transference responses to the patient's material was seen as a major source of information about what was going on in the analysis and in the patient—and analyst—as well (Heimann, 1950; Little, 1951; Racker, 1974; Searles, 1979; Rosenbaum, 2009).

As the psychoanalytic movement grew and matured, then, Freud's one person, drive-centered psychology was supplemented with two-person versions on his inner need position. The most notable forms of this extension were built around relational needs and issues on the one hand (Mitchell, 1988) and narcissistic needs on the other (Kohut, 1971, 1977; see also Langs, 1998; Good, 2006; Rosenbaum, 2009). While there has been some dispute as to which of these need systems is most crucial to psychological development and its pathology, it has been possible for peacemakers to step in and argue that the two sets of needs form a complementary series of developmental requisites and issues (Pine, 2003; Rangell, 2006). Reality therefore does come into play in a broad and secondary manner in this line of thought because these theorists tend to see relational and empathic failures by caretakers and other harmful realities as doing direct damage the psyche. Nevertheless, while these investigations dissect the nature of the effects of such traumas on the child's psyche as they influence, for example, the patient's adult dysfunctions and direct the nature of the healing process, there is a failure to similarly dissect the intricacies of the external events that facilitate these dysfunctions. Similarly, later-day classical Freudians, who at times acknowledge triggering incidents in relationships with others, continue to stress the primacy of drive-related unconscious fantasies and needs and the role of intrapsychic conflict in the development of emotional ills.

On the whole, the main thrust of second paradigm thinking is to explore the status of the patient in the present as revealed in the analytic interaction and to trace his or her developmental failures and inner mental conflicts to a mixture of current needs and past cumulative and acute traumas. Freud's inner mental focus, then, gave a cast to psychoanalysis in which current symptoms and interpersonal disorders are explored in light of the early life experiences that are said to be the root source of later-day dysfunctions. Many dimensions of early human development have been examined through clinical reconstructions and direct observations, and the therapeutic effort has been concentrated on identifying the early life conflicts and developmental failures that contribute to later-day maladaptations. On this basis, the goal in therapy lies with the endeavor to repair and resolve these difficulties through both interpretation and the curative and ameliorative aspects of the analyst's interaction with the patient—the so-called corrective emotional experience. Emotional problems are said to lie within the mind of the patient and the role played by others is secondary, yet certainly a factor. Balmary (1979) and others have taken issue with this position largely because they see the primary source of emotional dysfunctions as existing in the behavior of significant others in the patient's early life—a critique of the classical instinctual drive theory that is shared by those who stress interpersonal factors in the development of emotional ills.

## FREUD'S MODELS OF THE MIND

As a scientist, Freud appreciated the role of models in scientific discourse. He therefore offered three models of the mind in the course of his work—a *neurologically based model* of mental functioning presented in his 1895 *Project for a Scientific Psychology* (Freud, 1895); a *topograhic model* in *The Interpretation of Dreams* (Freud, 1900), in which the *state of an idea or wish, conscious or unconscious,* defined the *two systems* of the mind; and a *structural model* in *The Ego and the Id* (Freud, 1923), in which the *functions of a system* defined the *three systems* of the mind—ego, id, and superego. The followers of Freud's second paradigm take the structural model as a settled delineation of mental activities, but by and large they do not make extensive use of the model in ways that affect their clinical and theoretical thinking.

*Chapter 4*

They also have not made any significant effort to revise or add to the model since Freud's presentation in 1923.

## The Topograhic Model

Freud's first definitive, entirely mental, psychodynamic model of the mind came after and was grounded in his mind-centered, second paradigm of neuroses; it views the mind as a need-centered entity. Based on his insight that dreams and emotional symptoms have similar underlying, unconscious structures, Freud introduced his topographic model in his landmark dream book, *The Interpretation of Dreams* (Freud, 1900). The model postulated two basic mental systems, the UCS and PCS-CS, each a collection of mental contents, one set unconscious and the other set conscious or capable of becoming conscious. Each system was characterized in terms of the nature of these contents and by particular features, attributed to the system itself, that gave these contents a distinctive set of qualities and attributes.

The system UCS was viewed as the seat of forbidden unconscious sexual and aggressive wishes derived from the earliest years of life—so-called *infantile wishes*. By virtue of their being unconscious, these wishes blindly and with a disregard for reality seek direct and immediate satisfaction. This quest may be activated by actual events—for example, the so-called *day's residues* for dreams—but these realities are of little consequence and they immediately fall to the wayside; it is the unconscious fantasies and wishes that they have aroused that are crucial to emotional life.

The other properties of unconscious contents derive from their forbidden wishful qualities. Thus, the contents of the system UCS and the system itself are devoid of negations and because forbidden wishes can never be fully satisfied, they are indestructible and timeless. Furthermore, because these wishes, which are incestuous and murderous, are forbidden satisfaction by the conscience—which Freud located in the system PCS-CS—they also are the essential instigators of conflict. The resultant *intrapsychic conflicts,* which pit the system UCS against the system PCS-CS, are the key sources from which neuroses arise.

Because forbidden wishes are prevented from achieving direct satisfaction by the defenses mobilized by the system PCS-CS—they are subjected to two levels of censorship—they are repressed and remain outside of awareness, but they also emerge into consciousness disguised in the manifest contents of dreams and fantasies. These disguises are effected though the use of the mechanisms of condensation, displacement, symbolization, and the use of reasonable representations. The result is a fluidity of representation in which one content or form of expression and satisfaction is substituted for another—again, without consideration of reality or logic. Freud termed these and other attributes of the system UCS, like the quest for immediate discharge, *the primary processes.*

The basic conflicts in mental life take place, then, between the systems UCS and PCS-CS. The latter system is the seat of the conscience and of the repressive defenses that oppose the satisfaction of a particular forbidden unconscious wish and block the pathways to awareness and behavior that would afford the wish its sought-for rewards. The allowance for only indirect satisfactions and the creation of a compromise formations leads to psychological mixtures in which the disguised wish and the defensive repressions directed against the satisfaction of the wish emerge as either a dream or an emotional symptom—or both.

Freud also described the essential features of the system PCS-CS and its contents. He saw the system as being fully capable of delaying the discharge of inner wishes and as being well grounded in and cognizant of reality, capable of negations, logical, and as making use of single, definitive representations of thoughts and feelings without any measure of symbolization or fluidity of expression. As noted, the system also was seen as the seat of the conscience and of the mental defenses that demand that forbidden wishes be suitably disguised before gaining satisfaction or entering awareness. Freud termed these features of the system PCS-CS *the secondary processes.*

Clinically, the topograhic model spoke for the interpretation of manifest dreams and emotional symptoms as conflict-driven compromise formations in which both the wish and the defense against the wish find expression. In the course of an analysis, the underlying unconscious wishes and defenses, which often appear as resistances to analytic progress, can be detected from patients' disguised manifest dreams and suitably interpreted. By undoing these disguises, the unconscious conflict becomes conscious and the patient is in a position to resolve his or her intrapsychic conflicts and renounce his or her troublesome forbidden wishes.

In this model, then, reality plays its main role in emotional life by activating unconscious wishes and it is this function that preoccupies the analyst. The focus is on the attributes, structure, and operations of the mind and not at all on the attributes, structure, and effects of reality on the psyche and on symptom formation. Most critically, when a dream is decoded in order to identify what Freud termed the latent (unconscious) contents of the dream, the search is for disguised forbidden wishes and not at all for disguised (unconscious) perceptions of external events. Even with the advent of the structural model, this trend has been sustained by second paradigm analysts.

As Freud continued his psychoanalytic studies, he found two major reasons that made it necessary for him to modify his topographic model. The first was his realization that patients' defenses and resistances, which he had located in the system PCS-CS, often operated unconsciously without the awareness of the patient. It therefore seemed necessary to relocate them in the system UCS, but this reassignment flew in the face of his basic conflict theory of neuroses. Locating both sides of a conflict in the same system was untenable. Similarly, Freud had located the conscience, which was opposed to the direct satisfaction of the forbidden instinctual wishes of the system UCS, in the system PCS-CS. But here too he began to see clinically that a patient's moral values and sense of guilt very often were experienced unconsciously rather than consciously. Unable to be satisfied with placing the conscience in the system UCS, Freud sought a new model of the mind—and it was slow in coming.

## Freud's Structural Model

Freud's revised model of the mind did not appear in print until 1923. It is a three-system, structural model. It was still based on his wish-centered theory of the mind, but it also included some dramatic changes in his view of the design of the mind and the basis on which its systems could be identified. This model persists to this day, although it does so mainly as a background feature of current psychoanalytic thinking rather than as a specific reference point for clarifications of the model or the theory it supports. This arises largely because each of the second paradigm subtheories tends to be centered on one of the three systems of the newly modeled mind and because model making as an aid to theory and practice has lost favor among second-paradigm psychoanalysts.

Freud proposed the existence of three systems of the mind, each with specific *functions* that gave the system its identity. Each system has conscious and unconscious components so this aspect of a system is of secondary, if any, importance. The three systems are: *The ego,* which is the seat of executive, mediating, reality testing, tension regulating, and relational functions; *the id,* which is the seat of the instinctual drives; and *the superego,* which is the seat of the conscience, ideals, self-image and self-worth, and additional tension regulating operations.

The ego is obliged to deal with reality and the later-day theories of ego psychology, object relations and other forms of relational thinking are focused on the need for healthy relatedness and the consequences of parental failures in this regard. With the ultimate focus on the mind of the child-patient, both psychic damage and intrapsychic conflicts are studied in light of interactions with both early-life figures and the psychoanalyst. The intersubjective theory which arose from these interpersonal considerations attempts to characterize the subtle exchanges of affect and meaning, and the shared view of reality—in analysis, mainly the reality of what is going on in the patient's psyche—developed by those who participate in dyadic relationships. Although it is assumed that many aspects of these interactions take place unconsciously, the therapeutic work derived from these approaches tends to be phenomeno-logical and to mix conscious and self-evident unconscious processes together (Stolorow, Brandshaft and Atwood, 1987)).

The concept of the id promoted a continuation of Freud's instinctual drive theory with its focus on Oedipal and pre-Oedipal issues in which conflicts between the id and the ego and superego characterize the battle within the mind (Freud, 1923, 1926, 1940). Finally, the introduction of the superego has led to self-psychology with its stress on the empathic support necessary for the development of a healthy self and self-image, as well as on issues of self-esteem, conscience, moral values, tension regulation, ideals, and the like (Kohut, 1971, 1977). By and large, the focus is on the failures of caretak-ers to provide the narcissistic supplies needed by the growing child and the damage done to the psyche and self as a result. As can be seen, as is the case for much of second paradigm thinking, reality comes into play as the source of need satisfactions and ego support, while issues of psychic damage also loom large.

All in all then, reality is said to play a part in the theories developed on the basis of the structural model of the mind through the role of others as instiga-tors and satisfiers or frustraters of id wishes and of relational and narcissistic needs. Failures along these lines are seen as the cause of neuroses. The clas-sical subtheories that have been proposed on the basis of the structural model are two-person theories in which the other person may become the source of support for or damage to the three systems of the mind in light of relational and narcissistic needs. However, these approaches maintain a focus on the inner mental effects of these traumas and seldom pay attention to the details of the specific triggering events that cause this damage—especially those that are initiated by the analyst in the analytic situation. Reality is viewed in general and superficial terms and as a result, these theories are not concerned with specific adaptations to particular environmental challenges. They are instead, mind-centered theories of the state of the self and the three psychic agencies, and of their relationship with each other.

In addition to reinforcing the mind-centered view of the second paradigm, Freud's structural model dramatically altered the concept of "the uncon-scious" in psychoanalytic thinking. The hallmark of psychoanalysis has always been—and should still be—the fundamental concept of *unconscious mental processes*. In Freud's topographic model of the mind, the status of a thought, feeling or wish—that is, whether it was experienced consciously or unconsciously—was the critical factor in placing it in a system of the mind and thus, in regard to its nature, attributes, and effects. There was a sharp differentiation between unconscious and conscious contents and dramatic differences between how each system—UCS and PCS-CS—operated. The role of repressed contents and wishes as a defining feature of the systems of the mind kept the focus on the study of the system UCS and its contents and on the unraveling of the disguised entry into awareness of these contents.

The situation changed dramatically with the structural model in which the systems of the mind were defined in terms of their functions rather than the state of awareness of the ideas, needs, or feelings with which they were concerned and operated. All three systems of the mind were seen to have conscious and unconscious features, and the term "unconscious" was downgraded to a quality of mental experience; it no longed was an essential defining feature of the systems of the mind. In time, the concept of gradations of awareness was introduced and analysts soon found it irrelevant to determine whether a given need or fantasy, narcissistic insult or empathic failure, was conscious or unconscious—the two modes of experience became conflated. Despite Freud's stress on the need to undo dream disguises so as to access repressed unconscious fantasies and wishes, his second paradigm sent psychoanalysis down a path in which its most basic concept was all but lost. Most second paradigm therapeutic work deals with manifest, conscious contents and their evident implications. As a result, psychoanalysis has taken on a phenomenological, cognitive cast; in adaptive terms, it has become a conscious system psychology.

Much of this has arisen because of the loosely structured, undisciplined listening and formulating process used by second paradigm psychoanalysts. These efforts tend to be theory driven with an emphasis is on vaguely defined processes like empathic attunement and intersubjective understanding. The trend is to be pattern-seeking as reflected in the purported implications of patients' manifest material. The focus tends to vary, set one moment on the direct meanings of patients' manifest comments, the next moment on their implications, then shifting to patients' behaviors and patterns of thinking and acting. Then, after formulating the current meanings and implications of this mélange of material, the analyst usually attempts to find links to patients' early life experiences as they are supposedly being reenacted and repeated in the analytic relationship—the patient's so-called *transferences*. There are few if any rules, guidelines, agreed-on definitions, or means of validation in connection with these efforts which are, on the whole, shaped by the theory to which the analyst subscribes. The communicated material itself is treated as being homogeneous; for example, no distinction is made between narrative and nonnarrative or intellectualized communications.

All in all, then, depending on an analyst's theoretical bias, a world of meaning is read into or extracted from the verbal material, affects, and behaviors of the patient. Diverse interventions of various kinds are advocated including the revelation of the analyst's own associations to the material from the patient; personal self-revelations by the analyst; questions, confrontations, reconstructions, and interpretations, genetic and otherwise; pattern recognition; manifest or direct queries as to connections between the present and the past; proposed links between past figures and current reactions to and feelings about the analyst; patients' and analysts' shared views of what is going on in the patient's mind or of what is happening between them in the analytic interaction; and many other kinds of nonvalidated comments too numerous to list. The unconscious aspects of the patient's material is either irrelevant or taken to involve anything of which the patient seems unaware—be it his or her developmental level; type of relatedness; narcissistic impairments; the meanings implied in the material at hand or from past sessions; connections between the present and the past; patterns of behavior; and whatever else the patient has missed and the analyst deems to be important.

It can be seen, then, that the second paradigm listening processes has no clear guidelines as to when, why, and how an analyst listens, formulates, and intervenes. The process is open to a most inviting arbitrariness which cannot be faulted or questioned by critics working within the paradigm because there are no standards to turn to. Interventions are made, the patient responds, and the analyst decides if the work seems to be moving forward or is not advancing. This decision generally is made on the basis of the patient's manifest response to an intervention and relies more on common sense and the analyst's biased judgment than on any psychoanalytic criteria of sound therapeutic work. This openness to competing and invalidated possibilities and the deterioration of analytic technique and thinking characterizes many of the evolved features of Freud's second paradigm. As a result, classical versions of psychoanalysis are bathed in a sea of uncertainty to this very day.

## FREUD'S FIRST PARADIGM IN AN EVOLVED FORM

The adaptive approach (Langs, 2004, 2006) is the only presently configured, comprehensive theory of the mind and emotional life that can be viewed as an extension and elaboration—with suitable revisions—of Freud's first paradigm of psychoanalysis. However, the approach was not developed through attempts to extend Freud's initial ideas about neurosogenesis. Instead, it was arrived at relatively independently, driven by clinical observations that indicated that second-paradigm psychoanalysis did not afford reality the role in emotional life that was its due. This dissatisfaction led to an alteration in listening to and formulating patients' material in therapy sessions through which external inputs into the psyche were afforded special attention. It was some time after the approach had been more fully developed both clinically and theoretically that, largely in the course of writing this book, it was realized that the adaptive paradigm was grounded in a modified set of propositions drawn from Freud's first, trauma-centered view of emotional life.

The heightened attention paid to reality by the adaptive approach was enhanced in four ways:

First, by recognizing that communications from others and the multiple meanings of external events are experienced by the human mind both consciously and unconsciously, that is by means of conscious and subliminal or unconscious perceptions.

Second, by the realization that patients experience the interventions of their therapists through both of these means of perception—that is, both consciously and unconsciously.

Third, by appreciating that the mechanisms by which repressed, anxiety-provoking latent dream thoughts and fantasies are encoded into manifest dreams—condensation, displacement, and symbolization—are also used to encode unconscious perceptions of the repressed or more precisely, obliterated, anxiety-provoking meanings of traumatic communications and external events.

And fourth, by realizing that not only dreams, but all of the stories patients tell in their sessions—that is, that all narrative forms—carry both manifest and disguised messages and meanings, while intellectualizations, speculations, interpretations and the like carry only single messages and a set of implied but not encoded meanings.

Application of these principles led to a focus on patients' views of and responses to the interventions of their therapists, understood primarily in terms of conscious and unconscious perceptions rather than conscious and unconscious fantasies. The latter arise secondarily; they are imaginative responses to valid unconscious perceptions and they entail all manner of interpretations, speculations, genetic connections and the like, links which arise after an actual meaning or implication of an intervention has been unconsciously registered. The connections between therapists' interventions and the narrative imagery from patients were established through the identification of *bridging themes,* images that are shared by both the meanings of an external stimulus and the encoded manifest dream or story with which the patient has responded to it.

To cite two examples, a male therapist forgets and misses a therapy session with a female inpatient. At her next appointment, she openly (manifestly, consciously) forgives him, but she then tells the story of how her boyfriend failed to appear, as promised, during visiting hours the previous night. He was trying to drive her crazy; she could murder him for it. He always had problems with women; they come from his relationship with his mother. When the therapist interprets the imagery as the patient's view of himself in light of his missing her previous session, she then adds that she doesn't care so much about her boyfriend because just before she was hospitalized, she met a guy who seemed to be really smart and reliable.

Notice the bridging theme of failing to keep an arranged appointment. And notice too that the patient's conscious reaction to the therapist's lapse is the exact opposite of her encoded, unconscious reaction—forgiveness which smacks of denial as compared to murderous rage which seems to be a reasonable response to the therapist's lapse. In addition, the patient offers what is called *an unconscious interpretation* (Searles, 1975) to her therapist regarding the unconscious source of his hostile absence. Then, after the therapist intervened, she tells him an encoded story of a new boyfriend who is smart and reliable. This last is a response to an intervention that is termed *deep unconscious validation*—patients' *encoded affirmation* of a therapeutic effort by the therapist. These are all aspects of psychoanalytic thinking and technique that are part of first paradigm therapeutic efforts but not found in second-paradigm endeavors.

Another therapist overcharges his female patient in the bill he hands to her—he had forgotten that he had missed a session due to a family emergency. In the next session she reports a dream in which her butcher is robbing her at gunpoint. Associating to the dream, the patient recalls catching the butcher with his hand on the scale—he is a cheater. She then turns to a recent newspaper story in which a butcher was apprehended as the murderer of a young child. The patient then calls the therapist's attention to his overcharge, adding that he evidently forgot that he had canceled one of her sessions the previous month. It's quite all right, she tells him, she makes mistakes like that all the time. Later in the session, the patient brings up an abortion that her mother had when the patient was a young girl.

The bridging theme here is stealing money—the butcher in the dream and the therapist's overcharge, which is the *triggering event*. While the patient consciously excuses the therapist for his error, unconsciously, she views the therapist as a cheater and also sees his error as an act of violence against her which she equates with an attempt at murder. A genetic link emerges later in the session in that the patient's mother's abortion seems to be the lens through which she unconsciously experiences the therapist's hostile error. The unconscious mind tends to take the most dire view possible of harmful interventions and patients react to these errors accordingly.

## UNIQUE FIRST PARADIGM INSIGHTS

Many new insights followed from the realization that patients respond to their therapists' interventions both consciously and deep unconsciously, and that conscious reactions are intermittent, while deep unconscious reactions are continuous—patients' encoded responses to their therapists' behaviors and comments emerge in virtually every narrative they communicate. It was found too that triggers evoke themes, and thus narrative themes organize around the meanings and implications of their triggers—there is method to the encoded madness of the emotion-processing mind. It was found too that the richness and complexity of external events and communications is missed entirely by the conscious mind, which tends to simplify and deny most of the anxiety-provoking aspects of external events. On the other hand, the deep unconscious mind perceives and responds adaptively to countless nuances and meanings of therapists' interventions, correctly detecting many grim implications of interventions that seem innocuous or are missed consciously, but are validly recognized deep unconsciously as devastatingly destructive. Likewise, the healing aspects of many interventions are not appreciated by the conscious mind but validated and acknowledged by its deep unconscious counterpart. Adaptive therapists had only to identify the triggering intervention that was evoking a patient's narrative themes and to trigger decode these themes accordingly, and they found themselves educated as to the kinds of interventions that are on target and healing as compared to those that are harmful and disruptive. The deep unconscious mind is humankind's most reliable guide when it comes to the evaluation of emotionally charged interventions and incidents that typically determine the course of human lives—and a given psychotherapy experience.

I shall now highlight some of the main lessons learned from the use of the adaptive orientation with its primary focus on the mind's reactions to external realities and their traumatic triggering events:

Adapting to reality is the basic function of the human mind. And adapting to unfavorable environmental changes—that is, to traumatic triggering events—is the primary function of the emotion-processing mind, the mental module that has evolved to adapt to these ultimately life-threatening challenges (Langs, 1996, 1997).

The emotion-processing mind is a two-system entity, with a *conscious system* that operates with direct awareness of its perceptions and its reactions to these inputs, and a *deep unconscious system* that perceives the world without direct awareness—that is, subliminally or unconsciously—and processes anxiety-provoking stimuli and their meanings outside of awareness as well.

The adaptation-oriented operations of the conscious system are expressed in conscious thoughts, that is, in intellectualizations and in the manifest contents of dreams and other narrative vehicles. The adaptation-oriented operations of the deep unconscious system are encoded or disguised in dreams and other narratives.

Recognizing the structural and functional differences between narrative and nonnarrative communications is vital to properly understanding the design of the emotion-processing mind and its efforts at adaptation. Narratives are the sole vehicles of unconscious communication; they are two-meaning expressions with manifest meanings linked to conscious system operations and encoded meanings that are reflections of deep unconscious adaptive responses. In contrast, intellectualizations are single message communications with manifest meanings fraught with implications that can be extracted from their contents, but they are not vehicles for encoded unconscious expressions and thus do not lend themselves to decoding efforts.

The encoded meanings of narratives can be identified solely by decoding their themes in light of the triggering events that have activated the emotion-processing mind and its deep unconscious system—a process called *trigger decoding.*

The conscious and deep unconscious systems of the emotion-processing mind operate relatively independently. Each system has its own mode of perception, adaptive knowledge and coping capacities, preferred mode of adapting and relating, defenses, value system, morals and ethics, self-image, instinctual drive needs, mode of tension regulation, and the like.

When it comes to the unconscious realm of experience, *unconscious perception,* which is incisive and relatively nondefended, is the basic unconscious operation of the emotion-processing mind. It is only after a trauma has been unconsciously perceived and processed—and the deep unconscious system does so with great accuracy and full knowledge of the meanings being conveyed—that *unconscious fantasies* come into play. These fantasies are not primarily biologically driven, but are reactions to perceived environmental threats. As such, they tend to conjure up the most grim possibilities imaginable and yet to be quite wise in their ideas about what is going on. These encoded fantasies, beliefs, and impressions involve efforts to understand why the trauma has occurred, what it truly means, and what has motivated the therapist to do or say what he or she has done or said. If the imagery is a response to a therapist's intervention, it will include a highly reliable assessment of whether the intervention is valid and if not, what unconsciously motivated the therapist to make the error—an unconsciously forged healing effort at interpretation. On the whole, these efforts are extremely sensitive, quite valid, and highly reliable.

The deep unconscious mind shows a remarkable ability to identify and express connections between current and past traumas, insights that are, however, transmitted to awareness solely in encoded form.

In carrying out its adaptive functions and generating encoded solutions to the impact of traumatic incidents, the efforts of the deep unconscious mind are governed by a powerful set of *archetypes*—universal perceptions, ways of coping, and the like. Many of these archetypes involve preferred modes of dealing with death, death-related traumas, and the death anxieties they evoke—meanings of stimuli to which the conscious mind is highly insensitive while the deep unconscious system is in constant touch.

Accurate, healing interventions by therapists are validated unconsciously by the wisdom subsystem of the deep unconscious mind. This kind of assessment and affirmation of interventions is reflected in responsive stories of wise, sensitive, helpful individuals. In contrast, an erroneous intervention is met with images of people who are blind, mistaken, insensitive, and unhelpful, while an actively harmful intervention evokes encoded themes of assault and violence.

Comparison of manifest-conscious and encoded-unconscious reactions to the same triggering event—for example, of patients' direct and encoded narrative responses to their therapists' interventions—reveal many striking features of the two systems of the emotion-processing mind, and they indicate that overall, the operations of each of these systems tend to be at odds with each other. Most notably, it has been found that the conscious system automatically obliterates and denies many anxiety-provoking traumas and many of the most troubling meanings of consciously perceived or remembered traumatic incidents. As a result, compared to their unconscious counterparts, conscious knowledge and wisdom are severely impaired and unwittingly biased towards the denial of painful realities and the death-related meanings of events such as the errant interventions made by psychotherapists. The conscious mind also is highly sensitive to and strongly affected by the presence of unconscious guilt and the need for punishment for harm done to others; as a result it tends unconsciously to skew its decisions and behaviors towards those that are self-punitive. All in all, then, the conscious mind is a poorly informed, extremely unreliable, and untrustworthy adaptive system when it comes to dealing with emotionally charged issues and the validity of therapists' interventions.

Among the many consequences of these universal features of the conscious system is that theories and therapies that are forged by conscious minds tend to be strongly influenced by denial mechanisms and needs for self-harm, and thus are likely to be flawed, incomplete, and self-defeating—and thus harmful to patients and therapists alike. These attributes are reinforced by the many lacunae in conscious system morality and the ease with which its moral principles are compromised. In contrast, deep unconscious adaptive wisdom is insightful and effective to an extent that lies far beyond any conscious-system capabilities—it is highly incisive and trustworthy. And deep unconscious morality is pristine, with adaptively ideal standards that are enforced through unconsciously mediated self-punishments for violations of, and rewards for adhering to, its invaluable basic tenets. Everyday life and the process of psychotherapy configured on the basis of conscious needs, values, preferences, wisdom, and adaptive capabilities is based on a severely compromised world view, while another, far more effective and constructive world view takes over when these endeavors are based on comparable deep unconscious faculties and viewpoints.

These realizations help to illuminate Freud's two paradigms of psychoanalysis in that the heirs to his second paradigm have a conscious system world view and thus operate on the basis of a highly uncertain, generally dysfunctional conscious-system psychology. On the other hand, the adaptive approach, which is heir to Freud's first paradigm, has been forged on the basis of the deep unconscious system world view and it has generated a psychology of great beauty and inordinate wisdom. The two paradigms are worlds apart.

In this context, two additional critical differences between the operations of the systems of the emotion-processing mind deserve mention. The first is that the deep unconscious system is extremely sensitive to rules, frames, and boundaries in both psychotherapy and life in general (Langs, 1998b). It recognizes and seeks the ideally healing, *archetypal frame* for all relationships, including those that prevail in psychotherapy. Thus there exists, and encoded communications support, a universally sought and unconsciously validated, optimal set of ground rules for a treatment experience. This position stands in contrast with the conscious system which is frame insensitive and inclined toward departures from the ideal frame, many of them unconsciously sought for self-punitive reasons (departures from the ideal frame are harmful to all concerned) and in order to gain relief from the secured frame existential death anxieties that arise when ideal conditions prevail (see below).

The second set of differences between the two systems arises with the discovery that *unconscious forms of death anxiety* are an ever-present, pervasive phenomenon and that these anxieties have enormous influence over emotionally charged decisions in everyday life and in psychotherapy—on everything from structuring the framework of treatment, the type of therapy a patient seeks and a therapist offers, to the way in which therapists intervene and patients respond to these efforts. Here too conscious reactions, which are adversely affected by the unconscious death anxieties that many interventions arouse, are markedly different from deep unconscious reactions, which tend to stand fast against these anxieties and point to ways to cope effectively with them.

There are three forms of death anxiety to which the deep unconscious mind is quite sensitive and the conscious system quite insensitive (Langs, 1997, 2006, 2008):

*Predatory death anxiety,* which is the fear of annihilation by natural disasters or through the acts of other living beings, especially other humans. The archetypal response to this anxiety is the mobilization of psychological and physical resources in order to combat the threat.

*Predator death anxiety,* which is the fear of annihilation as punishment for having harmed others. The archetypal response to this anxiety is one of deep unconscious guilt and the unconscious orchestration of self harmful acts and decisions.

And *existential death anxiety,* which is the fear of ultimate demise, that is, of personal mortality. The archetypal response to this anxiety is the use of denial which takes a myriad of behavioral and mental forms.

There are archetypal connections between frame conditions and the arousal of death anxiety. For example, all departures from the ideal, archetypal frame are experienced deep unconsciously as predatory even though they tend to be welcomed consciously because they are a way of defending against the entrapping, existential death anxieties evoked by ideal, secured frames. Unconscious predator death anxiety is aroused in therapists when they depart from the archetypal frame, thereby causing them to experience a deep unconscious sense of guilt and as a result, to engage in self-punitive behaviors that are reflected in the self-defeating ways they conduct psychotherapy and handle their personal lives.

## SOME FRESH PERSPECTIVES

Freud's creation of his second paradigm implicitly and explicitly offered several ways to deny death's enormous power over emotional life and the psychoanalytic process. He did this by claiming that sex, not death, and fantasy, not reality, are the primary issues in human life; that we have a death instinct, that is, a wish to die rather than a fear of dying (Freud, 1920); and that death is not represented in the unconscious (Freud, 1923). Even so, he did at one point acknowledge the importance of death for human life in a well known closing comment to the B'nai Brith: "We recall the old saying: Si vis pacem, para bellum. If you want to preserve peace, arm for war. It would be in keeping with the times to alter it: Si vis vitam, para mortem. If you want to endure life, prepare yourself for death" (Freud, 1915, p. 300).

There are two features of this wise comment that are relevant here. First, despite his claim that unconscious Oedipal fantasies are the core issue in emotional life, Freud was able to step back and see that dealing with life in an effective manner requires being prepared to cope with the prospect of death—the ultimate external trauma. To use Freud's own idiom, cited in the previous chapter, this was, however, his way of merely flirting with death and not an insight that he was ready or able to fully commit to and develop further. In addition, it is well to notice that Freud speaks of *preparing* for war and death, but does not mention developing strategies for *engaging* in the actual battle against death, be it in war or in life.

In this light, it can be said that Freud's second paradigm—and classical analysis to this very day—explores ways in which humans arm themselves for the archetypal war against death with which life eventually is preoccupied, consciously at times and unconsciously without let up. Learning how to relate effectively, satisfy sexual needs and resolve sexual conflicts, obtain narcissistic supplies, and interact well with others intersubjectively are ways that humans can build the ego strengths and strong sense of identity that will serve them in all manner of adaptations and most critically, in adapting to the inevitability of personal death.

It is, however, left to Freud's first paradigm to identify the nature of the battle and come up with strategies with which a skirmish or two can be won against an ultimately overwhelming enemy so powerful that defeat is inevitable. Indeed, the preoccupations of the second paradigm serve in part to create the denial-based illusion or delusion that defeat is not inevitable—even though it is and must be factored into one's adaptations to particular death-related traumas and life as a whole. The first paradigm tells us up front what this war of wars really is about, and it also offers realistic, albeit unconsciously forged, adaptive strategies for gaining temporary individual and collective victories and coming to terms with the certainty of eventual defeat. We see again that Freud's first paradigm is grounded in the archetypal realities of life on earth, while his second paradigm is in its own way a wishful fantasy system that is certain to be responsible for an unneeded amount of personal and collective emotional pain.

## SUMMING UP

This list of distinctive features of the emotion-processing mind which can be recognized through extensions of Freud's first paradigm make clear that we are in fact dealing with two very different views of the mind, emotional life, and the world in general. As for psychotherapy and psychoanalysis, it also is clear that the way that you understand the emotion-related mind and conduct psychotherapy is dramatically different depending on which paradigm guides your thinking and practice. Freud's second theory is a conscious-system paradigm, invented by conscious minds and reflective of the defenses and denial-based and self-punitive needs of the conscious system. Freud's first theory, as reflected in the adaptive approach, is a deep-unconscious paradigm that has been built on the basis of deep unconscious insights and the need for openness to all emotional issues, especially those that are death related (Langs, 2006, 2008).

All things considered, then, there appears to be a solid case for the thesis that Freud's flight from reality into fantasy, from real traumas into imagined traumas, and from environmental threats to basic biological inner needs, was misguided and thus strongly affected by unconscious needs and motives. This idea is supported by the finding that there are two sets of negative consequences to Freud's shift in focus: The first involves errors in formulating, theorizing, and the practice of psychoanalysis, while the second involves the use of the paradigm to deny and avoid critical aspects of external reality and the serious psychological dangers they pose, much of it evident only in the encoded narrative imagery to which the classical analyst is blind. Let's look now at each of these detrimental developments.


## WHAT FREUD LOST THROUGH HIS PARADIGM SHIFT

Having established that the classical and adaptive theories and their elaborations constitute two very different paradigms of the human mind and emotional life, I turn now to showing that the first theory is far superior to the second theory and that the elaborate researches and writings of second paradigm analysts, although valid in many ways, serve as well as a type of denial of death even as they offer some essential insights needed for sound emotional health.

In Rorty's (1989) terms, I am claiming that the metaphors and language of the reality-centered theory of the mind should replace the metaphors and language of the need-centered theory. This change is called for because the new language is far more explanatory, predictive, and suitable for today's world than its predecessor. Rorty indicates that this kind of change always meets with opposition from those who are accustomed to using the prevailing language, but he does not take into account psychological factors in this resistance which, in this case, involve *a shift from a benign fantasy-based language to a grim language of death.* That said, empirically speaking, much of this need for change arises because it appears that the mind-centered paradigm has taken analysts and others down a path strewn with relatively insignificant findings and not a few misconceptions. To show that this is the case, I turn now to the insights provided by the first paradigm regarding the flaws in second-paradigm thinking.

## THE FLIGHT FROM REALITY INTO FANTASY

Some previous writers (Balmary, 1979; Good, 2006) have simply argued that Freud's turn away from reality toward fantasy was inherently erroneous and thus defensive and driven by inner need rather than clinical observations. Because many later-day analysts have claimed that Freud and his followers actually did not abandon the consideration of reality factors in neuroses, we need to carefully spell out the nature of Freud's shift and its failings. These are some of the more critical considerations:

Freud's paradigm shift was based on the proposition that emotionally, fantasies are stronger and thus more influential than reality. At face value, this is an untenable contention. A later-day version of this proposition is that everyone experiences traumatic events differently, that it is not so much that the trauma *per se* is damaging, what counts is how that trauma is experienced mentally.

This viewpoint reflects a failure to recognize the existence of archetypal experiences in human emotional life, a characteristic of conscious system thinking especially as it pertains to adaptations to environmental challenges. These archetypes operate on the highly affecting deep unconscious level of experience, a realm that has not been addressed by second-paradigm psychoanalysts. The adaptive view is quite different: It has found that there is a universal core to how humans deep unconsciously experience a given type of trauma. Individuals vary in their constrained conscious responses to these universal meanings and they respond selectively to such meanings based on sensitivities derived from earlier life experiences and their current life situation. The inner-mental world view also tends to overlook the power of a trauma, especially one that is contemporaneous, to directly damage the human psyche.

There are several additional erroneous ideas to be found in second-paradigm thinking. For one, there is the belief that reality serves mainly as a source of the proper satisfaction of biological and interpersonal needs or as the trigger for the arousal of inner mental needs which, when forbidden, will activate unconscious intrapsychic conflicts. These contentions deprive reality of its role as the instigator of conscious and deep unconscious adaptive activities that have pervasive effects on the human psyche and the course of an individual's life. By implication, this proposition also serves to deny that the most powerful role played by reality in human life is the fact that humans always eventually die.

Another deficit in second-paradigm thinking is its failure to recognize the complexities of external events. There is an analogy here to the early view of the protoplasm that makes up much of the body of a living cell. Protoplasm originally was thought to be a homogeneous mass, but with advances in microscopy and chemistry, it was discovered that protoplasm is a complex entity with many different subsystems and functions previously unknown to early researchers. Much the same applies to reality, which is treated naively and superficially by second-paradigm psychoanalysts even though there are many critical nuances to the actual make-up of a real event—much of it comprehended solely by the deep unconscious system of the mind. Second-paradigm psychoanalysts occasionally consider the broad manifest meanings of an environmental event, but they take the words and actions of others at face value instead of examining them for implied and more critically, encoded, meanings.

Other contentions of dubious validity include Freud's claim that reality events trigger inner mental fantasies, needs, and conflicts and then fall to the wayside, while the aroused needs take over and dominate the psyche. This position has led to the creation of the concept of "psychic reality" which is a combination of external inputs and inner mental propensities—with the stress on the inner mental aspects. This is another way of placing emphasis on the individual experience of reality without a consideration of the existence of universal, archetypal meanings.

Also of note is the finding that the second paradigm operates on the basis of the thesis that, in contrast to all other living beings, humans are compelled to adapt first and foremost to their own inner strivings and needs. The primary adaptive concerns of all other organisms, which is to cope with environmental challenges and traumas, are believed to be secondary adaptive issues in humans. It is however quite unlikely that we are exceptions to this archetypal rule of nature and clinical research developed within the framework of the adaptive approach indicates that in fact, this is not the case.

All in all, then, buttressed by supportive research findings and consciously wrought but unreliable clinical evidence, the second paradigm appears to make use of its superficial truths to serve the human need for conscious-system denial and defense, which, by definition, renders the theory as a basically flawed approach to the human psyche. By underplaying the role of reality in emotional life, the paradigm has facilitated an approach to the human psyche in which death and its encumbrances are all but absent—even though they are in fact at the center of adult emotional life, much of it on the unconscious level of experience. Freud does indeed seem to have gone astray in forging his revised paradigm of psychoanalysis.

## The Misguided Fate of the Second Paradigm

Further evidence that Freud had made a misstep can be found by another look at the path down which his second paradigm has taken psychoanalysis, much of it inherent to Freud's new position and solidified when he invoked his structural model and theory of the mind. The result was a strong commitment to investigating the inner mental conflicts that arise between the ego and the id at the behest of the superego, and thus a further diminution of the role of reality in emotional life. Similarly, the turn to the study of developmentally focused researches, which have produced some important insights, also served to reinforce the avoidance of the role of specific external traumas in emotional life. Deceptively, the success of these efforts, which have been based on the study of manifest behaviors and communications, has tended to limit the expansion of second-paradigm thinking into new areas of study.

The structural theory also has fostered a deterioration in thinking about the realm of unconscious experience and this has led to a rejection of the critical role played by unconscious factors in emotional life. The systems in the structural model of the mind are defined by their functions rather than the status of their contents—conscious or unconscious. Thus, the idea of unconscious mental operations has faded away and because all three systems of the mind have conscious and unconscious components and functions, the actual level of awareness inherent to a given thought, fantasy, or need is believed to be of little if any consequence. The term "unconscious" is still in use to some extent but it alludes to so many different phenomena—for example, brain processes, need systems, fantasies, and the like—that it is of little import or usefulness.

The turn to mind-centered theories also has made psychoanalysis all but irrelevant to the broader issues in the world today. The problems facing societies and nations are clearly death-related with a stress on the use of violence and the religious justification of much of this violence. For most people on earth, reality imposes itself on their lives in ways that overwhelm their minds and themselves, but psychoanalysis has almost nothing to say about these realities. All in all, these limitations have contributed to the legitimate rejection in many quarters of psychoanalysis as a meaningful theory and form of therapy in today's world.

In light of the insights generated by the first paradigm into the operations of the emotion-processing mind, we can see too that the critical adaptive human capacity for *unconscious perception* has been overlooked by second-paradigm analysts. Ill-defined ideas about unconscious attunement and empathy do not do justice to the human ability to be in touch with the feelings and issues of another human being. Technically, this vagueness arises because of a failure to recognize the differences between narrative and nonnarrative communications, a missing insight that would facilitate the recognition and appreciation of distinctive deep unconscious experiences and adaptive processes. Given that the deep unconscious world of experience is the realm in which the most grim and affecting meanings of potentially disruptive traumatic events are registered and dealt with adaptively, and in which the most effective solutions to adaptive challenges are generated, the loss in human resources, individually and collectively, is enormous. Second-paradigm psy-choanalysts hear only one half of their patients' messages and of their own communications to their patients as well—and it is the lesser half. They live in a universe comparable to Abbott's *Flatland* ([1884] 1984) where missing dimensions of the universe go unrecognized. There is then a great void in the listening process and psychological understanding that can be derived from Freud's second theory of the mind. Dealing with inner needs pales in com-parison with dealing with the telling impact of external events. Indeed, the increasing richness and intricacies of the adaptive resources of living beings as they have evolved into more complex organisms, including ourselves as humans, testifies to the ever-increasing nuances of experienced environmen-tal threats and to the need to evolve sound, equally complex means of dealing with these external dangers.

## The Basic Causes of Neuroses

Psychoanalysts who adhere to Freud's second paradigm are at odds concern-ing the basic causes of emotionally founded disturbance. This lack of a uni-fied theory is in itself an indicator of an incomplete or erroneous paradigm. The main contenders are (Langs, 1998a; Pine, 2003; Good, 2006; Rangell, 2006; Rosenbaum, 2009) forbidden instinctual drives (classical Freudians), narcissistic needs (self-psychologists; Kohut, 1971, 1977), relational needs (those who adhere to object relations and intersubjectivity; Stolorow, Brand-shaft and Atwood, 1987; Mitchell, 1988; Rosenbaum, 2009) and maturational needs (Jungians; Jung, 1968, 1972). While each of these classes of needs do indeed contribute to emotional health or illness, much of it according to how they are dealt with by caretakers and others, one reason why none of these subtheories has become dominant in second-paradigm thinking is that, by the standards set by the first paradigm, the most fundamental cause of emotional maladaptations—death and its attendant anxieties—is not a central concern of any of these subtheories. Put another way, each of these theories may be viewed as a highly sophisticated *denial of death system.* Indeed, death is seldom mentioned in these writings, is never a focal point for analytic ideas, and even when patently at issue clinically, it is pushed to the side in favor of other considerations or interpreted upward as not really alluding to death *per se* but serving as a representation of some other issue like a patient's iden-tity or self-image and the like (see Langs, 2006; Rosenbaum, 2009). This observation suggests that symptom relief in second-paradigm therapies may stem in large measure from the analyst's avoidance of their patients' death-related issues and of the traumatic sources of their personal death anxieties. Other forms of paradoxical, unconsciously mediated relief also have been identified in connection with second-paradigm forms of treatment (Langs, 1985). They include relief due to patients' unconscious needs to idealize their analysts and their therapeutic results, patients' finding support through analysts' unconscious sanctions of their pathological behaviors, and from patients' unconscious comparisons with their analysts through which they realize unconsciously that they are far more healthy than their analysts. In one study (Langs, 1985), it was found that all but one of the twenty patients who were interviewed after their therapy was terminated found relief in one area of functioning but suffered fresh symptoms in another area. There is much work to be done to determine the actual extent to which second-paradigm patients do or do not achieve lasting symptom relief and improved emotional functioning based on their work with their analysts.

Another area of oversight involves the extensive role played by rules, frames, and boundaries in emotional life and the therapeutic process (Langs, 1998b). The adaptive approach has revealed the existence of an archetypal frame which is universally and consistently sought and validated by the deep unconscious system of the emotion-processing mind through its encoded narratives. The second paradigm overlooks the pervasive role played by these aspects of the psychoanalytic situation because they are encoded in narrative communications and must be trigger decoded in light of frame-related interventions to appreciate their importance and profound effects.

Working with manifest contents and their implications and without a sound method of validating their frame-related efforts, second-paradigm psychoanalysts have failed to make use therapeutically of sound interventions related to this aspect of the therapeutic experience. Because of the existential death anxieties that are evoked by the ideal archetypal frame, classical analysts, whose therapeutic efforts are designed unconsciously to defend against such anxieties, lean towards a variable-frame approach. In contrast, therapists who make use of Freud's first paradigm strongly favor secured frames because on the deep unconscious level of experience, they are the only frames to obtain validation and they have enormous healing powers. Adaptive therapists also have found that modified frames—that is, departures from the deep unconsciously sought archetypal, ideal condition for therapy—are universally and rightfully experienced as harmful and damaging in ways that are largely unconsciously perceived and mediated—and thus of real consequence.

The prevailing ideas and techniques that pertain to the ground rules of treatment differ markedly in the efforts made by analysts working within the framework of each of the two paradigms. This vital area of therapeutic experience is the domain of many second-paradigm misconceptions, especially in regard to the harm caused unconsciously by therapists' self-revelations to their patients and other noninterpretive interventions. In addition, because of the failure to recognize universal frame-related archetypes, second-paradigm analysts have no means of arriving at a consensus as to the nature of sound principles of frame management. All in all, guided by deep unconscious validation, first-paradigm therapists tend to work in optimally secured frames, while second-paradigm therapists, guided by patients' often misguided conscious reactions to frame-related interventions, tend to vary in their approach to the ground rules of treatment and to be quite lax in this regard—and unknowingly harmful to their patients and themselves as a result.

## Some Consequences of Freud's Paradigm Shift

Psychoanalysis is a biological science and as such, issues of survival and sound ways to adapt should be of primary concern. But because of its adaptation-avoiding aspects, Freud's second theory actually includes many patently maladaptive behaviors among its norms. Let's look at some of these evidently errant ideas.

### The Concept of Transference

A prime example of a second-paradigm concept that defies biological norms is the concept of transference, which posits that patients basically misperceive the intentions and interventions of their analysts, thereby staking a claim for an essentially maladaptive mind. The transference concept implies that the human mind is inclined to misread immediate reality in a manner that threatens rather than serves survival. Because there is no evident survival value to such mistakes, the thesis of transference goes against fundamental evolutionary and adaptive principles.

Freud gingerly introduced the concept of transference in his contribution to *Studies on Hysteria,* written with Josef Breuer (Breuer and Freud, 1893–1895). Even though he was in his trauma-centered phase of thinking, he posited that his patients, without due cause on his part, transferred their beliefs and fantasies towards figures from their childhood onto him as their analyst. This suggests that evidently without realizing it, Freud was already sowing the seeds of his second, mind-centered paradigm. As such, the evident flaws in the transference concept also foreshadow the flaws that would be inherent to second-paradigm thinking. Thus, while followers of Freud's second paradigm view his propositions regarding the nature of transferences as one of his greatest discoveries, critics of the concept, such as Chertok

(1968), Little (1951), and Szasz (1963) see it as a largely defensive, denial-based invention.

The key idea as formulated by Freud (Breuer and Freud, 1893–1895) was—and still is—that patients enter analysis with unconscious memories of early harm from caretakers and project the resultant view of the caretaker onto the analyst even though the analyst has done nothing to deserve it. Later on, Freud (1912a, 1914a) proposed that transferences are based on fantasies that distort the patient's picture and experience of the analyst. In current practice, there is some acknowledgment that the analyst may evoke a transference reaction, but the stress remains on the patient's intrapsychic experience and interpretation of the triggering comment or behavior—the image is of an innocent analyst and a misguided patient.

Since many discussions of transference are poorly grounded in clinical data, it is important to note that Freud invoked the concept only when a patient spoke directly of him and of matters and people connected with him (see Freud, 1918). Thus the concept is grounded in conscious, manifest allusions to the analyst which are seen as unjustified and based on earlier life experiences, and which are either inferred by the analyst or revealed in a patient's subsequent associations to the transference idea or image. Conscious perceptions prevail and unconscious perceptions, as defined by the adaptive approach, are not a consideration.

The criticisms of the concept offered by Little (1951) and Szasz (1963) are centered around issues pertaining to the powers of reality compared to those of fantasy. They stress the fact that the transference concept assumes that the analyst is in reality innocent of wrong-doing, but is seen or fantasized as doing wrong by the mistaken patient who confuses the past with the present. Based on their own clinical experience, they regarded this position as untenable.

The circumstance surrounding the invention of the concept of transference, as described by Freud (1914b) and presented in historical detail by Chertok (1968) and Good (2006), is of relevance to the present discussion of Freud's two paradigms and the issue of which factor is dominant in emotional life—reality or fantasy. The defining moment for the invocation of the concept arose when Freud, who was seeing therapy patients in sanitaria and in their homes, gave a body massage to a young woman patient in her bed at home and then put her into a trance. When the patient awoke from the trance, she threw her arms around Freud and exclaimed her love for him. Convinced that he hadn't done anything to arouse this love, he decided that the patient's father must have been seductive and was the real object of her ardor. Thus was born the concept of transference in the guise of an the innocent analyst who is the undeserving victim of the patient's imagination and past seducers. This need to believe in their own innocence has persisted among second-paradigm analysts to this day. Their only nod to reality lies with the minimally interactive idea that the analyst may in some vague and general way provoke transference reactions, but the patient misreads these provocations or recruits them for their own pathological inner reasons.

The first paradigm has developed a more complex and tenable position in this regard. It finds that within a relatively secured frame, conscious distortions by patients of the efforts of their therapists are quite rare. The approach also introduces an aspect of the therapeutic relationship and interaction that is missing from the second paradigm, namely, the existence of patients' valid unconscious perceptions of the soundness of their therapists' constructive interventions and a related unconscious appreciation for therapeutic errors in regard to both frame management and efforts at interpretation. Remarkably, the deep unconscious system has the capability of accurately evaluating the soundness of an intervention and encodes its assessment in narrative communications. The system's evaluations offer a reliable guide to sound therapeutic techniques—interpretive and frame-related.

This is another example of the differences in viewpoint as seen through the two Freudian paradigms: The second paradigm sees the patient as someone who often mistakenly attributes negative qualities to a therapist's realistically helpful interventions, while the first paradigm sees the patient as mistakenly idealizing the therapist consciously when in truth, as unconsciously perceived by the patient, the therapist is making interventions that are harmful and disruptive.

Thinking in the context of the second paradigm tends to be ahistorical in that it posits basic fixed inner needs that are expressed and projected into situations that have little or no bearing on their activation. While this approach tends now to be interactionally cast, it is not definitively adaptive nor does it acknowledge responses to the universal meanings of therapists' interventions. Instead, it leans towards identifying the individual conscious perceptions and beliefs implied in a patient's behaviors and communications. In addition, in a relativistic manner, the patient and therapist attempt to create mutually constructed, shared views of the realities and distortions inherent to their interaction and to the patient's experience of its features. However, because the paradigm is a conscious-system approach laced with denial mechanisms, both patient and therapist tend to idealize the analyst as an essentially empathic and healing individual. Studies of patients' deep unconscious experiences of the interventions used by these analysts give lie to this picture. The deep unconscious mind perceives many empathic failures at times when analysts are consciously convinced that they are quite in tune with the needs and meanings of the communications of their patients (Langs, 2006). Much of this confusion prevails because there is no arbiter of the truth value of second-paradigm interventions and propositions.

## The Role of Death and Death Anxiety

Functionally, the various subtheories derived from the second paradigm distract both patient and analyst from the death-related issues in patients' lives and in the material communicated in their sessions. There are countless clinical examples in the literature in which death-related imagery is either ignored or interpreted upwards to allude, not to death, but to narcissistic and relational needs (Langs, 2006; Rosenbaum, 2009). The unrecognized, unconsciously driven determination of the conscious mind to deny death and its encumbrances—the very stuff that the first paradigm is made of—wreaks havoc with second paradigm thinking.

The differences between the two paradigms is especially clear when we compare the basic position that each has regarding death and death anxiety. The first paradigm sees death-related traumas and human mortality as the ultimate challenge and most disruptive—and creative—force in emotional life. It recognizes through its use of trigger decoding that *unconscious death anxiety* is a silent but ever-present force in human existence. In contrast, the very notion of unconscious death anxiety is absent from second-paradigm thinking—it is a factor that operates beyond the range of its radar. This blind spot is, as noted, reminiscent of *Flatland,* the book by Abbott (1884) about geometrical beings who live in a two dimensional world without the least awareness of a third dimension.

## Other Limitations

Another limiting feature of the second paradigm is its stress on individual uniqueness and on the differences between individuals and their analytic experiences. This view arises because while the design of the conscious mind is archetypal, its operations—that is, conscious choices and behaviors—are far more individualized than universal. There is of course the universality of the Oedipus complex as posited by Freud and the series of archetypes proposed by Jung (1972)—those of the hero, warrior, victim, anima and animus, and the like. But these are behavioral patterns rather than unconsciously determined perceptions and adaptive responses to life's most fundamental challenges. Missing from the second paradigm are the critical universal ways humans experience certain kinds of common traumas as well as a recognition that archetypes constrain and unconsciously direct individual reactions.

Missing too are the many adaptive archetypes that have been discovered by first paradigm therapists, including a group of powerful, behavior-predicting, death-related archetypes that have an enormous influence on human choices and actions.

As a final indication of the vulnerability experienced by second-paradigm practitioners, consciously and unconsciously, there is the way in which their paradigm supports a closed system approach that erects impenetrable barriers to any form of psychology that questions or threatens its basic tenets. I have already alluded to the efforts by Freud and others to suppress the attempts by Abraham and Ferenczi (Masson, 1984) to redress the relative neglect of reality factors in emotional disturbances and their treatment. Similarly, despite the adaptive approach's commitment to viable healing secured frames and to sound therapeutic techniques, its extensive writings and unconsciously validated tenets have been ignored by second paradigm analysts. As Rorty (1989) has pointed out, the absence of free discourse speaks for a nonliberal society with compromised morals.

In sum, then, while the first paradigm readily endeavors to test out the validity of the ideas of the various schools of psychoanalysis that have been established on the basis of second-paradigm thinking and to make use of the propositions they have proposed that are supported by encoded, unconscious validation, adherents to the second paradigm, virtually without exception, have turned a deaf ear to the ideas developed by those who have contributed to the development of the first paradigm. Despite the evident validity of many of the propositions of the first paradigm, they have not cited or made use of its model of the mind and its unique insights have not been afforded the least consideration. They have erected a stone wall of silence set against first paradigm thinking for underlying reasons of which they are, whatever their conscious rationalizations, entirely unaware. Their denial of first paradigm findings and principles is not only anti-scientific but also an expression of their deep and unresolved need to deny reality and death, much as it must have been for Freud at the time of his paradigm shift.

This brings me to another failing of Freud's second paradigm. The inner mental approach not only prevents psychoanalysis from unearthing much needed insights into the hidden forces driving world affairs, past and present, it also directs students of human life, such as the biographers of great leaders, to investigate minor and inconsequential factors in their lives such as their sexual conflicts, relational problems and narcissistic wounds. This has resulted in the generation of extremely clichéd psychoanalytic biographical formulations and mundane historical insights. The adaptive approach calls for a very different search, that is, for the death-related traumas and other realistic factors that took place in the lives of the prominent individuals who affected the course of human history—and others of note as well. From this vantage point, the search must be made for early- and later-life death-related traumas because the approach has shown that these incidents—their nature, the conditions under which they were experienced, as well as when and why they took place—are the source of the unconscious motives that drive human life and the vicissitudes of our civilization.

Finally, I come back to the question as to why second paradigm psychoanalysts are so impervious to the wisdom of the first paradigm. This is tantamount to asking the key question raised in this book: Why did Freud abandon his most promising first paradigm and why did he fail to engage in a detailed study of the complexities of both realms—inner mental and outer reality? For the first paradigm analyst, this is tantamount to calling for a search for the early-life traumas that unconsciously drove Freud to abandon reality and to use the Oedipus complex as a means of looking away from the real world and focusing on the inner one. Because these forces evidently operated unconsciously, we can assume that these traumas must have been, either in their entirety or in regard to their most critical meanings, repressed and obliterated. If we can discover the nature of these traumas in the life of Freud—and he does offer us an enormous amount of narrative material to facilitate the search for encoded representations of these far-reaching, hidden incidents—we can then make use of our knowledge of archetypes to develop some likely hypotheses as to why he turned away from reality into fantasy—and why present-day analysts continue to do so. Indeed, the blind acceptance of the basic aspects of Freud's second paradigm suggests that these trauma-evoked defensive needs are a universal feature of the emotion-processing mind and indicates that if we are able to solve the mystery of Freud's obliterated traumatic past we will be well on the road to understanding the trauma-relayed issues of psychoanalysts—and humankind—in general. This in turn should tell us why there is for all therapists, classical and adaptive, such a desperate need to deny the potentially devastating emotional impact of external events on our lives and the lives of our psychotherapy patients—and why one very small group has overcome this need while the other has not. It also will help us to clarify the archetypal need for second-paradigm analysts and others to exclude those who try to wake them from their misguided but unrecognized state of slumber.

To begin our historical search, then, let's turn again to the story of how and why Freud's paradigm shift came about.

# Chapter 5

# Freud in Conflict

As we have seen, the death of Freud's father in 1896 seems to have played a significant role in his shift in focus from actual seductions to fantasied seductions and then to wishes to seduce—and murder. Nevertheless, like all tragedies—and the turn away from reality is tragic because it was a wrong turn—there is a powerful back-story to this tale and it begins, like the tragedy of Oedipus, before Freud's birth and extends into his earliest years of life. If I am correct in this conjecture, we can be quite sure that these traumas affected his maturational years and choice of profession, his shift from neurology to psychiatry, and within psychiatry from the study of hereditary and physical causes to those that are psychological. These adverse events also must have evoked a strong need in Freud to unravel the mysteries of the mind and its dysfunctions as they would illuminate the lives and neuroses of both his patients and himself—the two being totally intertwined.

Freud's personal story inevitably is linked to the history of his psycho-analytic thinking. And here we shall be concerned mainly with that part of the story that built to a climax with the aging and deteriorating health of his father, an experience that Freud went through as he turned forty. Whatever the unconscious disturbing ramifications of this situation were for Freud, they seem to have intensified to an unbearable degree with his father's death—and even more so with the first anniversary of that death. It is likely that the theo-retical missteps that Freud took at that time were based to a significant extent first, on long repressed early-life traumas and second, on additional recent traumas of which we have little or no record.

The specific exciting incident for this world class drama is, then, the anni-versary of the death of Freud's father which was soon followed by Freud's letter to Fliess in which he announced that he no longer believed his *neurotica*

(Freud , 1954, Letter 69, September 21, 1897, pp. 215-218). Freud's intense reaction to this first anniversary was foreshadowed by two developments whose role in his decision to abandon reality have not generally been recognized by others.

## HOW DREAMS ARE DISGUISED

The first development involved an insight that came to Freud in one fell swoop on July 24, 1895, four years before the death of his father (Freud, 1900). It was of such monumental proportions that Freud himself imagined the placement of a marble tablet that would commemorate his achievement. He envisioned that the tablet would be inscribed with these words:

> In This House, on July 24th, 1895 the secret of dreams was Revealed to Dr. Sigm. Freud. (Freud, 1954, Letter 137, December 6, 1900, p. 322)

Freud was alluding to his discovery or sharpened realization that dreams are the carrier of two messages; that they embody two sets of meanings. One set is manifest—the dream as dreamt—and the other set is disguised within the very same images. But in addition to recognizing that dreams have manifest and latent contents, Freud had unearthed the Rosetta Stone that held the key to breaking the dream code. Having identified the means by which the latent contents of a dream is transformed into a manifest set of dream images, he had only to reverse or undo this process of disguise in order to be able to detect the camouflaged messages contained in manifest dream sequences.

Shifting to the present for a moment, second-paradigm psychoanalysts accept these ideas in principle, but nevertheless tend to work solely with manifest dream contents and their themes as if they were not disguised but instead point directly to a patient's emotional issues and fantasies. For example, efforts to undo disguised instinctual drive wishes are rare in the literature, while extracting the implications of manifest dream themes is in common practice. In contrast, actually undoing the disguises that camouflage the unconscious meanings of a manifest dream and thereby gaining access to a dream's latent meanings, largely in terms of unconscious perceptions (rather than unconscious fantasies) is standard practice in adaptive psychotherapy—it is at the heart of the process known as *trigger* decoding (Langs, 2004).

In any case, it is well to appreciate that Freud's discovery involved a basic archetypal property of the communicative capabilities of the human mind—the ability to express two or more messages in a single narrative image. Also archetypal is the specific mechanisms that he identified as the means by which unconscious contents are encoded into a dream—the use of condensation (the capacity of a single image to convey multiple meanings), displacement (the use of images about one subject to convey unconscious messages about another, related subject), and symbolization (the use of a universal manifest image to represent another, related unconscious image). To these mechanisms he added secondary revision and concerns for representability—mechanisms that render most dreams intelligible.

In 1895, then, Freud discovered the means by which he and future analysts could undo the camouflage built into dreams and thereby access the unconscious realm of mental experience. Freud emphasized that these mechanisms of disguise apply equally to dreams and emotional symptoms, which meant that he had thereby unearthed the secret to symptom formation as well.

With these insights in hand, he began to develop the psychoanalytic techniques through which the secrets of emotional symptoms could be brought into awareness by undoing the disguises that helped to create a symptom-related manifest dream. His focus was on the unconscious conflicts that are caused by forbidden, censored unconscious wishes and fantasies which press for discharge and expression. The therapeutic goal was to expose these disguised conflicts to conscious awareness, doing so for both the wish and repressive defenses against their expression. This would then enable the patient to knowingly resolve his or her previously unrealized issues.

But these insights, which Freud applied to inner mental wishes and needs, also can be broadened into a basic archetype that holds true for his rejected trauma theory as well. The four mental mechanisms that Freud identified as the essential means by which the human mind disguises anxiety-provoking, unconscious fantasies are the same mental mechanisms that the human mind uses to disguise anxiety-provoking traumatic experiences—unbearable realities past and present. Within this framework, the undoing of these disguises is guided by the triggering event to which the patient is reacting. The rather arbitrary decoding process that characterizes the rare efforts at decoding carried out by second-paradigm analysts—without an anchoring trigger, multiple interpretations are common—is replaced by a procedure that is constrained and guided by the nature and meanings of the triggering incident for a given dream image. In addition, examining patients' narrative responses to trigger decoded interpretations allows for an assessment of the validity or nonvalidity of these efforts and keeps them on track. The wide range of possible dream interpretations and the absence of an unconscious means of validation are features of the second paradigm that motivate analysts to favor Freud's *laissez faire* second theory over the more stringent but also more reliable trauma-centered paradigm and its techniques.

During the time that Freud wrote *The Interpretation of Dreams* (Freud 1900), the disguised secrets embedded in dreams were thought to be unconscious fantasies, wishes, and such. We do not know to what extent Freud initially used his landmark insights to explore and interpret his patients' and his own dreams during the time he was convinced that early-life seductions were the main source of adult neuroses. He may well have made considerable progress along these lines. These advances would have moved him closer to exposing the hidden truths of his own early-life traumas and would have increased his anxiety over their being finally revealed to him through his decoding efforts—a most unbearable prospect. These are the kinds of critical issues that affect basic decisions in the emotional realm. Constellations of early traumas that operate unconsciously and that reach awareness in encoded form, which is usually the case, have an enormous influence on a psychoanalyst's choice of profession and preferred theoretical orientation—and all of our lives in general.

Following his 1895 discoveries, then, Freud had two sets of insight to work with: First, his seduction hypothesis and second, his ability to decode the unconscious messages embodied in dreams. A look at his writings before his paradigm shift in 1897, especially his case reports in *Studies on Hysteria* (Breuer and Freud, 1893–1895), reveal that Freud was to some extent trying to apply his insights into the mechanisms of dream disguise to his patients' free associations and using this technique to gain access to the unconscious aspects of their early experiences of seduction. Whatever efforts he also applied to his own dreams, it seems likely that he intensified these efforts when his father became ill and even more so after the anniversary of his death in 1897 when Freud began his formal self-analysis.

During this period, Freud did not however look into the distinction between patients' direct recall of an early childhood seduction and their recollection of such traumas as encoded in their manifest dreams. In working with dreams, Freud's goal was the lifting of the repressive defenses that barred a traumatic memory from directly entering awareness and thus he strove to facilitate a breakthrough of the memory, whole cloth, into conscious awareness. As a result, the search was made for either an existing memory that had eluded censorship or a repressed memory that could be coaxed into direct awareness through interpretations that resolved the use of defenses.

The adaptive approach has shown, however, that consciously remembered early traumas either screen other, more disturbing traumas or have aspects to them that are not recalled directly; these aspects are especially anxiety-provoking and they emerge solely in encoded form in patients' dreams and stories. The traumas that can be gleaned solely through trigger decoding need to be reconstructed based on these decoding efforts and they must obtain unconscious validation to assure their accuracy and cogency. This last effort, when successful, is especially healing because the repressed and obliterated aspects of early traumas exert far more influence than the parts of memories that are consciously recalled.

The probability that Freud was unconsciously experiencing a conflict of this kind is supported by adaptive studies which have shown that patients in psychotherapy not only create intense unconsciously driven resistances against the direct recall of significant early life traumas, they also strongly resist communicating the encoded dreams and stories that convey these events in disguise. Everyone—patients and therapists alike—has a set of communicative defenses with which they unconsciously oppose and interfere with the generation of a full network of meaningful, trigger-evoked narrative expressions. One of these defenses is the inability to associate dream elements with narratives of actual past events. This blockage is important because these associated incidents tend to be more powerful emotionally, and far more revelatory when trigger decoded, than the elements of the dream itself.

With his discovery of how to decode dreams, Freud's past undoubtedly was moving in on him. And because his father appears to have been a central figure in the repressed traumas that were threatening to become available for trigger decoding, quite naturally, his father's illness and death would have increased the likelihood of a dramatic breakthrough. In general, current traumas and the anniversary of these traumas tend to create increasing pressures for less and less disguised expressions of these events. Thus, Freud's communicative defenses may have been diminishing during these trying times and an emergency defensive measure became sorely needed. The shift of the locus of the pursuit from reality to fantasy was ideally suited for this purpose.

Archetypically, obliterated traumas always are death-related. As a result, by virtue of evolved design, the conscious mind is naturally opposed to and resists any movement towards their revelation—disguised or undisguised. As second-paradigm psychoanalysts bear witness to, everything possible is done to avoid trigger decoding the aroused, encoded expressions of these traumas—such efforts are not part of their techniques of psychoanalysis. Towards this end, death related themes are ignored and interpreted to have benign meanings other than those that are grimly death-related. And in their work with dreams, there is no appreciation of the importance of narrative guided associations to their elements—stories of actual events that tend to be less disguised and more openly death-related than the images in the average manifest dream. Finally, efforts at reconstructing these death-related traumas based on triggering decoding patients' narrative images is either not attempted or is abandoned before it bears fruit.

It seems likely, then, that Freud's communicative defenses began to weaken under the pressure of the death-related anniversaries he was experiencing, events that were connected with his repressed and obliterated early-life traumas. For this reason, his encoded imagery may well have been becoming less and less disguised. If so, he would have been compelled to resort to a new defensive strategy. This is quite likely the immediate unconscious reason he gave up his seduction theory of neuroses—if his unconscious mind would not stop encoding translatable representations of actual past traumas, his conscious mind would treat them as unreal fantasies.

## EIGHT POSSIBLE TRAUMAS

It seems to have taken Freud some six weeks or so after losing his way to restore his communicative defenses to a point where he could feel safe to move forward again. But before we get to that moment in history, let's go back over his story, keeping in mind these new ideas about what was likely to have been going on.

Four weeks after the death of his father, Freud informed Fliess that he had made a major revision in his seduction theory (Freud, 1954, letter 52, December 6, 1896, pp. 173–181) in that he now proposed that it was fathers who almost always were at fault. This shift in his position evidently moved Freud a step closer to the early-life traumas he had suffered at his father's hands in his earliest years.

Four weeks earlier, around the time his father died, Freud revealed the other side of his ambivalent feelings about reconstructing his own past. In a letter to Fliess written a few days after the death of his father (Freud, 1954, Letter 50, November 2, 1896, pp. 170–171), Freud described a dream which he later reported again in *The Interpretation of Dreams* (Freud, 1900). It was dreamt the night before or the night after his father's funeral—he gives conflicting dates in connection with the two descriptions of the dream. The dream, which I shall explore in detail in the next chapter, involves Freud seeing a sign that has two simultaneous messages: Thou shall close the eye; thou shall close the eyes.

Among the dream's likely multiple meanings, it seems to hint at the solution to his dilemma in regard to revealing or concealing his traumatic past—one that Freud will openly turn to a year later . The instruction he issues to himself is to shut his eyes twice over, to not see rather than see. As suggested by Krull (1979), we may think of this as a message sent in some manner to Freud by his father, but it must be Freud's message to himself as well.

It appears, then, that in the midst of his unconscious efforts to defy nature by sustaining his reality-centered theory of neuroses, Freud was beginning to show signs of weakening his resolve and caving in to the universal need for a not-seeing, death-denying theory. The closing of the eyes can be thought of as preparing the way to a death-denying paradigm in order to combat the evidently mounting pressures that he was experiencing to express and deal with his early life traumas on the occasion of the death of his father and its first anniversary. Nature, archetypal and personal, conspired against his holding firm with his seduction hypothesis and remaining open to decoding the narratives that embodied these hurtful incidents. This pressure is evident in the contents of the dream which, as I shall conjecture in chapter 8, through condensation, probably encoded clues to the very traumas he was trying to prevent entry into his conscious awareness.

The pressures on Freud to shift away from reality and its ties to past traumas were enormous. To further appreciate the intensity of his situation we have only to list the possible or likely early-life traumas that he may have been dealing with unconsciously—there are few if any indications that his struggle with his past took place within his conscious awareness. There are eight powerful, death-related early-life traumas that have been or can be postulated as having occurred before Freud's birth and during the earliest months and years of his life—and his father was involved in each of them. Seven of these postulated incidents have been mentioned or explored in the literature (Balmary, 1979; Krull, 1979) and one of them, perhaps the most powerful incident of them all, has been explored in a limited manner in a previous book of my own (Langs, 2008).

The Eight possible traumas are:

First, the death in their infancy of two of Jakob Freud's children from his first marriage to Sally Kanner, long before Freud was born.

Second, the death of Sally Kanner in 1852, again well before Freud was born.

Third, the possible suicide of Jakob's second wife, Rebekka, whose existence was concealed from Freud and the world at large. This took place some two to three years before Freud's birth.

Fourth, the possible infidelities of Jakob Freud during his marriage to Freud's mother, Amalie. A weaker variation on this theme is that Jakob masturbated and in some way had let his son know about it and had indicated that it should be kept secret.

Fifth, that Freud was born on March 6, 1856 and not as family lore has had it, on May 6, 1856. This would have made Freud a bastard child.

Sixth, that Freud's mother, Amalie, had an affair with her step-son, Phillip, who was much closer to her age than her husband, Jakob.

Seventh, that Freud was never sure of the identity of his biological father, that is, whether it was Jakob or Phillip Freud. Indications are that this trauma could have been the most powerful unconscious determinant of Freud's paradigm shift and the most disturbing death-related trauma in his early life.

Eighth and last, the death of his brother Julius when Freud was less than two years old. This is the only trauma of the group regarding which we can be certain that Freud was fully aware of consciously. His reaction to this loss involved conscious feelings of guilt caused by his wish to be rid of this rival for his mother's love. While a consciously recalled trauma may have many critical unconscious ramifications, a review of Freud's life and his missteps suggests that this loss, however terrible, did not have a major impact on his psychoanalytic thinking.

## FREUD'S COMMUNICATIVE DEFENSES

It appears, then, that Freud was compelled throughout his life to deal with a massive series of traumas and that he did so largely on the unconscious level of experience. Archetypically, his conscious mind would devote itself far more to obliterating the clues to these incidents than it would to supporting their revelation. Here too a compromise would be wrought: Moments in which Freud generated encoded imagery that lent itself to trigger decoding and the revelation of one or more of these past traumas alternating with the development of a strong set of obliterating communicative defenses.

Whenever a current event activates the memories of a damaging incident, the conscious mind will react in ways that defy prediction. At times, there is an unconsciously wrought diminution of the use of disguise with emergence of encoded themes that are far less disguised than in previous dreams and stories. Usually, this reduction in communicative defense lasts only for a brief period of time and is generally followed by a shoring up of these defenses with the generation of more heavily disguised encoded imagery which is especially difficult for the patient to associate to and for the therapist to decode. In effecting this shift towards stronger communicative resistances, the conscious system resorts to a series of typical communicative defenses: A failure to remember current dreams; a seeming inability to associate narrative incidents called forth by any dream imagery that does emerge; in the absence of a current dream, an inability to make up a story that could serve as a dream equivalent—a so-called origination narrative (Langs, 2004) and as the source of narrative associations; and if all else fails and a potentially revelatory network of thinly disguised narrative themes does emerge, there is an inability on the part of the patient to trigger decode the narrative material in a way that facilitates the reconstruction of the early trauma to which it pertains.

The expression of these defensive communicative archetypes are found in both psychoanalysts and their patients, and in the opposition among analysts and some therapy patients to the adaptive approach which facilitates this kind of trigger-decoded reconstructive work. In therapy sessions in which a patient's early trauma has been activated unconsciously, we often see an archetypal flight from reality of the kind made by Freud. Thus, patients tend to ignore or deny the activating, currently traumatic events that have triggered their narrative imagery, but in addition, they tend to offer self-interpretations focused on inner needs and conflicts, the implications of their manifest material, repetitive patterns of behavior, and such—all of this in lieu of interpretations that are trigger decoded and reality-centered. Much the same applies to the therapeutic work carried out by their therapists. With his flight from reality and shift to inner mental issues, then, Freud was embracing an archetype that is, at its core, an effort to build and reinforce communicative defenses set against the recovery of early-life traumas and the devastating death anxieties that are evoked by both their encoded and conscious expression.

Freud's denial of the crucial role played by reality in both dreams and emotional symptoms is definitively stated in his dream book of 1900. He wrote there that realities in the form of day's residues evoke inner unconscious fantasies, memories, and wishes and that they then fall to the wayside—that is, that actual events activate inner needs and create psychic realities but have little direct impact of their own on the psyche. This dropping away of reality and its replacement with inner beliefs and fantasies places the human psyche in the unique and unnatural position of being the only organ system in living beings that is not in some lasting manner directly affected by the damage caused by traumatic environmental events. This is a biologically untenable position that has been invoked in the service of denial rather than as an expression of a sound insight.

The core of denial involved in this default position is most clearly seen in adaptive psychotherapy when it is indicated to patients seen in consultation that they will, in their therapy, be working with their dreams and other narratives in order to access the unconscious traumas and issues that are driving their emotional ills. These patients have no choice but to make a choice: They may decide consciously to go forward with the therapy and communicate narratives like dreams to which they associate further narrative material. Or they may instead either decide against entering this form of therapy or begin treatment but become frozen with a seeming inability to remember their dreams or make up a story. Instead, they stay fixed on their manifest communications and engage in need-centered intellectualizations, ruminations, naïve self-analyses and self-interpretations, and the like—that is, they do almost anything but communicate in the narrative mode. Such patients, and they are quite common, do not last long in this treatment mode; their dread of the recall and reactivation of their death-related, unconsciously remembered experiences is more than they can bear.

Adaptive psychotherapy offer patients the unique gains, insights and emotional relief that comes from meaningfully reworking and coming to terms with prior traumas—self-inflicted and inflicted by others as probably was the case with Freud. Years of clinical experience shows that almost no one can on their own carry out the steps of the adaptive trigger decoding process that takes a person from a manifest dream to a trigger decoded insight—the help of an adaptive therapist is essential.

There is but one known therapeutic pathway down which this journey to recollection and insight can be effected—any divergence from this pathway is a communicative resistance (Langs, 1993, 2004, 2006). The path is entered by remembering a current manifest dream (or making up a story—a dream-equivalent); responding to its elements with guided narrative associations about actual past incidents; moving on to identifying the triggering events that have evoked this pool of images; and finally, linking the triggers to the themes. Thus, the process culminates in the trigger decoding of patients' valid unconscious perceptions of the therapists' interventions and the reconstruction of past traumas—all subject to encoded, unconscious validation. It is then this pathway which is blocked again and again by communicative defenses and other archetypal forms of resistance such as taking flight from reality.

Freud stood on the threshold of moving deeply into this most compelling pathway, but he turned away from it at the very moment that he seems to have been on the verge of a major breakthrough. Then, after pausing briefly to catch his breath, he entered a far less important, yet alluringly far less meaningful alternative pathway, one down which most humans were—and are—prepared to follow him, far more so than had he stayed on course. Paradoxically, then, his flight into a denial of reality and death met his own archetypal needs and those of other psychologists and as a result, enabled him to develop the psychoanalytic movement—albeit one that was founded on conscious-system denial. Denial of death made psychoanalysis possible, but in an impossible form.

This discussion brings to mind the fairy tale of the emperor's new clothes. The population is in denial, refusing to acknowledge that the emperor is naked—that is, vulnerable to death, much as they are. Only a naïve, innocent little child sees the truth—that is, that no one, even a king, is exempt from death. One individual against the masses, one truth teller among many liars (Bion, 1977).

The story speaks to the situation in psychoanalysis where the masses buy into Freud's second, denial-of-death paradigm, and here and there one individual stands against the masses and sees that not even psychoanalysts and their patients are immune to the inevitability of death. And by the way, archetypically, contrary to the happy ending of the fairy tale in which the people accept the boy's view, we can be sure that the true story is that the child was stoned to death by the populace. This is how humans handle harbingers of death and how Freud created psychoanalysis—by silencing the Freud that knew on some level that death is the ultimate issue in life.

For a month or two after repudiating his seduction theory, Freud was without a position on the nature of neurosogenesis. But then, based largely on his ongoing self-analysis, he discovered the Oedipus complex which proved to be his main thrust into the world of archetypes—and a limited and misconceived one at that (see chapter 8). Freud's interpretation of this complex turned his initial thinking on its ear (Balmary, 1979): Instead of being the victim of a seduction, the patient became the perpetrator—in fantasy. With an unconscious universal need of minor emotional import in hand, and an extremely biased interpretation of the myth that effectively screened out critical aspects of reality, Freud could proceed with his self-analysis. And for the world at large, he could continue his study of dreams and their latent, unconscious meanings and his investigations of the nature of neuroses and the psychoanalytic experience. Each of these efforts would be focused on inner mental needs, fantasies, motives and conflicts to the relative exclusion of the impact of actual events and when traumatic, their power to damage the mind and cause emotional symptoms. Unwittingly, Freud had made a choice between decoding reality and decoding fantasies and he could proceed with his efforts to develop psychoanalysis only after he had assured himself that the decoding would be inner- rather than outer-directed.

This analysis of the pivotal moment in Freud's life and in the history of psychoanalysis, by which I mean the psychodynamically oriented study of the human mind and emotional life, once more takes us back to the central question to be answered in this book: What was it that unconsciously motivated Freud to turn away from his first paradigm of neuroses and drove him to create a second, far less viable and less reliable paradigm? The adaptive study of the evolution and design of the emotion-processing mind and its archetypes indicate that unresolved, deep unconscious death anxieties must have played a critical role in this decision. I turn now to the reported details of Freud's early life that provide us with likely incidents that embody clues to the answer to this most vital question.

# Chapter 6

# Psychoanalytic Detective Work

In writing about his patient Dora, which was his first extended case study, Freud introduced the concept of symptomatic acts which give expression to unconscious thoughts and impulses. In that context, he made the following observation:

> There is a great deal of symbolism of this kind in life, but as a rule we pass it by without heeding it. When I set myself the task of bringing to light what human beings keep hidden within them, not by the compelling power of hypnosis, but by observing what they say and what they show, I thought the task was a harder one than it really is. He that has eyes to see and ears to hear may convince himself that no mortal can keep a secret. If his lips are silent, he chatters with his finger tips; betrayal oozes out of him at every pore. And thus the task of making conscious the most hidden recesses of the mind is one which it is quite possible to accomplish. (Freud, 1905, pp. 77-78)

As we turn to the effort to extract encoded and other types of clues to past traumas revealed in Freud's writings, it is well to appreciate that adaptive studies indicate that unconscious unresolved death anxieties are among the strongest unconscious factors in analysts' needs to present—that is to chatter with—their case material and their own dreams, including those that pertain to their patients. Freud did so with an over-abundance that is in keeping with an unconscious urge to work through yet resist processing the unusually large number of early-life, traumatic incidents he seems to have experienced.

In principle, *predatory death anxiety* unconsciously motivates analysts to expose those who have harmed them in the past in order to find them guilty of crimes of uncalled for trauma and have them duly executed—in a sense, punished and murdered—for their misdeeds. Freud seems to have had strong unconscious motives of this kind that prompted him to generate encoded narratives that reveal in disguise the long series of incidents that had caused him harm.

*Predator death anxiety* evokes deep unconscious guilt which drives analysts to confess their own errors or "sins" through which they unconsciously reveal that they have unduly harmed others. There is an accompanying deep unconscious need for punishment which takes the form of unconsciously orchestrated self-harm—the equivalent of self-execution and suicide. For Freud, at first look, this need appears to have been a secondary motive for his encoded self-revelations because his crimes against others were overshadowed by the crimes others had perpetrated against him. However, as I shall show in chapter 8, Freud evidently took on the role of executioner vis-à-vis those who had harmed him and thus, even though the punishments he meted out were justified, they nonetheless evoked in him an unconscious sense of guilt that called for his punishment as well.

Another way in which predator death anxiety may have played a notable role in Freud's confessions involved his identification with those members of his family who had harmed others—including Freud himself. This would have been especially true of his father's predatory acts because as the Bible tells us—referring to another archetype—the sins of the father are brought down upon the sons. Thus, the sons are heirs to the father's crimes even as they also are called on to avenge and punish, and be punished for, the father's transgressions. Freud's unconscious identification with his father as a perpetrator of harm against others most certainly would have caused him to experience predator death anxiety and seek self-punishment through some form of self-harm.

Finally *existential death anxiety* plays a role in encoded self-revelations related to both supervision and personal traumas because there is an archetypal need in all humans, believers and non-believers, to set the record straight and put their lives in order before they die. As we shall see, this need was quite evident in Freud's last original book, *Moses and Monotheism* (Freud, 1939), which had all the earmarks of a deathbed confession that was centered around the greatest trauma in Freud's life (see below and Chapter 8).

These ideas are a variation on a well known comment made by Winnicott (1947) to the effect that analysts write papers and books in order to complete their analyses. Adaptive studies have generated more sanguine insights, showing that they do so based on the unconscious need to expose those who have harmed them, often by having made them into their helpless victims. The vengeful side of this need to confess is self-evident, but there also is a healing side reflected in the unconscious need to bring closure to these past traumas so their detrimental effects are significantly diminished—short of that, they can wreck a life. Unresolved traumas in the life of an influential personage like Freud also can wreck a science, as seems to be the case with psychoanalysis.

The adaptive aspects of recovering early traumas and working them over consciously lies with the satisfaction of knowing the truth about the actions of others and about one's own life. While there is satisfaction in meting out punishment to those who have offended you, there also are benefits from gaining fresh perspectives on what happened—and why. There also is a unique opportunity to mete out genuine, unconsciously grounded forgiveness of others for harm done to oneself based on trustworthy trigger decoded insights.

In respect to situations that have been repressed and obliterated because one has caused harm to others, gaining trigger decoded access to these incidents facilitates the achievement of fresh, healing insights into what had happened. More importantly, such efforts can facilitate the expression of unconsciously wrought, genuine atonement for the harm done and an insightful resorting to sound reparative acts. These ways of expiating guilt and reducing or resolving deep unconscious needs for self-punishment are the only means available to us to genuinely make peace with our "crimes" against others; conscious atonement has little or no effect on the deep unconscious system of morality and ethics and does little to alleviate unconsciously driven acts of self-punishment. In addition, in cases in which borrowed guilt plays a role, unconsciously atoning for the harm others have caused is crucial for the healing of the relationship from which the guilt has been borrowed and to deep personal healing as well.

The confessions made by psychoanalysts touch on actual happenings that are laden with conflict, anxiety, rage, depression, and guilt. Real traumas call for real solutions and as a result, there are real impulses to murder an offending predator or to commit suicide if the analyst has been the perpetrator of harm. As a result of the danger posed by these grim impulses, there are communicative needs to both remember and forget, reveal and conceal, confess and pretend innocence, tell the truth and lie. Thus, many of the most troubling family secrets that have affected the course of a life, such as those we seek to uncover in the life of Freud, are seldom available directly, that is, in a manifest and undisguised form. In fact, a directly recalled trauma is likely to serve as a screen memory (Freud, 1899) which covers over and disguises another even more painful and critical incident that has been fully repressed and obliterated. Freud himself offered a memory of playing with his cousins as a child which he believed served this screening function, although he contended that the earlier memory screened a later, more painful one.

Another likely example of a screen memory, which Freud did not take as having a screening function, is his recall of the story his father told him of having had his hat knocked from his head by a non-Jewish boy while the father was walking on the sidewalk (Balmary, 1979; Krull, 1979; Rizzuto,

1998; see below). In general, almost all consciously retained memories from early childhood, and a fair percentage of striking later-day memories, have a significant screening and disguising function, and thus they both reveal and conceal the repressed aspects of actual events—the more traumatic the incident, the heavier the disguise.

## THE NATURE OF DISGUISED CLUES

In turning to the early years of Freud's life, then, we are searching for clues to the nature of his significant early-life traumas so we may examine their effects on his paradigm shift. We do so because archetypically, the influence of incidents of this kind is inextinguishable. The clues we seek may take a variety of forms. There may well be an accurate, manifest, undisguised conscious memory of an actual trauma that is of significance, even though it also has a screening function. Much like a dream, the manifest memory has meaning per se, but it also generally serves to disguise a repressed incident as well. Freud's memory of the death of his brother Julius may well be a case in point.

Other ways in which an obliterated early trauma may find expression include the existence of an inexplicable behavior that suggests that an active, hidden trauma has contributed to the incident in question. A possible example is the Freud family crisis that took place soon after the birth of Freud's sister Anna, when Freud was approaching three years of age (Krull, 1979). The crisis, whose sources are unknown, led to the break up of the family with Freud's two half-brothers moving to England and Freud's nuclear family moving from Frieberg to Vienna—all of it for reasons that are unclear but suggest a major family debacle.

Other clues to hidden traumas include emotionally founded symptoms, peculiar habits, odd behaviors, single inexplicable actions, other adaptive failures, and fixed ways of thinking that imply the presence of a hidden traumatic driving force. In these cases, however, the event in question and the meanings that are being betrayed by these clues are especially difficult to unravel—Dora playing with her reticule being a case in point. Language-based clues are far more definitively decodable than those that are conveyed through actions and habitual behaviors. This takes us to the most promising source for indications of obliterated events, that of narratives of all kinds—dreams, recalled incidents, made up stories, stories about incidents in the lives of others, and the like—and their double-message functions. One message is manifest, while the other is latent and encoded in the first; there is, then, a consciously intended tale that simultaneously expresses a consciously unintended but unconsciously wrought tale—in this case, the story of a past traumatic incident. While Freud saw these encoded messages as expressions of forbidden unconscious wishes, the adaptive approach sees them as disguising anxiety-provoking incidents, past and present. This means that Freud's manifest dreams and other storied communications, especially the stories of the incidents that were brought to mind by his manifest dream elements, almost certainly encode the secret traumas to which he was subjected to as a child and at other times in his life as well.

Properly *trigger decoding* these disguised communications is the key to identifying these obliterated yet highly influential traumatic incidents. Meeting this challenge is facilitated by searching for *bridging themes*—images that link a manifest narrative to an underlying, encoded trauma. This search is facilitated by the adaptive finding that triggers evoke narrative themes and that these themes in turn reflect the nature of a triggering event. This means, for example, that the themes in Freud's narratives will put us on the trail of the traumatic triggers he endured and was unconsciously attempting to work over in his psychoanalytic work and life.

Freud was a prolific narrator as shown by his communication of multiple reported case histories, his own dreams and associations to them, and the other kinds of tales he recounted and analyzed—for example, the Oedipus myth (Freud, 1900, 1917, 1924), the lives of Leonardo DaVinci (Freud, 1910a), Moses (Freud, 1939), and Schreber (Freud, 1911), the story of Gradiva (Freud, 1907), and more. This means that whatever the practical justifications, driven by deep unconscious needs, he has given us a rich heritage of encoded clues to his personal and family traumas. But in many ways his heritage is too rich, filled with such a plethora of clues that no one can possibly detect and decode all of them and everyone must struggle to identify those clues that are most cogent to his life and work. One of Freud's major communicative defenses was his tendency to offer so many narratives that it is a daunting task to separate the wheat from the chaff—that is, the revelatory narratives from those that primarily serve to avoid and deny his underlying traumas. It can be truly said that *Sigmund Freud was an archetypal over-narrator.* And because the material he generated is so florid, it also is difficult to organize the themes he generated around a particular triggering event. It takes a lot of ingenuity to outwit Freud's communicative defenses, but it nevertheless is possible to do so.

The situation is like a crime scene: Freud and the members of his family have been both victims and perpetrators of a series of harmful acts—"immoral crimes," as they are experienced by the candid deep unconscious mind. But the exact nature of these crimes and the identity of their perpetrators are quite uncertain and in addition, there are so many clues strewn about here and there, there is great difficulty in sorting things out. Nevertheless, it is our job as psychoanalytic detectives to identify and decode those clues that will tell us with a strong measure of likelihood who was responsible for carrying out the most serious crimes and who were their most damaged victims. That done, we then need to trace how these crimes affected the lives of those involved—and here, specifically, how they unconsciously affected Freud's paradigm shift.

In the best spirit of psychoanalytic detective work and with an eye to obtaining unconscious validation whenever possible, I shall proceed methodologically by deciphering a particular set of encoded clues reported by Freud in a narrative generated in his psychoanalytic writings in order to arrive at one and another probable trauma. I shall then examine and decode encoded clues in a different narrative to see if they validate, refute, or call for revisions of my initial hypothesis. The more extensive the support offered by the mounting narrative evidence in hand, the stronger will be my confidence that I am on the right trail. All along, I also shall take pains to not ignore or avoid a clue that seems to challenge my thinking in some way. At stake is not only gaining deep and critical insights into the driving forces in the life and work of Sigmund Freud but also into the basic archetypes of the human mind.

Put another way, given the existence of a large number of biographies of Freud and of the history of psychoanalysis written on the basis of his second paradigm, I shall be writing a fresh, partial history of Freud's life and of Freudian psychoanalysis based on his first paradigm of emotional life. Where others have written conscious-system histories, I shall be writing a deep unconscious-system history, using the vision and wisdom and other resources of the profoundly wise deep unconscious mind instead of the extremely defensive conscious mind. Where others have used inference making and tried to extract implications from his writings and the personal history he has left behind, I shall be focusing on trigger decoding the major narratives in Freud's writings—that is, on trying to identify the themes in his stories that appear to bridge over and provide clues to the specific traumatic triggering events to which Freud was subjected. Where others have looked mainly into Freud's sexual, relational, and narcissistic needs and issues, I shall be looking into his likely death-related traumas. And all in all, the history that I give word to will be significantly different from the history that has already been told by others, and mine will be, I fully believe, a history that is far more revealing, cogent, and fateful than that told on the basis of second-paradigm perspectives.

## FREUD AS SUBJECT

A few introductory words are called for about subjecting Freud to his own, however greatly modified, psychoanalytic process (see also Balmary, 1979). Given that he has attracted so many unjustifiably hostile and irrelevant *ad hominem* criticisms, most of them without an informed, thoughtful evaluation of his theoretical position, I want to make clear that, as I have striven to do for many years, the critiques and discussions I shall offer will be based on accepted biographical and empirical data, however selectively utilized. To the best of my knowledge and ability, the conjectures and formulations that I shall make will be rational and logical, and above all fair to and justified by the data at hand and offered with full respect for Freud's genius and sincere, labored efforts. Given the speculative nature of my discussion and the possible errant pathways that they may have taken, and the high risk of misconceptions or mistaken inferences, it is well to consider this work as the best I can offer based on what is presently known within Freud's first paradigm and the adaptive approach. As with any quasi-scientific study, the results are open to revision if fresh material that points in new directions becomes available.

That said, there is a great deal of internal consistency in what I shall offer and a notable amount of support from the handful of others who have researched aspects of the subject matter of this book. I share with Freud himself, who, as he approached his study of Leonardo DaVinci, wrote of the following spirit of investigation:

> When psychiatric research, normally content to draw on frailer men for its material, approaches one who is among the greater of the human race, it is not doing so for the reasons so frequently ascribed to it by laymen. "To blacken the radiant and drag the sublime into the dust" [Schiller] is no part of its purpose, and there is no satisfaction for it in narrowing the gulf which separates the perfection of the great from the inadequacy of the objects that are its usual concern. But it cannot help finding worthy of understanding everything that can be recognized in those illustrious models, and it believes that there is no one so great as to be disgraced by being subject to the laws which govern both normal and pathological activity with equal cogency. (Freud, 1910a, page 63)

## BACK-UP RESOURCES

Lives as remembered and lives as described by others are complex reconstructions subject to personal bias and distortion which, in psychoanalysis, stem in part from an observer's theoretical orientation which serves as the lens through which what is seen and not seen is determined and directs the interpretation of the incidents involved. Even at the very moment that we are living a fragment of the story of our lives, the purported facts of what is happening and their meanings will vary depending on the orientation and perspectives of the observer—be it oneself or another person. There is as a rule a core of archetypal or universal certainty about the nature of a dramatic event around which there always is a cloud of uncertainty. This lends itself to selective perceptions and variations in understanding that render the observer as important as the observed—even when they are the same person.

All of Freud's mainstream biographers (for example, Gay, 1988) have viewed the story and psychodynamics of his life through the lens of Freud's second paradigm. Krull (1979), who argued that Freud inappropriately fled from reality and from the real causes of neuroses when he gave up his seduction theory, nonetheless configured her arguments and conclusions based largely on second-paradigm thinking. The only exception to this trend is Balmary (1979), who used a Lacanian framework of neurosogenesis based on the secret faults of the father—and at times, the mother—for her carefully detailed review of the causes of Freud's change of heart. From her vantagepoint, Freud's shift in theory was a way of moving from facts to myth, from observations to unfounded belief; from health to neurosis (see below).

This brings me to my own frame of reference, the eyes through which I shall be searching, selecting, and interpreting the events of Freud's early life. As I have indicated, my basic position is that of an updated version of Freud's first paradigm—*the adaptive approach.* As noted, its basic thesis is that external life traumas are the most powerful activators of emotional responses in humans and that among these activating incidents, death-related traumas are especially compelling and most likely to evoke maladaptive reactions. In this light, extensive use will be made of the death-related archetypes discovered clinically through the adaptive approach because the universal tendencies that are active in today's psychotherapy patients were active by and large in the past for Freud. These archetypes include the nature of the most telling traumatic incidents a person can suffer from, as well as the typical responses that are made when they transpire, including the common pool of defenses and other adaptive reactions that they evoke.

It was in fact discoveries about human mental life made using the adaptive approach that prompted me to take a fresh look at the myth of Oedipus which in turn prompted a fresh look at Freud's second paradigm of psychoanalysis. My clinical data indicated that violence, death, and death anxiety are the main sources of human conflict and suffering, a finding that caused me to reexamine the Oedipus story to see if these issues were a significant part of the tale. It turned out that there are eight major incidents of murder, suicide and violence in the tale compared to the single incestuous relationship between Oedipus and his mother, Jocasta. This discovery, which ran counter to Freud's interpretation of the myth, made it imperative for me to take a closer look at the other themes in the myth and a fresh look at Freud's thinking as well. In time, this took me to Freud's paradigm shift which appeared to be a grave and costly but well rationalized error. It then behooved me to discover the unconscious roots of this error and my own clinical material made clear that archetypically it had to involve death-related traumas in his earliest years of life. I was prepared to guard against any undue prejudices that this hypothesis might create and to not allow them to inappropriately bias my research and conclusions. There is a fine line between testing an hypothesis and not realizing that it is blinding you to the most evident implications of the data at hand.

Another facilitating factor for the new insights that I will be offering lies with my adopted Socratic teacher, Marie Balmary, whose book *Psychoanalyzing Psychoanalysis* (Balmary, 1979) presented me with a detailed and erudite study of Freud's shift in his theory of the origins of neuroses and with a set of reality-centered etiological ideas of her own that I responded to as if I was in the presence of a very wise mentor. To my knowledge, Balmary is the only psychoanalyst to offer extensive evidence for the claim that Freud's thinking led psychoanalysis astray. As I shall soon describe, her primary thesis involved the death of Jakob Freud's second wife, Rebecca, whose existence was kept secret from Freud and who may well have died by jumping from or in front of a train. Balmary saw this incident as a basic fault of Freud's father and argued that Freud was unable to articulate and deal with this fault. This in turn was seen as the main unconscious reason Freud needed to move psychoanalytic thinking away from reality, which is the locus of the faults of significant others and which played a role in Freud's initial seduction theory. The shift as we have seen was to the realm of fantasy in which the individual himself—his own incestuous wishes in particular—was viewed as the cause of his emotional ills; the role of others in these syndromes became a secondary matter.

As I studied the evidence that she presented for her thesis, I responded in significant part as a student who had already begun to entertain a different but related thesis—that the key early-life trauma that Freud suffered was his uncertainty as to the identity of his biological father. I was able, then, to develop and initially test my hypothesis by using Balmary's clinical and historical findings—and added my own evidence later on. Through my interactions with her ideas and writings many compelling new ideas began to dawn on me. Most of these insights were supported by my burgeoning clinical findings regarding archetypal reactions to death-related traumas and by further research into Freud's writings. These unique forms of validation lent credence to my reconstructions and conjectures.

Other useful perspectives that supported this research included my training as a classical analyst, steeped in ideas drawn from Freud's second paradigm. While in time I discovered many flaws in this version of psychoanalytic theory, its propositions nonetheless gave me a grounding in psychodynamics and an initial understanding of the unconscious realm of experience. Most importantly, it provided me with an abiding appreciation for the means by which the human mind disguises unconscious transactions and thus an ability to decode the hidden messages in narratives like dreams and clinical anecdotes—messages about actual incidents instead of inner needs and fantasies. Without the realization that narratives encoded the identity and meanings of traumatic events, the research I was pursuing could not have taken place.

Also advantageous for this pursuit was my contact with researchers engaged in exploring in a psychological laboratory setting the dynamics of *subliminal* perception (Silverman, Lachman, and Milich, 1982). This created a mind-set and sensitivity on my part for how reality is perceived outside of awareness, another basic idea that facilitated my search for the actual traumas Freud had experienced in his early life. In addition, readings in science and especially in evolutionary biology helped to ground my thinking in the theories of evolution and adaptation, and as a result, to think about Freud's life in terms of the universal challenges to survival that he seems to have had to endure. This reality-based perspective also enabled me to appreciate that the mind can be damaged by harmful environmental events as much as any body organ—so be it with Freud.

Finally, there was my own history of remembered early (and later-day) traumas whose encoded unconscious implications and meanings I had, with much effort, been able to some extent to trigger decode through an adaptation-oriented self-analysis that I undertook after my formal training analysis had ended. No one digs into issues pertaining to reality, trauma, and death without strong cause. The problem is that archetypically, such incidents tend to cause an individual to flee rather than explore reality. For reasons still unknown to myself, I defied this archetype and this exploration is one of the many studies that eventuated on this basis (see personal note).


## SOME BASIC ARCHETYPES

To enhance our understanding of the conjectures that lie ahead and to enable us to be acutely aware of the obstacles that will confront us, it will be helpful to identify the archetypes that pertain to both emotion-related human communication and dealing with death-related traumas. These archetypes were unearthed through adaptive clinical investigations and by means of a series of formal, quantitative research studies sponsored by the approach (Langs, Badalamenti, and Thomson, 1996). Fundamentally and by genetic-biological design, when humans communicate freely, they naturally and lawfully alternate between narrative and non-narrative or intellectualized modes of expression. Simply put, allowed free rein, we all tell encoded stories and then stop telling such stories only to begin to tell them again in an endless cyclical dance.

Within this basic pattern, there is a continuum consisting at one end, of individuals who are inclined to tell many stories, so-called *strong narrators,* and at the other end, those who tell few stories, so-called *relative non-narrators.* Narratives are the carriers of encoded, unconscious messages and some of the most powerful stories we tell encode the history and perceived meanings of our death-related traumas. This suggests that strong narrators, such as those who frequently remember their dreams and associate freely to their elements, have a notable need, and are inherently unafraid, to encode the story of their repressed and obliterated traumas. Relative non-narrators on the other hand dread encoding the story of their traumas and in most cases, they will flee adaptive psychotherapy when the opportunity to communicate narrative material is offered to them.

This does not, however, mean that relative non-narrators do not have a story to tell. In fact, they typically have suffered from a series of extremely damaging traumas and they show an unconscious fear of being overwhelmed psychologically by the encoded expression of these incidents—and even more so, of their being trigger decoded and recalled even in part. This dread is based on the anxieties created by the murderous rage and suicidal urges evoked by such developments and as a result, they shut themselves down communicatively.

Despite their readiness to tell encoded stories, it has been found that strong narrators also have palpable communicative resistances. Indeed, the natural ratio between their communicative efforts at revelation versus concealment is about 1:10. Everyone has their communicative defenses—it is only a matter of their intensity and at what point in the communicative cycle they appear. Strong narrators tend to alternate between brief moments of encoded revelation and long periods of non-revelation. In psychotherapy, they initially react to a sound trigger decoded interpretation with encoded, unconsciously validating narratives only to shift into an obscuring mode of expression for a strikingly long time thereafter. As a rule, these communicative resistances persist until, spontaneously or after therapeutic effort, they are momentarily resolved and a new cycle of encoded expression followed by extended obliteration is initiated.

It is striking to see the extent to which significant repressed early traumas or the most critical meanings of consciously recalled traumas are obliterated from awareness and do not gain direct but only encoded expression. Furthermore, a remarkably large number of traumatic incidents do not register consciously at the time they transpire. A prime example is seen when a therapist develops visible signs of a physical illness or disability: Patients almost never consciously register this kind of event, but they do perceive it unconsciously and then convey these perceptions in their encoded narratives. The unconscious need to deny reality in these situations arises because the deep unconscious mind always reacts to such observations by imagining and expecting a worst case scenario—most often, that the therapist is dying and that they are and will be the cause of his or her pending demise.

In addition, many traumatic incidents that do register in awareness are quickly erased from conscious memory, never to be recalled directly again. As for traumas that are consciously registered or remembered, many of their most significant meanings and implications will not have been recognized consciously at the time of the incident, meanings that therefore will not be recalled directly when the incident itself is recovered in analysis. These meanings are accessible solely through efforts at trigger decoding and this possibility arises only when a fresh traumatic incident arises, one that is linked to and activates the old trauma and the encoded themes that are pertinent to identifying its implications for the patient. I shall be using our knowledge of these communicative archetypes and principles in our efforts to track down Freud's early traumas and their effects on his paradigm shift.

It is, by the way, common parlance to speak of repressed traumas, but this usage stems largely from Freud's second paradigm which stresses the role of forbidden or anxiety-provoking fantasies and wishes in neurosis formation. In this context, the primary cause of anxiety is a pathological inner need and thus a failure to recall a memory linked with that need is seen as the result of repression; as per Freud's topographic model of the mind, the inner need is barred access to awareness. It is in this context that repression is seen as the basic mental defense in human emotional life.

*First paradigm,* reality-centered approaches view the matter of psychological defenses in a different light. Because the mind is dealing first and foremost with actual traumatic incidents, *denial* is the mind's basic psychological defense. Denial or obliteration are terms used to refer to not perceiving a significant aspect of reality—of barring from conscious awareness a disturbing event or its most anxiety-provoking meanings. In the context of the second paradigm, denial has been taken to imply a psychotic break with reality, but in the first paradigm it is seen as a universal unconscious defense against a perceived external danger. Thus, the term *repressed trauma,* which alludes to the obliteration of an actual incident, is a misnomer; *denied or obliterated trauma* is the more appropriate term.

The adaptive approach sees the defenses of *denial and obliteration* in response to an endangering traumatic incident as the basic defenses of the emotion-processing mind; repression is viewed to be a supportive secondary defense. This implies that the most accurate means of reconstructing a past trauma comes about when a therapist recognizes that a current traumatic trigger has taken place and then listens to the patient's encoded narrative responses seeking to identify clues to the reactivated early trauma to which the current incident is linked. In a suitably altered form, I intend to apply this methodology to Freud's traumas by identifying an important later-day trauma, such as the death of his father, and then attempting to trigger decode his responsive narratives to the current event in order to identify the early-life trauma with which it is linked unconsciously. This is feasible because archetypically, an early-life death-related trauma lays down encoded representations of its existence and meanings which remain in the deep unconscious mind throughout one's life—in a sense waiting for a current incident to activate its disguised expression. These residuals always are one of the root causes of an emotional dysfunction. The timelessness of these effects is a first-paradigm version of Freud's claim that unconscious wishes are timeless; this may be so, but the enduring effects of victimization and victimizing others are far more endlessly critical to human life.

## FREUD NARRATIVE STYLE

To return to the subject of communicative archetypes, let's look at Freud's position on the narrator-non-narrator scale and in addition, review and elaborate on the type of communicative defenses of which he seems to have made most use. We have only to examine Freud's early writings and the storied lives he later wrote about to realize that he was a remarkably prolific narrator—an abundant dreamer and raconteur. Indeed, this propensity may well have contributed to the undoing of his psychoanalytic thinking in that once he discovered how to decode dreams, he could do so only as they applied to needs and fantasies. Archetypically, patients who are offered the adaptive form of psychotherapy and who are told that they will be asked to work with their narratives consistently react in ways and with images that indicate that unconsciously, they have an intuitive sense of where decoding these narratives will take them. Quite unconsciously, they realize that this is the sole means of meaningfully accessing their most telling and disturbing traumas and their most anxiety-provoking meanings. The archetypal response to this unconscious realization is that patients who cannot tolerate this first-paradigm quest will either seek another therapist who will not engage in a narrative form of treatment and not make use of trigger decoding, but will instead make use of some version of Freud's intellectualized, conscious-system, second-paradigm form of therapy, or they will seek a non-dynamic, cognitive therapist with whom narrative communication is not an essential part of the therapy.

In his own way and with an influence that extended well beyond his own work and life, Freud seems to have behaved archetypically in this regard, although he did so in a manner that is quite unusual. Undoubtedly protected by his paradigm shift, he continued to be a strong narrator, but he tended to restrict his associations to his dreams to limited allusions to actual past events (which in extended narrative form are the ideal guided associations to dream elements). He frequently made use of intellectualizations and direct analyses (both are non-narrative in nature and thus forms of communicative resistance). He also tended to recall extremely long dreams that were so flooded with dream imagery as to render their proper trigger decoding an almost impossible task.

In his first thirteen years or so of writing, Freud produced an unprecedented, probably never to be repeated by a psychoanalyst, flood of narrative material. His stories are to be found in his letters to Fleiss (Freud, 1954), *Studies on Hysteria* (Breuer and Freud, 1893–1895), the dream material in *The Interpretation of Dreams* (Freud, 1900), the stories recounted in *The Psychopathology of Everyday Life* (Freud, 1901) and in his four major case histories—Dora (Freud, 1905a), the Rat Man (Freud, 1909c), the Wolf Man (Freud, 1918), and Little Hans (Freud, 1909a)—and a series of lesser case histories. There also are multiple narratives in his book, *Jokes and Their Relation to the Unconscious* (Freud, 1905b), the story in his paper on Jensen's Gradiva (Freud, 1907), studies of the lives of Leonardo DaVinci (Freud, 1910a), Michaelangelo (Freud, 1914d), and Moses (Freud, 1939), the analysis of Schreber (Freud, 1911), and many other vignettes, case histories, and allusions to narratives that are found in literature, theater, the Bible, and such.

In essence, then, as noted above, Freud's communicative resistances were grounded in an over-abundance of narratives. He managed to offer so many dreams and stories with manifest and encoded personal ramifications that no human mind—neither his own nor that of anyone else—could easily process their contents towards trigger decoded reconstructions and insights. This is a common communicative defense found in the strong narrators who are seen in adaptive psychotherapy; these patients are naturally inclined to flood their sessions with narrative images and themes which most often serve to overwhelm rather than edify.

Therapists who follow the principles of Freud's second paradigm are, as was Freud himself, blind to the presence in narratives of encoded clues to actual traumatic events. Freud unwittingly took advantage of the evolved design of the emotion-processing mind that causes us as humans to blur the nature of the secret traumas, present and past, that we begrudgingly wish to reveal. This natural conscious-system defense makes the critical work of reconstructing early traumas a difficult process indeed. Because of the defenses built into the conscious system, humans only rarely can carry out an effective form of self-analysis. Using second paradigm principles, this effort to achieve truly insightful self-healing is bound to succumb to conscious-system defensiveness. The seeming insights gained in these efforts tend to be superficial, over-intellectualized, and far more in the service of defense, self-harm, and the denial of death than in the service of achieving a measure of deep understanding. All of this speaks for the limitations and certainty of failure of Freud's self-analysis which he undertook only after his paradigm shift—that is, only after he could be certain unconsciously that his efforts would not take him to the real source of his neurosis.

## RESOURCES AVAILABLE AND LOST

In seeking the unconscious reasons for Freud's paradigm shift, five interrelated tasks stood before me:

First, to try to identify the *historical indications* of early traumas in Freud's life.

Second, to trigger decode the narratives from Freud's writings that reveal the aroused deep unconscious anxieties and conflicts that he was *dealing with at the time of his paradigm shift.*

Third, to further explore Freud's narrative material for encoded clues to the obliterated *early-life traumas* he had endured.

Fourth, to trigger decode those segments of Freud's narrative material that appear to convey his unconscious experiences of his most significant early-life traumas.

And fifth, to explore how these revelations enable us to understand the unconscious sources of Freud's seemingly errant paradigm shift.

The resources available to me included the largely resistance-serving, over-abundant narrative material from Freud which nevertheless is frozen in print and can thus be carefully explored and mined. While adaptive studies have shown that recording a dream or story tends to interfere with the expression of guided associations to dream elements—associations that are as a rule stronger and more meaningful than the dream elements *per se*—we are compensated by nonetheless having extensive dream material and other narrative vehicles to draw on and decode. Freud does at times offer personal associations to some of the dreams and stories he tells, but they tend to have limited narrative qualities and often lean toward intellectual analyses. On rare occasions, he refers to an activating triggering event for a dream, which he calls a *day's residue.* However, he does not in principle make use of these incidents as a guide to trigger decoding his dreams because he views these realities as activators of inner mental wishes rather than important in their own right. In adaptive thinking, however, meaningful day's residues are traumatic incidents with manifest or implied death-related meanings which evoke emotionally critical mental activities, much of it on the deep unconscious level of experience. These incidents are not innocuous sparks, but are themselves dangerous conflagrations whose identification is critical to the trigger decoding effort.

As for Freud, his failure to make available many of the most telling triggering events for his dreams is another limiting factor in our pursuit. With the exception of gross traumas, like the death of Freud's father or the anniversary of his death, we seldom have access to the immediate triggering events in his day-to-day life and work—incidents that must have been the immediate stimuli for the unconsciously driven paradigm shift he undertook. This means that efforts at decoding some of Freud's major narratives will be the main source of the reconstructions I shall make.

## SOME MISSING MATERIAL

In addition to his communicative defenses, Freud carried out at least three actions that definitively precluded revelation and served concealment. Despite his hunger and expectations for personal fame, twice in his life—in 1885 and 1907—Freud destroyed his personal papers (Krull, 1979). The triggers for these decisions are not known even though we can be sure, based on archetypes, that they were death-related. In addition, efforts to understand Freud's personal psychology were dealt a great blow in the course of his writing his masterpiece, *The Interpretation of Dreams* (Freud, 1900). And therein hangs a tale:

Having expressed a variety of ideas about Freud's version of psychoanalysis and his life (Langs, 1978a, 1982, 1984, 1985), I became interested in his early life soon after I had completed a series of books devoted to the theoretical structure and clinical ramifications of the adaptive approach (Langs, 2004, 2006). Because I had acquired a strong interest in archetypes and saw parallels in Buddhist thinking and the adaptive approach, I began to study the Bible and religion in light of adaptive insights (Langs, 2008). In the course of this work I came to see that one reason for religion's failure to bring peace to many individuals and to the world at large was that religious thinking lacked a sound understanding of human psychology. I realized that psychoanalysis was the only theory of the mind that could have provided religion with this missing element and it was easy to see why, despite some minimal efforts in this direction, psychoanalysts had failed to do so. The problem arose largely from Freud's rejection of religion as reflecting a passing neurotic wish for an omnipotent father (Freud, 1927) and what amounted to his outright dismissal of religious thinking as a subject for psychoanalytic investigation and clarification.

I began to look into writings that had attempted to clarify Freud's attitude toward religion (Vitz, 1988; Rizzuto, 1998; Yerushalmi, 1991) and these writings took me back to the details of Freud's life and his ideas about the myth of Oedipus. As mentioned above, it occurred to me that the psychoanalytic theory that I had crafted empirically was trauma- and death-centered and that in this context, sexual issues and themes, while undoubtedly a potential source of conflict, are viewed largely as of secondary import and primarily as defenses against death anxiety. In this light, I decided to re-examine the myth to see if it supported a sex/incest-centered or a death/violence-centered theory of emotional dysfunctions. I saw this exploration as one way of trying to validate the adaptive position and I was quite reassured when I discovered that the myth contained eight acts of and allusion to violence and death to the single act of incest committed by Oedipus with his mother. The odds were strongly in favor of adaptive thinking (see chapter 8) and of the death-related archetypes it has identified. It was only a small victory for the adaptive approach, but it encouraged me to dig deeper.

I turned next to *The Interpretation of Dreams* (Freud, 1900) and to a reexamination of the Irma dream with which Freud begins this masterful book. Given that the dream book contains Freud's opening statements on the psychoanalytic theory he was in the process of creating, I had hypothesized that the first dream that Freud presented to the world would, as is believed of first dreams from psychoanalytic patients, encode significant information about his unconscious issues and mental state at the time. I also expected that the dream and his associations to it would contain encoded clues to the early-life traumas that were driving significant aspects of his psychoanalytic thinking. Having explored this dream years earlier (Langs, 1984), I eagerly turned to a reexamination of its contents and Freud's associations, intending to use my most recent ideas about the emotion-processing mind to probe their contents.

The dream in question is the well known and extensively researched "Irma dream" which was dreamt in July of 1895 (Freud, 1900). Freud responded to the dream by associating to its elements and then comparing his unconscious dream thoughts with the manifest dream. This approach to the dream enabled him to discover the critical mechanisms by which dream thoughts are disguised in the surface of a dream.

As for my search for encoded indications of current and early-life traumas, I was able to identify scattered death-related elements in the day's residues for the dream and found that there were a few themes in Freud's dream-associational network that also appeared to support adaptive thinking. But I also was quite aware that the pool of narrative themes derived from the dream itself and from Freud's associations to its elements was lacking in images that could easily be thought of as disguising death-related traumas. There was no sense of a coalescing network of themes that organized around death-related issues nor did the themes seem to point to a likely specific death-related triggering event from Freud's current or past life. Meaningful encoded narrative imagery tends to gather around a central death-related issue and to evoke an intuitive feeling for its likely accumulated unconscious meanings. This kind of experience arose later on when I examined the dream that Freud dreamt the night of or night before the death of his father and when I explored the stories he recounted regarding Oedipus and Moses (see chapter 8). But this was not my sense with the Irma dream.

All in all, then, while the Irma dream had something to offer in the way of validating adaptive observations and ideas, there was no sign of a smoking gun. The preamble to the dream fittingly begins with an allusion to a violation of the archetypal frame or ground rules, namely that Freud had a personal relationship with his patient, Irma, and her family. He commented that their mixed relationship had caused him many disturbed feelings and noted that a therapeutic failure would threaten his relationship with her family. This mixture of relatedness, professional and personal, may weakly encode Freud's unconscious experience of the mixed relationship between Freud's mother and his half-bother, Phillip—familial yet incestuous—but this is a formulation that is more of a stretch than a likelihood. I began to feel that I had lost an important battle for the adaptive cause and for Freud's first paradigm.

I reviewed the dream several times hoping to find something important that I had missed. The immediate day's residue for the dream was a visit by a colleague named Otto at Bellevue where the Freud family was vacationing. Otto had told Freud that Irma—whose analysis, although incomplete, had been terminated—was better but not quite well. Freud detected a reprimand and wrote out the case history to show to a colleague—his co-author Breuer (Breuer and Freud, 1893–1895)—as a way of justifying himself. That night he had the dream which he wrote down immediately on awakening. In it, he is receiving guests in a large hall, takes Irma aside, blames her for still being ill, examines her and has three of his colleagues do the same. They find an infiltration, an infection, and decide that dysentery will intervene and the toxin will be eliminated. They blame Otto for having thoughtlessly given Irma an injection of propionic acid with an unclean syringe.

This is a brief summary of a very long dream of the kind reported by strong narrators who overwhelm themselves—and their therapists—with encoded, storied imagery. Freud's first association to the dream is to the large hall and the planned celebration of his wife's birthday at which Irma was expected. (He does not mention that his wife was pregnant at the time.) He goes on to associate to the elements of the dream and many of them are explanatory rather than narrative. This is another common communicative defense seen in strong narrators and it limits the development of the meaningful and coalescing pool of narrative themes needed for trigger decoding. Indeed, Freud's focus is on his conscious concerns about Irma's not accepting his solution to her ills and how it is affecting his reputation as a budding analyst. The idea in the dream that Irma has an organic illness would, he explains, exonerate him entirely. He realizes that this explanation indicates that he has a wish to have a different patient who would be more amenable to cure. All this is conscious-system processing of evident issues; it is lacking in the powerful narrative themes that characterize dealing with grim, deep unconscious traumas and issues.

Themes with some power finally do emerge when Freud associates to the white patch in Irma's throat, in that it brings up his daughter's serious illness two years earlier (we do not however get a detailed narrative) and his own use of cocaine and how his misuse in prescribing the drug had hastened the death of a dear friend of his. He also associates to a woman patient who had succumbed to what he had thought was a harmless remedy that he had prescribed and to a male patient whom he had sent on a journey which had led to his becoming ill. Along different lines, Freud has a sense that the dream also was intended to deride his colleagues in their ignorance of hysteria. The chemical injection eventually leads Freud to a discussion he had with a colleague regarding the sexual origins of neuroses.

Most notable here are themes in which Freud caused harm to, and the death of, patients whom he had treated. In discussing the dream, Freud ignored these powerful, death-related themes and quickly changed the subject to the sexual origins of neuroses. The sequence suggests that death and death anxiety are prominent issues in the latent, unconscious contents of this hallmark dream, but there is little to indicate the triggers and past traumas to which they refer. The shift to sexuality has all the earmarks of a flight from and defense against the encoded images related to harming and killing others. This is a typical example of the use of sexuality to support the second-paradigm denial of a death—a type of defense that persists to this very day.

There were other associations to the dream, most of them explanatory and intellectualized and only occasionally narrative in nature. All in all, Freud interpreted the dream as fulfilling his wish that he not be responsible for Irma's continuing ills, a wish that is openly implied if not frankly stated in the manifest contents of the dream and which ignores the more serious, grave themes of causing patients to die, the sexual roots of neuroses, and the cure through dysentery—that is, through physical illness.

In sum, the dream and Freud's associations to it involved themes related to both death and sexuality. The material seemed to be indecisive regarding which issue is more critical for emotional life. In addition, my growing suspicion that Freud had doubts regarding his biological father found little support from this dream-associational complex.

Was I wrong in my thesis? Were there clues here to another early-life trauma that I had missed? Nothing seemed to jump off the page as I had thought it would. Other writers had suggested that there had been an affair between Freud's mother and her step-son, Freud's step-brother, Phillip, that his father had committed adultery, and that his father's second wife had killed herself. But there was very little in these encoded dream themes to support any of these hypotheses. There had to be a key trauma that organized this dream, but its nature eluded me.

For the moment my main satisfaction came from being able to learn a lot about Freud's communicative resistances and the limitations of his approach to dreams. It was clear that Freud did not distinguish intellectualized from narrative associations to dreams, that he did not engage in reality-based trigger decoding but pursued the identification of active inner needs, and that he arrived mainly at quite superficial, conscious-system interpretations of his manifest dream material—trends that are evident among psychoanalysts to this day. But I also had received a measure of validation of my adaptive findings that the nature of the ground rules of psychoanalysis and departures from the ideal, archetypal frame are fundamental issues in the psychoanalytic experience. It was, it seemed, by unconsciously driven archetypal design that Freud had selected for this first dream a patient with whom the archetypal frame was basically modified—he not only knew Irma socially, he also had borrowed money from her father. In addition, in terms of the unconscious need to confess one's "sins," he had made his work with her a matter of public knowledge.

That said, I was nevertheless very disappointed by the absence of the kind of validation I was seeking from this landmark dream. I took this as fair warning that in attempting to trigger decode Freud's dreams and identify the early-life traumas with which they dealt, it was important to take care to not read too much into the available imagery and to not allow a thesis to force the imagery into compliance—to not try to force a square peg into a round hole. As disappointing as it was, recognizing non-fits and non-validation is as important to me as finding thesis-supporting imagery. It is a way of keeping myself "honest" and recognizing a need to revise my thinking accordingly. However, as I eventually learned, it turned out that this did not prove to be necessary in this situation.

Further reading about Freud's paradigm shift eventually helped to relieve my concerns that I was on the wrong track with the adaptive approach and my thinking about Freud's early life. I discovered that in preparing the opening chapters of the dream book, Freud had sent sections of the drafts of the manuscript to his correspondent. This material included a fully analyzed dream—"the big dream" as Freud called it—that Freud had planned to make the centerpiece of the volume. Fliess advised Freud to not use this dream in the book and Freud complied (Freud, 1954, letter 113, August 1, 1899, p. 288; Schur, 1966, 1972; Krull, 1979). Schur also reports on a letter that the disappointed Freud wrote to Fliess after he had "condemned" the dream to oblivion, asking what it was about the dream, which evidently contained highly autobiographical material, that had prompted the advice to drop the dream from the book. Was it his anxiety, his wife Martha, the *Dalles* (a Jewish word for poverty) or his being without a fatherland? This terse question offers few clues to the dream's contents. Freud's last word on the matter was that he had had a substitute dream in which a house constructed of building blocks had collapsed. Clearly, something fundamental had been lost in the doing. But as far as is presently known, the specific reasons for Fliess's advice are not documented and the dream material has not survived in any form.

Krull has suggested that the allusion to Martha involved the idea of being married to another woman. As for the reference to being without a fatherland, Freud's comment in writing a preface for the second edition of the dream book, published in 1908, seems to echo that allusion: "For this book has a further subjective significance for me personally—a significance which I only grasped after I had completed it. It was, I found, a portion of my own self-analysis, my reaction to my father's death—that is to say, to the most important event, the most poignant loss, of a man's life. Having discovered that this was so, I was unable to eliminate the traces of the experience" (Freud, 1900, p. xxvi). As we shall see, there is far more to this impassioned statement than meets the eye.

The loss of the big dream is, then, a monumental setback for those who would deign to decode Freud's secret traumas from his dream-associational material. Archetypically, it is all but certain that this dream and Freud's associations to its elements contained thinly disguised clues to the traumatic triggering events and deep unconscious experiences that were active at the time that Freud dreamt the dream and decided to write his dream book. The dream also must have touched on the most critical early-life traumas to which Freud had fallen victim. A thinness of disguise is suggested by Fliess's outright rejection of the dream and Freud's own comment regarding the dream to the effect that he had lost the feeling of shame required of an author.

*The Interpretation of Dreams* (Freud, 1900) contains Freud's first relatively independent psychoanalytic pronouncements and as such, the material in the book is of great significant on both the manifest and encoded levels of communication. Freud himself viewed the book as an unconscious effort to come to terms with the loss of his father, but clearly, additional trauma-induced unconscious motives and needs must have played a significant role in his selection of this dream as the centerpiece of the book. We have reason to suspect that the missing dream would have served as a harbinger of the past, reflection of the present, and predictor of the future. It is likely that Freud himself had no awareness that this was the case, yet his decision to do as Fleiss advised him suggests that he unconsciously intuited that the dream network was far too revealing of his actual traumas for him to tolerate its publication. Here too it seems that the initial impulse to reveal soon gave way to the stronger impulse to conceal.

The Irma dream was, then, a replacement dream, a substitute for a dream that would have almost certainly yielded many profound insights into Freud's life and work. The impression that the unconscious underpinnings of this substitute dream are quite obscure is in keeping with the adaptive finding that when a therapist misses an opportunity to trigger decode a thinly disguised, readily decodable dream, the patient will in the next session tend to report a dream that is far more dense and difficult to decode than its predecessor. A similar flight from encoded meaning seems to have occurred in the situation with Freud.


## FREUD'S SELF-ANALYSIS

This discussion has a bearing on Freud's self-analysis which he began soon after the death of his father and which was instrumental in his writing his dream book (Schur, 1972; Anzieu, 1959). The highpoint of his efforts—and they led to many new insights—was the solidification of his second paradigm and the rejection of the universal role played by childhood seductions in neuroses. The self-analysis soon led him to his own Oedipal wishes and to the generalization that the Oedipus complex is the central dynamism in neurotic symptoms (Freud, 1954, letter 71, October 15, 1987, pp. 221–225).

Adaptive studies have shown that because of the evolved, inherent defensiveness of the conscious system of the emotion-processing mind, unconsciously validated or true insight is possible only with a rigorous application of the use of trigger decoding. Narrative imagery provide the only known means of accessing deep unconscious experiences and the impeccable adaptive wisdom of the deep unconscious mind. On its own, the conscious mind is incapable of side-stepping or resolving its own defenses and arriving at these kinds of valid, deeply meaningful insights—it is geared towards self-deception and self-harm far more than self-knowledge. Even when attempts are made to engage in trigger decoding—efforts that

Freud did not undertake—the conscious mind seldom properly decodes its own dreams. We are all natural born encoders but we are not natural born decoders. The evolved design of the emotion-processing mind is such that the conscious mind is inherently disinclined and opposed to engaging in the process of trigger decoding, which is one reason why Freud did not intuitively attempt it and why this vital decoding process is not as yet part of standard analytic technique.

In adaptive psychotherapy, especially in its extended ninety-minute-session version (Langs, 1993, 2004, 2006), patients are taught the steps that can take them from a manifest dream to a trigger decoded insight. They learn to report a dream early in each session or to make up a fictional story—that is, create a dream equivalent; to associate to the elements of the dream with narratives of actual incidents from their own lives or from other sources drawn from the real world of experience; to identify and list the active triggers; and to connect the narrative themes to the meanings and implications of the most pertinent current triggering events. In most instances for patients in psychotherapy, the key triggers are interventions made by their therapists, many of them pertaining to the management of the ground rules and framework of treatment. The patients' narrative themes are decoded as valid unconscious perceptions of the implications of the triggering interventions made by their therapists to which are appended interpretations of patients' reactive thoughts and fantasies. To the greatest extent possible in light of the available narrative imagery, the effort is then made to connect these responses to current triggering events with experiences related to past traumatic incidents in the life of the patient. This is at present the only known path from the surface of a dream to deep unconscious experience and to the decoded processing of obliterated traumatic incidents.

Clinical practice indicates that making this journey on one's own is all but impossible—it takes a great deal of skill and luck to overcome the conscious-system defenses that have evolved to sabotage this kind of therapeutic effort. In most cases, then the assistance of an adaptive therapist is essential. This is the case because the underlying traumas and memories are so severely death-related and anxiety-provoking that they are utterly unbearable to the conscious mind. Patients who are able to carry out parts of this process typically arrive at formulations that reflect self-evident, conscious-system thinking that tends to involve relatively weak and unempowered issues. Despite the fact that they are in a first-paradigm form of therapy in which the decoding of encoded traumas is paramount, patients' self-interpretations tend, then, to be in keeping with Freud's second paradigm and to deal with issues of inner needs and conflicts. In creating his second paradigm of psychoanalysis, Freud did indeed lock himself and the world at large into a defense-dominated form of treatment that taps into the archetypal human need to deny death and its encumbrances.

The consistency of these findings speaks for two points of relevance here: First, that the archetypal preferences of the conscious mind conforms to Freud's second and not his first paradigm of emotional life. Freud moved from a paradigm that goes against human nature to one that, however defensive and weak its focus, is natural for the human mind. Second, there is the realization that Freud's self-analysis was all but certain to take him to some kind of inner need theory of the mind and move him away from the death-related traumas that the conscious mind finds so intolerable to experience and cope with.

The outcome of Freud's self-analysis was, then, sealed by evolution ages before he searched for and found what he was looking for regarding the etiology of neuroses. Any chance he had of staying the course in his fight against his natural inclinations to deny death and its encumbrances appears to have been lost because of the intense pressures to deny reality that were created with the anniversary of his father's death.

## MATTERS OF LIFE AND DEATH

Before writing this book, I borrowed from classical Freudian theory the thesis that the basic reason we defend ourselves against the recall of traumatic incidents or their reconstruction through trigger decoding is that these efforts, if successful, are certain to evoke unbearable anxieties and terrible depressive symptoms in the bearers of these secrets. Indeed, classical psychoanalytic theory is an anxiety-centered theory, and avoiding unbearable anxieties and resolving them in analysis are seen as prime goals of treatment. It also is a depression-centered theory in which the dread of abandonment and loss, and of narcissistic wounds, are central dynamisms. These seemed to be reasonable ideas and my main dispute with classical thinking lay with the basic sources of these anxieties—again, whether they derive mainly from realities or fantasies.

In the course of working on this book, however, I began to see these matters in a different light. Based in part on new insights into death-related archetypes that were emerging from my clinical work with patients and in part, on the material I was decoding in Freud's writings, a new thesis regarding the sources of resistances in psychoanalysis began to emerge. The outcome was that as I endeavored to ascertain why Freud needed to obliterate the major traumas in his life, I began to see signs that at the very moment when he decided to shift paradigms, the anxiety and depression he probably was experiencing was based on deeper issues—that what was at stake were matters of life and death! I developed the thesis that Freud's flight from reality and his paradigm shift were unconsciously driven by his being on the verge of suicide and/or homicide—each in some real but derivative manner. That is, I began to conjecture that

Freud was about to engage—or might have already engaged—in behaviors and in making decisions that would be or were going to be extremely self-destructive and/or devastatingly destructive against others. Encoded themes of murder, self-harm, and suicide were quite common in the narratives that he explored and generated on his own during this time in his life and career. The belief that they encoded his unconscious struggle with actually harming himself and others in some way began to find support and take hold.

Formulating matters in this vein became possible because I was realizing that for many years I had been observing clinical material that indicated that patients who have deliberately or inadvertently harmed others—for example, parents with genetically damaged children or who have been party to spontaneous or elective abortions—tend to obliterate and deny the ramifications of these death-related traumas and to avoid encoded expressions of these incidents as well. It emerged that they do so because they are utterly and deeply convinced that the trigger decoded recall of these incidents will cause them to punish themselves by committing suicide!

Clinically, whenever a reactivated, encoded recollection of this type of trauma arose in their material, themes of suicide would appear somewhere in their narratives. They were expressions of deadly encoded, unconscious impulses that had no counterpart in awareness. What's more, these impulses were not treated as fantasies—as I at first thought was the case—but as impulses that would lead to actual enactments. These patients tended to be chronically self-destructive, but they dreaded most the acute encoded expression of their "crimes" and they activated intense communicative defenses against this taking place. They behaved as if their lives were at stake and clung to their communicative defenses in order to save their lives!

Those patients who had been victims of death-related traumas caused by others—for example, being abandoned by their parents, children of mothers who had attempted to abort them, inadvertent victims of a congenital defect—reacted unconsciously to the possibility of recovering their obliterated traumas with fears that they would enact a talion form of revenge on those who had tried to harm or actually had damaged them. While many of these patients tried to consciously deny or minimize the harm done to them, their deep unconscious minds took the very opposite view of the situation—encoded themes of attempts to murder were quite common. And their level of anxiety was quite high not only because it stemmed from their homicidal impulses, but also from the deep unconscious guilt they experienced in response to their murderous intentions. This guilt created a need to punish themselves for their contemplated or actual murderous acts—again, by committing suicide. Archetypically, then, the turn to self-harm is the outcome of recovered traumas for both the victims and perpetrators of the harm involved.

These situations are difficult to resolve because the deep unconscious system of morality and ethics, which has an inbuilt, pristine set of moral standards, is extremely sensitive to the harm we cause others. The system unconsciously and insistently orchestrates rewards for moral behaviors and metes out severe punishments—usually by means of some equivalent of suicide—for transgressions. The system also is extremely unforgiving and self-punishing; indeed, helping patients to insightfully achieve *deep unconscious atonement and forgiveness for themselves and others* is one of the most difficult challenges encountered in adaptive psychotherapy—and in life as a whole. In like vein, with victims of harm, the system tends to insist that they mete out the talion punishments due to the offending parties. This is where the idea that the son must avenge the crimes of the father comes into play—an inner demand that seems to have played a notable role in Freud's life story.

There is considerable evidence that Freud was the victim of a series death-related traumas. He thus had good cause unconsciously to want to murder several members of his nuclear family—his father, mother, and half-brother in particular (see chapters 7 and 8). Quite outside of his conscious awareness, the death of his father and the arrival of the fateful first anniversary of his death seems to have rendered these intentions unbearably strong, intensifying his need to take vengeance on his predators after which he would feel pressures to commit suicide, probably in some attenuated form. It follows from this conjecture that Freud was desperately trying to save his life and prevent himself from wrecking his marriage and career by rejecting his seduction theory. In so doing, he was detoxifying the reality-based dangers he was experiencing by shifting the arena of his struggles—and those of his patients—from reality to fantasy. It appears, then, that it was for reasons of self-protection and survival that Freud turned away from the most compelling truths of emotional life and he did so in a way that had great appeal to his followers—and all of humankind. Who among us has not been victimized by, and the cause of harm to, others? For Freud personally and the world at large, survival was being served by his paradigm shift, even though the loss of personal and collective peace and wisdom was—and still is—enormous. Survival first, knowledge second, especially when that knowledge is life endangering.

As is usually the case, however, given the intensity of his unconsciously experienced traumas and conflicts, Freud's efforts at denial and defense did not—and could not—entirely suppress his need to expose those in his family who had harmed him and to confess to his own murderous response to them as well. This grim drama is encoded in his narrative material which he could not refrain from communicating to the very end of his life; it is present in his final effort at creative writing, *Moses and Monotheism* (Freud, 1939).

As I indicated earlier in this chapter, a reading of his dream book (Freud, 1900) shows the extent to which Freud made use of conscious-system defenses in negotiating these issues. Again and again, he tried to present his unconscious mind as populated with common, everyday needs and wishes while overlooking themes of theft, frame violations, violence, suicide, and murder which speak for far more gruesome problems in his life and work. Freud made use of his unconsciously wrought defenses in his analysis of the Oedipus myth by viewing incest as the primary issue while overlooking the multiple allusions to violence and death that are so dominant in the story. He did not know it consciously, but he was by evolved design fated to engage in these defenses and he built his psychoanalysis on that particular foundation.

In so doing, Freud managed to save his life, but he led the world down a primrose path when it needed, as far as psychoanalysis was concerned, to journey down a path strewn with the grim truths of life and death. Had he not done so, there might not have been a psychoanalytic movement, but there probably would have been a version of the adaptive approach, however few its followers. In time, someone else undoubtedly would have created an inner-need form of psychoanalysis which, because of the archetypal unconscious needs it satisfies, eventually would have flourished. But even as the analysts committed to this form of psychoanalysis were trying to deny reality and death, they would be haunted unconsciously by Hamlet's thought, which is quoted by Freud in the letter in which he introduced his second paradigm of emotional life: "So conscience doth make cowards of us all" (Freud, 1954, Letter 71, October 15, 1897, p. 224).

Freud seems to have known unconsciously that he had fled his past in a state of hidden fear and as a desperate life-saving measure. There is consolation in knowing that his flight was archetypically determined, but there also is pain in knowing that it is a retreat engineered by unrecognized human weaknesses. Facing up to the discovery that classical psychoanalysis is a basic defense against suicide and murder calls for courage to face this truth and asks us to come up with better ways to cope with the death-related traumas that inevitably come our way. Freud did not move in that direction; his genius was humbled by reality. It's time now to investigate just what those awful realities were.

# Chapter 7

# Freud's Early Traumas

Based on universal archetypes, the traumas that Freud experienced in his early years can, in principle, be expected to have left traces of consciously recalled fragments, but their main representations would have taken an encoded form. The most significant aspects of these traumas would operate deep unconsciously and would find expression only when a related current trauma reactivated these earlier incidents. The resultant encoded narratives would, in their imagery, condense the unconscious nature and meanings of both of these traumatic experiences—present and past. It can be seen, then, that trigger decoding is vital to the recovery of death-related traumas, especially those that have arisen early in a life. These traumas operate like the inextinguishable background radiation that was generated with the origins of the universe at the time of the big bang—their effects are everlasting, that is, they persist within a given lifetime. They can function as unconscious sources of creativity, but they also serve as the basic source of emotional dysfunctions such as emotionally founded symptoms and errant views of the emotion-processing mind and human condition.

Gaining access to these repressed, obliterated traumas is quite difficult. They do not break through whole cloth into awareness and their reconstruction tends to be met with great resistance from both patients and their psychoanalysts. Nevertheless, when encoded themes related to the past are activated by a current trauma, there usually are disguised markers of the earlier incident such as allusions to the time period in which the trauma took place. Therapists need to be prepared for such material from their patients and they should keep in mind the task of reconstructing the traumatic past if they are to offer that type of formulation. Patients will respond consciously to these interventions in various ways, positive and negative, but their narrative associations, which encode validating or non-validating reactions, are critical to the therapist's assessment of the accuracy of his or her reconstruction. A relatively complete understanding of a current symptom, whatever form it takes, is possible only when the links to an earlier trauma have been identified and the relevant themes trigger decoded in light of both the present triggering incident and the past, death-related trauma.

## THE GAME PLAN

It is in this spirit, but with full awareness that this kind of methodology is applicable to biographical explorations only in a limited way, that I shall now endeavor to identify and discuss the most likely traumas in Freud's early life. I shall present the known manifest clues that suggest that these traumas did in fact occur; explore trigger decode narrative material available in Freud's writings that seems to encode and confirm the existence of these traumas; discuss how Freud seems to have coped with these death-related incidents; and finally, indicate how these analyses clarify the unconscious sources of Freud's errant paradigm shift.

In delineating the direct and encoded evidence for the existence and influence of these traumas, I shall examine four different sources of information:

- Freud's *direct recall,* if any, of a given trauma as he consciously experienced and remembered it.
- Freud's *encoded recall* of a given trauma as he unconsciously experienced and remembered it.
- Freud's *encoded unconscious perceptions* of, and reactive fantasies to, the trauma in question.
- The *unconsciously mediated* effects of the trauma on Freud's paradigm shift.

In principle, a trauma may be consciously experienced, remembered consciously in part and the rest obliterated and repressed, or it may be entirely obliterated at the time it takes place or some time after it actually happens. Whatever the mechanisms, most or all of the incident is thereafter unavailable to conscious recall and the recollection of the event will surface solely in encoded form when it is reactivated.

In addition to the conscious or deep unconscious registration of a traumatic incident *per se,* there are conscious and especially unconscious thoughts, fantasies, beliefs, and memories that arise in connection with what has happened, why it happened as it did, and what it means. These fantasies are not biologically driven from within the mind based on unconscious sexual and other needs; they are instead reactions to an external trauma and serve as part of an individual's conscious and unconscious efforts to adapt to the damage that the trauma has caused. Archetypically, the conscious mind tends to obliterate much or all of a death-related trauma and surround it with barriers to recall that are constituted as forms of communicative defense and denial and repression. Conscious assessments of these incidents therefore are incomplete and unreliable, and not to be trusted. On the other hand, the deep unconscious mind processes these incidents with great wisdom and insight, but its view of these events is always extreme; it tends to stress the most horrendous implications of these incidents and imagines worst case scenarios as well.

To cite a hypothetical, archetype-based example, Freud may have been told about, and thus known of and thought about consciously, the death of two of his father's children during his first marriage. There may have been some consciously mediated effects of this information. But in addition, Freud most likely would have developed a series of unconscious beliefs about what had happened and processed these fantasies entirely outside of awareness. For example, he probably would have entertained the idea that the two children were murdered by their parents who had then cannibalized them. Freud fainted during his brief effort to psychoanalyze Victor Tausk when Tausk reported a dream in which he cut Freud's body into pieces and devoured them piece by piece. This later-day event may well have been based on Freud's unconscious, reactive fantasies about this earlier trauma which had remained active in Freud's deep unconscious mind and imagination.

## CONTRIBUTIONS FROM KRULL AND BALMARY

The most extensive studies of Freud's early traumas were reported by Krull (1979) and Balmary (1979). Krull's position is that Freud erred in abandoning his seduction theory instead of extending it to include non-sexual traumas. In her view, the unconscious roots of this decision lay with an unconsciously communicated mandate from his father to conceal the father's transgressions. In support of this contention, she cites the double-image dream that Freud dreamt the night before or after the day of his father's funeral (Freud, 1954, Letter 50, November 2, 1896, pp. 170–171; Freud, 1900). In the dream Freud sees a sign telling him: Thou shalt close the eye; thou shalt close the eyes.

Krull takes this to mean that Freud must not look into his father's religious and sexual transgressions. The former took shape as a liberalization of the father's religious position and his abandonment of many of the orthodox beliefs and practices of his nuclear family (Rizzuto, 1998). The latter may have involved adulterous infidelities while the father was away on business—that is, transgressions of both a religious and sexual nature; there may have been secret, religiously and socially unacceptable masturbatory practices on his part as well. Based on extensive indirect evidence that indicated that Freud had an unconscious awareness of his father's infidelities, Balmary (1979) also believes that one reason why Freud turned away from the reality of his patients' early seductions was because they inevitably would have led him to the anxiety-provoking seductive acts of his father (see section on Rebekka Freud).

Regarding other issues, Krull does not take up the question of Freud's date of birth; she accepts the date claimed by his parents, much as does Freud's mainstream biographers (Gay, 1988). On the other hand, Balmary accepts the evidence found in local records, whose validity is challenged by some researchers, including Krull, namely, that Freud actually was born on March 6 rather than May 6, 1856. Balmary includes the falsification of his birth date among the three great secrets in Freud's early life: the other two being Jakob's marriage to Rebekka, his second wife, who probably committed suicide by jumping from a train, and the likelihood that Freud's mother had an affair with her step-son, Phillip—an affair that Krull also believes to have taken place. However, Krull leaves room for doubt that Rebekka actually existed; to the extent that she acknowledges the possibility of her existence, Krull does not explore the possibility that Rebekka committed suicide.

Both authors agree that whatever actually happened before and soon after his birth, Freud seems to have been unaware consciously of these traumas which were not spoken of by the family and were concealed from him by all concerned. Nevertheless, both writers point to recollections of his early childhood that suggest that these traumas did in fact take place. In a limited manner they also have tried to decode dream and other narrative material published by Freud that seems to support their conjectures. The possibility that Phillip was Freud's father or that Freud believed that this was the case is briefly mentioned in passing by Krull but not developed as a thesis; Balmary does not raise this issue at all.

Let's look now more closely at these purported and known early traumas and see what can be said of their nature and effects.

## THE LOSS OF SIBLINGS

Of the eight possible early-life traumas experienced by Freud listed in the previous chapter, the deaths of his half-siblings seem to have had the least unconscious impact on him; themes of infanticide and fratricide are relatively rare in Freud's narratives. The available historical material does not tell us if Freud knew about the death of the two children, a boy and a girl, who were born to his father and

Sally Kanner, his first wife. Freud interacted with their two surviving sons, Emmanuel and Phillip, but there are indications that they were inclined through some kind of family conspiracy to keep secrets from their much younger half-brother. Thus, they must have known about their deceased siblings, but they do not seem to have mentioned them to Freud. Little is known about their own reactions to these deaths. However, in the service of denying one's personal vulnerability to death, this type of death-related trauma tends unconsciously to be dealt with through violations of the ideal, archetypal frame—rule-breakers believe unconsciously that they are exceptions to the existential rule that life is followed by death (Langs, 2006). Thus this trauma may have played a role in the likely liaison between Phillip and Amalie, Freud's mother. Freud's step-brothers also must have known Jakob's second wife, Rebecca, and what had happened to her. But here too there is no indication that they spoke about her to their half-brother. Freud seems to have been consciously unaware of her existence; there is however evidence that he knew about her unconsciously.

As for the death of his brother Julius at age six months when Freud was two years old, Freud seems to have been consciously aware of his illness, which involved bowel infections, and he was well aware of his death. Freud mentioned it from time to time in his correspondence and writings. This loss did not consciously bring up the loss of his half-siblings before his birth; instead, Freud mainly expressed his guilt over his conscious wish to be rid of his rival for his mother's love. But in other comments, Freud expressed skepticism regarding the extent to which a two-year old can experience jealousy of a rival, so it appears that much of what he recalled may have been constructed consciously in later years.

Another source of anxiety which undoubtedly operated unconsciously may have been derived from Freud's knowledge that his father's younger brother, Abae, had four children, of whom one daughter appeared to be "normal," whereas another daughter and one of his sons became psychotic in their late teens; the other son was hydrocephalic and mentally impaired. Even though they were his cousins, archetypically, these impairments would tend to evoke a survivor type of guilt in Freud and unconscious anxieties related to having children who might suffer similar fates. Nevertheless, Freud's narrative material does not appear to have unmistakable encoded indications that these traumas were a prominent unconscious concern for him. Even so, I would conjecture that these traumas did affect Freud, even if in a secondary fashion. Family histories of this kind tend to make reality unpalatable and create needs to flee its relentlessly disturbing qualities.

Along different lines, Freud is likely to have unconsciously believed that Julius was murdered by Jakob and Amalie. Jakob in particular is likely to have been viewed in this way because he also would have been seen as the murderer of the two dead children from his first marriage and as the murderer of his second wife, Rebekka's, as well. The loss of Julius also would have been experienced unconsciously as a punishment to Jakob for these earlier crimes. Furthermore, as his father's son, Freud would have experienced an archetypal unconscious need to take on the sins of his father and seek punishment in his father's place—ultimately through being executed for these crimes and thus, through suicide or its equivalent. This may have been one of the unconscious constellations of death-related memories and reactions that were aroused with the death and its anniversary of his familial father, Jakob. As we shall see, the extended version of the myth of Oedipus entails Oedipus's taking on the sins of his father which had involved the seduction of a brotherly figure that had caused the sibling-like figure to commit suicide. In this context, Oedipus's murder of his father, which was ordained by the gods, can be seen as a talion punishment for the father's crime—a crime that is repeated in the father's attempt to murder Oedipus. As for Oedipus, with whom Freud identified, it needs to be appreciated that even a justified executioner experiences unconscious guilt and need for punishment for carrying out his divine mandate. Indeed, in the myth Oedipus is punished for having killed his father and not for having had incestuous sexual relations with his mother.

There are however only a small number of indications that Freud unconsciously processed these shadowy events. Archetypically, the psychotic state of his cousin probably created an unconscious fear of madness in Freud. In addition, although the relatives involved were distant relations, there also would be a fear that working over and decoding his deep unconscious memories of his early-life traumas would drive him insane. Freud showed signs of anxiety in connection with working with psychotic patients and reported only one major case of this kind—the Schreber case which was derived from his autobiographical writings rather than from direct clinical experience. Freud's analysis of Victor Tausk, an older student of his who showed signs of psychotic problems, was short-lived and Freud anxiously referred him to a junior colleague, Helene Deutsch. This decision was made after Freud had fainted when Tausk reported a dream of cannibalizing him (Roazen, 1969; Langs, 2000). Thus, an unconscious fear of madness may have played a role in Freud's flight from reality at the time of his paradigm shift.


## REBEKKA FREUD

Rebekka Freud is the mystery woman in Freud's pre-life history. During his lifetime, family lore had it that his father, Jakob, had been married to two women, Sally Kanner and Freud's mother, Amalie. However, historians have found seemingly irrefutable documentation in municipal records that Amalie was in fact Jakob's third wife and that his second wife was a woman named Rebekka.

Jakob's first spouse, Sally Kanner, bore him four children, two of whom died in childhood. The remaining children were Emanuel, who was born in 1833 and Phillip, who was born in 1834. (Amalie was born on August 18, 1835.) Sally died in 1852 and later that year a woman named Rebekka was listed as Jakob's current wife. By 1854 Rebekka was no longer listed as a member of the Freud household and because there is no local record of her death, it has been speculated that Jakob might have divorced her because she was childless (Krull, 1979) or that she had died somewhere other than in Frieberg. The first hypothesis is highly unlikely (Schur, 1972), although it may be encoded in Freud's (1910a) study of Leonardo DaVinci (see chapter 8), and the second hypothesis highly probable. Indeed, Balmary (1979) offers the thesis that the death of Rebekka some three years before Freud was born was the main hidden trauma of his early life, and that while Freud had no conscious awareness of this event, he did have a strong unconscious awareness of what had happened. She goes so far as to offer evidence that Rebekka probably committed suicide by either jumping from or in front of a train—probably the former. She argues that Freud's unconscious experience of this trauma was at the heart of what she sees as his neurotic flight from reality at the time of his paradigm shift and that this incident also was the unconscious source of Freud's severe train phobia.

Balmary's (1979) main support for these conjectures is taken form the myth of Oedipus, in which the first murder and first sexual crime are committed by the father rather than the son. That is, the basic fault is an act of the father, and the son then identifies with the father, introjects his crime and the need for punishment for the ill deed, and reacts to the father accordingly. Her main point is that Freud's seduction theory took into account the fault of the father—the primary seducer—which therefore called for the investigation of the father's role in the child's neurosis. After the death of his father, however, Freud was unable to tolerate the pursuit of his father's faults nor could he continue the exploration of how they had affected him as his father's son. The result was a shift from his trauma-based theory, in which both the father and the son are seen to play a role in the son's neurosis, to a wish-based theory in which the son, as an Oedipal figure, is held solely responsible for his suffering. Thus, this change of viewpoint constituted a denial of the role of the father in the son's emotional problems.

Balmary sees this shift in thinking as a turn to an untenable position, one that Freud adopted without good reason in that he did not indicate that it was based on fresh clinical observations that justified his new way of thinking.

Instead, Freud merely described his subjective impression that he had been wrong about the role of seduction in neuroses and suggested that emotional problems actually stem from forbidden wishes, largely incestuous in nature. In sum, then, as Balmary sees it, Freud had a neurotic need to forgive his father and deny his transgressions, and he transformed this need into an unfounded, new theory of neuosogenesis that exonerated the guilty parent. Freud's second paradigm therefore is an unconsciously driven neurotic symptom rather than an empirically documented insight.

With these formulations in mind, Balmary searched for both clues to the trauma or traumas that Freud's father secretly bestowed on his son and for indications that Freud's paradigm shift was gravely misdirected because of these early-life incidents. She focused on the Oedipus myth and the prehistory of the myth (Devereux, 1953) in which Oedipus's father, Laius, experiences the death of his father and his regent is killed. Laius seeks refuge with King Pelops and in time, he develops a passion for the king's son, Chrysippus with whom he runs off and seduces. In response, Chrysippus kills himself and Pelops puts a curse on Laius who, after his marriage to Jocasta, is warned by the oracle to not have a son because the son will murder him and marry his wife—the son's mother.

It is not known if Freud, who knew a great deal about Greek mythology, was familiar with this pre-story; he did not allude to it in his writings. Nonetheless, Balmary believes that it is quite likely that Freud had knowledge of the entire myth. She then points out that the pre-story strongly supports her contention that the faults of the father are the prelude to the symptoms of the child. In the myth, the fault is the seduction of Chrysippus which causes him to kill himself. A second fault identified by Balmary lies with Laius going against the oracle's prohibition against his having a son.

In these terms, then, the seduction theory, broadly defined, is affirmed and any theory that excludes the role of the other—that is, the parent or other caretakers—is in error. Balmary stresses the transmission of the fault from the father to the son and the unconscious need of the son to both atone and be punished for his father's transgressions—and for his own transgressions as well. In the myth, Laius's sin is punished by his being murdered by his son and Oedipus's sin is punished through his causing his own blindness and in the ways in which, afterwards, he sends his own sons to their deaths.

Balmary offers an extensive discussion of the Oedipus myth in which she questions Freud's choice of this myth as representing the core issue in emotional life and neuroses. She challenges what she sees as Freud's misguided emphasis on Oedipus's incestuous relationship with Jocasta to the neglect of other themes in the story. Balmary also suggests that Freud was quite defensive in interpreting the meanings of the myth in that he took its contents at face value, manifestly, without attempting to psychoanalyze and decode its contents in order to ascertain its unconscious meanings. She makes special note of the allusion to the second seduction that results in a suicide: Oedipus's seduction of his mother, Jocasta who, on discovering the truth of their relationship, kills herself. Balmary sees this as an encoded representation of Freud's belief or knowledge that Rebekka Freud committed suicide.

To comment briefly, the main problem with this conjecture is that it is difficult to justify a connection between the incest-based suicide that takes place in the myth and the evidently legitimate marriage of Rebekka to Jakob Freud. There is no indication that Rebekka was a member of Jakob's family, so the test of validation through the presence of bridging themes seems to fail. The human mind usually tells an integrated encoded story as it pertains to and describes a past trauma—each element of the story supports the other elements. This does not seem to be the case here—unless it is discovered that there was a blood link between Jakob and Rebekka.

Balmary does however cite other encoded evidence for the thesis that Freud had somehow, however unconsciously, learned about and processed the traumatic news of his father's marriage to Rebekka and her eventual suicide. For one, she points to Freud's unusual interest in Mozart's opera, *Don Giovanni*—Freud was quite unmusical. She connects this with his interest in mushrooms and his aversion to umbrellas, linking them through the theme of statues. Don Juan is the great seducer of women, while Leporello is his servant and the observer of these seductions. Balmary presents evidence that Freud unconsciously saw his father as a seducer of women and that Freud viewed Jakob's marriage to Rebekka as a dishonorable seductive act.

The Mozart opera tells the story of Don Juan's intention to forcibly seduce a young girl, Anna, whose father tries to defend her and who, as a result, is killed in a fight with Don Juan. Leporello and Don Juan spend a night in the cemetery where the father is buried and they see the inscription on the father's pedestal which promises to avenge the impious one who killed him. Don Juan mocks the threat and Leporello invites the father to dinner. He accepts the invitation and when he appears, Don Juan refuses his proposal that he convert. The statue takes his hand and the ground opens up and swallows Don Juan who is already in the grip of the terror and torments of hell.

Balmary links this dinner scene to the thesis that Freud (1913b) offered in *Totem and Taboo* to the effect that the origins of morality and religion lay in the past when a father possessed all of the women and allowed none to his sons. The sons rebelled and devoured the father, and then, in their guilt, forbid the eating of the totem animal who represented the devoured father—a theme that also may have been related to Phillip Freud's seduction of Jakob's wife, Amalie (see below). Unconsciously, Freud is said to have had a comparable attitude towards his father whom he saw as the seducer and the indiscriminate possessor of women. In this connection, Balmary believes that the questions Freud asked unconsciously about the secret date of his birth—"When was I born?"—was a disguised version of the question: "Who was Rebekka and when and how did she die?"

Along different lines, Balmary connects Freud's inhibition regarding visiting Rome to his interest in the statue of Moses, the law-giver of the Jews, and to Rebekka, who is represented there indirectly (Freud, 1914d). The Moses statue sits atop the tomb of Pope Julius (whose name is the same as that of the brother whom Freud lost as an infant). There are two other statues present with Moses, those of Leah and Rachel, the wives of the biblical Jacob whose mother was named Rebecca.

Balmary sees these links as reflecting the unconscious reasons Freud avoided Rome, much as he avoided confronting the sins of his father. She also suggests a possible link between the death (and fantasied murder) of Julius, the purported second child of Jakob and Amalie, to the death (and fantasied murder) of Jakob's second wife, Rebekka—all of which calls for punishment by death for the offending parties. While once again the connections here are quite loose and speculative, the implied conclusion once more is that Freud was unconsciously aware of his father's crimes and that he experienced a deep unconscious need to be both the executioner and executed for these misdeeds.

Another speculation comes to mind in this connection. While Balmary does not raise the question, we may wonder if Freud unconsciously believed or fantasized that Rebecca was his biological mother. This belief would have made her death a far more personal tragedy for Freud than his belief that his father had seduced and married her and then contributed to her death—that is, murdered her. This fantasy also would have intensified Freud's need to avenge Rebekka's death by killing—that is, devouring—his father, a justifiable homicide for which Freud nevertheless would then have condemned himself to death.

This line of thought also hearkens back to the Oedipus myth. Not only did the son murder the father, he also was the cause of the suicide of the mother. This is one of the reasons why Oedipus blinds himself and wishes to return to Mt. Cithaeron where his father had left him to die as a newborn. In this decoded reading of the myth, Freud unconsciously holds himself accountable for the death of Rebekka, a belief that is condensed with his evident wish to murder his actual mother, Amalie, for reasons that will be further discussed in the next chapter.

While these are highly speculative possibilities, they are in keeping with the extremely jaundiced aspects of deep unconscious experience and the tendency of the deep unconscious mind to react to traumatic incidents with flourishes of horrendous fantasies and beliefs. These are the kind of unconscious imaginings that embroider realities in ways that Freud, as is true of all humans, would have wanted to avoid bringing into conscious awareness at all cost. In any case, they speak for the need for denial-based barriers of a kind that few would dare to transgress, and thereby, they may account for the barriers that analysts in general have set against reality-based theories of the mind and neuroses. This danger is captured in a quotation of Shakespeare made by Freud in his letter announcing his discovery of the centrality of the Oedipus complex: "use every man after his desert, and who should 'scape whipping?" (Freud, 1954, Letter 71, October 15, 1997, p. 224). Freud meant this one way; I mean it quite another—that is, that the consequences of sinning in reality far outweigh those of sinning in fantasy.

As for other possible encoded allusions to Rebekka in Freud's writings, Balmary turns to Freud's "I no longer believe my *neurotica*" letter written nearly a year after the death of his father (Freud, 1954, letter 69, September 21, 1897, pp. 215–218). She reports that in the weeks prior to writing this letter, Freud had begun his self-analysis, picked out his father's headstone, traveled to Salzburg, the home of Mozart, with his sister-in-law, Minna, and suffered from his railway phobia while traveling to Orvieto to view the frescoes of the Last Judgment by Signorelli.

It is noteworthy that, although Balmary does not allude to it, that there are historians who believe that Freud had an affair with Minna (Swales, 1982; Maciejewski, 2007). Even if this was not the case explicitly, there is clear evidence that Freud was deeply involved with Minna whom some saw as his second wife, thus his journey with his sister-in-law must have had a strong incestuous quality to it. This incident therefore would have activated two of Freud's likely early traumas—his unconscious experience of having had two fathers and the affair between his mother and half-brother—thereby unconsciously recreating realities with unbearable consequences for him. This situation could have motivated him to decode his dreams in order to reconstruct these past traumas, but at the same time it also would have motivated him to not do so and to flee reality for insurance against the recovery of these memories. This may well have been one of the more compelling immediate triggers for his paradigm shift.

As for the frescoes, Freud's forgetting the artist's name was the subject of a paper he wrote in 1898 (Freud, 1898b). It is the first anecdote in his book, *The Psychopathology of Everyday Life* (Freud, 1901; see chapter 8) where the themes that Freud connects with the paintings are those of divine judgment, sexuality, and death—including the death of one of Freud's patients by suicide. Condemnation of his father for his sexual and murderous transgressions is implied in this encoded narrative. But it also may encode Freud's own guilt over his relationship with Minna and the presence of an impulse to commit suicide as the punishment he too deserved—killing off Freud's wife, Martha, also is implicit to this story. This is one of many indications that Freud was at a precipice when he decided to flee reality—that suicide in some derivative form was a real possibility had he not found a strong enough defense to bury the entire matter deep in the recesses of his mind.

## THE BIBLICAL REBECCA

Toward the end of the letter that Freud wrote to Fliess on September 21, 1997 renouncing his *neurotica,* Freud commented:

> I vary Hamlet's remark about ripeness—cheerfulness is all. I might be feel-ing very unhappy. The hope of eternal fame was so beautiful, and so was that of certain wealth, complete independence, travel, and removing the children from the sphere of worries which spoiled my own youth. All that depended on whether hysteria succeeded or not. Now I can be quiet and modest again and go on worrying and saving, and one of the stories from my collection occurs to me: "Rebecca, you can take off your wedding-gown, you're not a bride any longer!" (Freud, 1954, Letter 69, pp. 217–218)

This is the first allusion to a Rebecca in Freud's writings and it arises at a point in his thinking when a void seems to have been created: Seductions are not real, but imagined and thus are not the source of neuroses, but fantasies have not as yet claimed their right to be the source he was seeking, so the mat-ter stands as a mystery and the culprit is unknown. There is then no essential understanding of hysteria. All is lost.

Slightly less than a month later, however, convinced that he has benefited from his self-analysis, Freud tells Fliess that he now believes that the Oedipus complex is the root cause of hysteria and other neuroses (Freud, 1954, Letter 71, October 15, 1997, pp. 221–225). The story of Hamlet receives a more extended mention in that letter and I shall return to it in greater detail in the next chapter.

For Balmary (1979) it is sufficient that the name Rebecca occurs to Freud at the very moment he is renouncing his seduction theory. This is taken as evidence that his not wanting to bring his father's transgressions with Rebekka into awareness is the unconscious source of Freud's change of heart. Balmary pays little attention to the other themes in the allusion to Rebecca so she does not account for their presence—she takes one part of the whole with-out meeting the requisite that the remaining themes also must be accounted for. Nevertheless, the mention of Rebecca is seen as a disguised allusion to the fault of Freud's father. Balmary suggests that the wedding gown quotation did not occur to Freud by chance, but did so because there was active unconscious processing going on as evidenced by Freud's indication that his change of heart involved belief trumping observation and unconscious need trumping empirically grounded and reasoned response.

Balmary sees Freud's paradigm shift as marking his transition from a scientist to an impressionistic believer, a psychoanalyst. We may add that it is much easier to be a believer than a critical observer who must find ways to test and validate his or her theories and convictions. This is one of the great appeals of the second paradigm which is without a sound means of validation, while the first paradigm has such a method, one that is based on unconscious responses from the very knowledgeable deep unconscious wisdom subsystem of the emotion-processing mind.

A look at Freud's manifest train of thought in this crucial letter supports the idea of unconsciously driven imagery. Freud has just bemoaned the fact that his admitting that he no longer understands hysteria will prevent him from realizing his dreams of fame and fortune. He inserts an allusion to the lack of money as the cause of his childhood miseries, a self-interpretation which in all likelihood substitutes a lesser consciously remembered problem for a much stronger death related issue which he seems to be processing deep unconsciously.

The subsequent anecdote about the wedding gown seems consciously intended to express Freud's loss of knowledge which will cause the world at large to no longer take him as their bride—that is, give him their love. On the face of it, this is a very strange if not completely inappropriate and thus unconsciously driven way to express his disappointment over his loss of insight. Freud sees himself as a woman who is about to be married who suddenly is no longer marriageable. This is a most peculiar way to represent the loss of a major psychoanalytic insight and the rewards he expected to receive on that basis. If there is an underlying identification with Jakob's second wife, Rebekka, it can only speak unconsciously for thoughts of suicide—again, for Freud at a precipice. And we can be quite sure that the implied or encoded suicidal thoughts are not simply a response to an expected loss of fame and income, but derive from deeper unconscious sources of the kind I have been pointing to.

An understanding of the Biblical source of this allusion makes it even more of a *non sequitur* on the conscious level. The reference unmistakably is to Genesis and to Rebecca as the future wife of Isaac, the son of Abraham who was the father of the Jews. The essence of the message is that she not a virgin and thus cannot marry Isaac.

This reading is based on Rabbinical interpretations of the biblical story of Isaac's marriage. The bible tells us that Isaac's father, Abraham, sent a servant to find a bride for his son in Canaan, their homeland. When Rebecca offered the servant some water at a well, she was chosen for the role. Although it is not part of the old testament, the Rabbis believed that when Rebecca came to Isaac, he was entitled to check to see if she was a virgin. When he did this he found that her hymen was not intact and thus he asked her to take off her gown as she no longer could be his bride. But Rebecca explained that she had gotten entangled in some brush which caused her hymen to be ruptured; Isaac accepted this explanation and the wedding took place.

The essence of the sentence then is that Rebecca is not a virgin and thus cannot be a bride. These themes also do not fit with the conscious use that Freud was trying to make of them as a show of disappointment that he no longer had a theory of neuroses. Instead, as a self-reference, the story implies that Freud is damaged and unfaithful in some way—possibly to psychoanalysis by giving up his seduction theory. As for the encoded message contained in this brief story, while Balmary does not state it as such, the implication for Freud's unconscious view of the Rebekka situation is that she was damaged in some way which made her unsuitable as Jakob's bride. It raises the possibility, as some have claimed despite the village records, that Rebekka had not married Jakob, but lived with him for a while and then disappeared. The attempt to decode this story in light of an unconscious memory of the death of Jakob's second wife produces strained results of a kind that make this connection questionable at best. In the next chapter I shall offer an alternative thesis regarding the unconscious meanings of this story in the context of Freud's flight from reality.


## REBECCA WEST

The only other mention of a Rebecca in Freud's writings appears in his paper on some character types met in psychoanalysis, in the section on those wrecked by success (Freud, 1916; Balmary, 1979). The reference is to Rebecca West, one of the main characters in Ibsen's play, Rosmersholm. Freud's comments are preceded by a reference to Lady Macbeth as someone who, like Rebecca West, was wrecked by success. Lady Macbeth found success by participating in the murder of King Duncan and placing Macbeth on the throne, but it is a crime for which she pays with her life by committing suicide. Rebecca West drives Beata, the childless wife of the pastor whom Rebecca loves, to commit suicide but then is unable to marry the pastor—that is, to become his second wife. Rebecca West also ends her life by killing herself.

For Balmary, these themes again point to Freud's unconscious working over of the death of his father's second wife, Rebekka, through suicide. Rebekka is portrayed in these encoded stories as being childless and as having disappeared without leaving a trace or a child. But Freud does not mention Rebecca West's suicide which harkens back to the suicide of Jocasta. The link here is that Rebecca West's hidden crime was that she had committed incest with the man who had adopted her; it turns out that he was her father. Balmary also picks up on Rebecca West's falsification of her date of birth and ties this to the falsification of the date on which Freud was born. Jakob's impregnation of Amalie after the death of Rebekka, which may have taken place before his marriage to Amalie, is seen as another hidden fault of Freud's father. Unconsciously, Freud would have held himself accountable for the suicide of Rebekka, fancifully seeing it as a crime that he had committed before he was born, one that would have caused him to take on a deep unconscious guilt which he did not deserve.

It is well to note that these themes also could represent Freud's conviction that his mother had had an incestuous affair with her step-son and that Freud viewed it as the murder and overthrowing of Jakob as the father-king. As we shall see in the next chapter, there is considerable encoded evidence that Freud's punishment for Amalie for this transgression is that she should die by her own hand.

Returning to Balmary's conjectures, she also sees an encoded allusion to the suicide of Jakob's second wife in the epigraph for Freud's (1900) *The Interpretation of Dreams:* "If I cannot bend the higher powers, I will move the Infernal Regions." The quotation is taken from Virgil's Aeneid and the words are spoken by Juno in response to Aeneas's seduction of Dido who then commits suicide—the abandoned woman who takes her own life. This is another link to the purported fate of Rebekka.

Along different lines, Balmary cites the dream that Freud dreamt the night before or after his father's funeral, the double image of being requested to close his eyes. As does Krull (1979), Balmary sees this as an injunction to Freud to close his eyes to his father's faults—a command that Freud evidently obeyed by renouncing his seduction theory.

Balmary goes through Freud's letters to Fleiss and his lectures to the profession, presenting what she sees as other disguised indications that the death of Rebekka was a major trauma for Freud and that it adversely affected his creation of psychoanalysis, but she addresses these problems largely in terms of Freud's unconscious fantasies and wishes. Most notable in this regard is the lecture that Freud delivered in May 1896 to The Vienna Psychiatric Society—the first public delivery of his burgeoning ideas. Freud (1896c) made up two case studies; both involved train accidents and fatalities. It is certainly strange that in giving this landmark paper, Freud chose to present fictional case material drawn from his imagination instead of actual patient data. Here too we may treat the narratives as the equivalents of a first dream in analysis and suspect that the fictional material has special unconscious meaning for Freud. Balmary mainly sees this decision as another indication that for Freud, his work as a psychoanalyst was closely linked unconsciously to the death of Rebekka Freud.

Summing up, Balmary's thesis regarding the fault of the father and the traumatic impact on Freud of the likely suicide of Rebekka seems to have some support in the encoded narratives that Freud generated in the course of his work as a psychoanalyst. Nevertheless, there are evident uncertainties that raise questions about the validity of the conclusions she makes based on the extensive evidence she has gathered to support her thesis. When we come down to it, there are only two allusions to the name Rebecca in Freud's communications—the take-off-your-gown anecdote and the story of Rebecca West. There also are encoded bridging themes scattered throughout Freud's writings that link up with the death of Rebekka—themes like second wife, death and suicide, murder, and mysterious disappearance. The problem with all of this is that the deep unconscious system is a story teller; pieces of encoded narratives should go well together, support each other, weave a tale. The same principle applies to the narratives in a letter or dream: There should be elements scattered throughout the imagery that come together to encode an integrated narrative story—in this situation, that of an early traumatic event and its unconsciously experienced ramifications. In the service of disguise, these encoded stories are fragmented and the elements, rather than being continuous, tend to be discontinuous—one part of the tale here, another part there. Nevertheless, if the triggering event has been correctly identified, a reconstructed story can be pieced together from the fragments, and the integrated story is logical, sensible, and quite grim.

Balmary's decoded material does not seem to lend itself to such a narrative. Rebecca's taking off her gown because she is soiled does not seem to fit as an encoded representation of Rebekka Freud's disappearance. The themes of childlessness that Balmary touch on lead in one story to suicide (Lady Macbeth) and in the other story (Rebecca West) to both to suicide and murder. They are however unlikely to have been connected Rebekka's death unless there is a missing trauma of a miscarriage or abortion, serious possibilities for which, however, there appears to be no palpable evidence.

Jakob's marriage to Rebekka was appropriate and not known to have been incestuous or unduly seductive, but the themes that Balmary turns to repeatedly touch on these issues, suggesting a disconnection rather than a linkage. The ideas that Rebecca West had committed incest, compelled another woman to kill herself, and then committed suicide herself when she could have married the man she loved do not come together in an easy way that ties them to the death of Rebekka Freud. Thus, even though Balmary offers strong indications that Freud's paradigm shift was unconsciously driven by an early trauma that he could not bear to bring into awareness, and even though the mysterious disappearance of Rebekka Freud is likely to have been an issue unconsciously for Freud, the circumstances surrounding this event and Freud's unconscious view of his father's fault in this connection are difficult to define. This drama seems to be best captured in a story that Freud did not allude to in his writings and thus may not have been aware of—that of Laiuis's seduction of Chrippidus and the latter's suicide.

Balmary's work is fascinating and promising, but without an encoded smoking gun. The questionable outcome of her extensive and well-researched efforts are a reminder that pursuits of this kind, which seek to discover well-guarded family secrets and call for the use of a sound decoding process, are quite difficult to carry to a satisfactory conclusion. It is always necessary to wonder if there might be another trauma whose encoded representations have been missed. That said, let's look now at another likely trauma that probably had a more compelling role in Freud's life and paradigm shift.

## THE PURPORTED AFFAIR BETWEEN AMALIE
## AND PHILLIP

There is considerable indirect historical evidence that Amalie Freud had an affair with her step-son Phillip and that it contributed to the break-up and departure from Freiberg of the Freud family, with Phillip and his brother Emanuel going to England and the rest of the family moving to Vienna. The material available includes family anecdotes, some of Freud's conscious early memories, and in addition, encoded imagery in his letters to Fleiss, his dreams, and his professional writings.

While Balmary (1979) alludes to some of this evidence, she does not see the affair as Freud's most important early trauma. On the other hand, Krull (1979) gives it considerable emphasis although she remains guarded in her belief that the affair actually took place; she leaves room for the idea that much of the evidence is based on Freud's fantasies. Nevertheless, several writers have accepted and elaborated on her findings as alluding to an actual liaison (for example, Vitz, 1988; Rizzuto, 1998).

Jakob Freud was forty years old and Amalie nineteen when they got married; Phillip was twenty one and he lived across the street from the Freud residence. Jakob traveled a lot for business and there are encoded suggestions of marital infidelities on his part, but no explicit evidence for this possibility and no indication that if it was true, that Amalie knew about it. The bulk of the evidence for the liaison between Amalie and Phillip comes from Freud himself, much of it in encoded form. We may recall that in the letter to Fleiss dated September 9, 1897 (Freud, 1954, Letter 69, pages 215–218), in which Freud announced that he no longer believed in his *neurotica,* he offered a few brief associations that undoubtedly bubbled up from his deep unconscious mind and its memory bank. There is a passing allusion to Hamlet, who, although not mentioned here but referred to in a later letter, is the avenger of his father's death at the hands of his father's brother, carried out in a way that eventually leads to Hamlet's own death as well. It is in that letter that Freud went on to tell the previously quoted story of Rebecca having to take off her wedding gown.

To comment briefly, Hamlet's father was killed by his brother who then took Hamlet's mother as his wife. It is this murder that Hamlet must avenge and it entails the murder of a father by a brother, an incestuous marriage between a mother and a brother-in-law, and vengeance taken by a nephew against his uncle. The basic bridging theme that links the play to the affair between Amalie and Phillip is clear: A frame-violating, murderous brother figure illicitly marrying—sleeping with—a mother figure. The murder of Hamlet's father by his brother encodes an unconsciously perceived meaning of the affair between Amalie and Phillip; it is one aspect of Freud's response to his unconscious perception of the trauma and not the expression of an inner mental wish. The understanding reflected in the story is that in having an affair with his step-mother, Phillip had murdered and replaced Jakob in her affections and bed. For that reason, Freud would unconsciously experience a mandate to take vengeance on Phillip, to punish him in kind by killing him in the name of their father. Because of this psycho-biological adaptive need, Freud would then be obliged to accept punishment as the executioner of another man. In talion fashion, the deep unconscious subsystem of morality and ethics demands and exacts a murder for a murder. Thus on some level, Freud is obliged first to murder an unconscious perceived murderer and to then murder himself for having done so. This is another reason why Freud was at a precipice when he chose to change paradigms.

In his next letter to Fleiss, dated October 3, 1897 (Freud, 1954, Letter 70, pp. 218–221), Freud mentions his self-analysis, denies that his father played an active role in the development of his neuroses—and by implication, that this will be a feature of his pending paradigm shift. He also introduces his nurse-maid, Resi Wittig, and holds her accountable for his neurosis; recalls seeing his mother nude on a train from Leipzig to Vienna—in reality, it is most unlikely that this was the first such occurrence given the close quarters in which the family lived in Frieberg (Schur, 1972); and alludes to the birth and death of his brother Julius and to the guilt he experienced when Julius died. An addendum to the letter speaks of Resi as his seductress even though he was less than three years old when she left the family for jail as a thief. Freud also mentions a dream in which he failed to find a skull on the Lido as Goethe once had—a dream Freud associates with his uselessness as a therapist. This characteristically minor self-interpretation may well reflect an unconscious perception of his view of his current flight from reality and towards the world of fantasy.

In the following letter (Freud, 1954, Letter 71, October 10, 1997, pp. 221–225), Freud tells Fleiss that his mother's response to his inquiries about Resi involved the story of how Phillip had the police arrest her as a thief and how she spent time in jail. He then recalls the one-eyed doctor who took care of him as an infant and alludes to an early memory of hitting his forehead and requiring stitches for a wound that left a life-long scar. Freud then gets to a scene from around the time his sister Anna was born (Freud was nearly three years old), one that has haunted him on and off for the last twenty-nine years—that is, since he was twelve years old. The theme of the disappearing nursemaid has brought up a conscious memory in which Freud is crying his heart out because his mother is nowhere to be found. His brother Phillip opens a cupboard for him and Freud finds that his mother is not there. He cries some more until she comes through the door looking slim and beautiful.

Freud comments in the letter that he must have feared that his mother had vanished like his nurse and been locked up too, but in later writings, he offers different interpretations of this same incident (see below). This leads Freud to say that his personal analysis has brought him nothing new, but he then contradicts himself by indicating that one idea of general value has occurred to him: That he and boys in general experience a love of their mother and jealousy of their father, which gives power to the myth of Oedipus Rex.

After proposing that this universal Oedipal fantasy causes everyone to recoil in horror and to repress in adulthood the infantile wishes enacted in the myth, Freud indicates that he sees the same constellation lying at the root of the story of Hamlet. In an evident contradiction of his thinking about fantasy, Freud ascribes Shakespeare's writing of the play to some kind of actual event that allowed his unconscious to understand the unconscious of his hero. Freud then goes on to recount aspects of the tale: So conscience doth make cowards of us all; Hamlet's hesitation to avenge his father's murder by killing his uncle even though he had sent his courtiers to their deaths and had dispatched Laertes so quickly; Hamlet meditating on the obscure memory that he himself had entertained thoughts of the same deed because of his passion for his mother—"use every man after his desert, and who should 'scape whipping"; his unconscious feeling of guilt; his rejection of his instinct to beget children with Ophelia; and his succeeding to bring down punishment on himself and suffering the same fate as his father—that is, being murdered by the same rival.

So even as Freud sees himself fantasizing a wish to possess his mother, he sees Shakespeare enacting an Oedipal-like drama based on an actual repressed trauma. The themes of the uncle killing the father and of Hamlet avenging his murder speaks unconsciously of issues between Freud and his half-brother who was the age of an uncle and who functioned as such. Thus the Hamlet story as described by Freud appears to encode the theme of a brother who kills his brother, Hamlet's father, in order to wed his brother's wife. It seem plausible to believe that at the very moment that Freud was laying claim to the discovery that fantasied incestuous wishes were the source of neuroses, he was working over an actual incestuous seduction of his mother by his half-brother which Freud knew about on some non-conscious level. Evidently, he had obliterated the relevant memories from his conscious awareness and he dreaded having access to through his self-analysis.

Freud's second report of the story of the missing mother appears in *The Psychopathology of Everyday Life* (Freud, 1901). There he offers an interpretation of the memory by trying to decode its symbolically encoded themes. Thinking at first that it was a memory of being teased by his brother, as Freud called Phillip, Freud eventually came to believe that the incident drew on the dishonesty of his nurse to whom he gave coins that had been given to him as presents and who stole money from the family and was sent to jail. Because his brother was involved in her disappearance, he was present in the cupboard memory and when his mother left him for a short while, Freud became convinced that Phillip had done the same thing to her—that is, had had his mother jailed—and thus he forced his brother to open the cupboard for him. The image of his mother's sliminess did however bring up the fact that his sister had been born at the time and that soon after, when he was three years old, he and Phillip ceased living in the same place.

To comment briefly, Freud's focus on Phillip and his nursemaid's crimes seems to be a defensive displacement away from Phillip and his mother and the crime they probably committed together. This displacement, which places stress on a lesser issue to convey in disguise and yet cover over a far greater issue, is a common communicative defense and is typical of Freud's efforts at self-analysis. The clue that Freud's interpretation of the memory is flawed is seen in his failure to explain the crime that his mother had committed, the one that had caused his half-brother to see to it that she was sent to jail. However, if Phillip did indeed seduce Amalie, he would have engaged her in a crime that in Freud's eyes would have merited her being incarcerated. At this juncture, Freud ignores the reference to his sister's birth.

In a footnote to his 1901 book written in 1924, Freud offered his final interpretation of the story. As a child of three, he wrote, he had not yet understood that his sister had grown inside his mother's body and he was mistrustful and anxious that his mother's body might conceal more children. The cupboard was a symbol for his mother's inside, so he turned to his big brother, who had taken his father's place as his rival, for clarification. Freud's suspicion that the brother had had the nurse "boxed up" in there was connected with the further suspicion that the brother had recently introduced the baby inside his mother.

Elsewhere Freud recalled asking Phillip to stop giving babies to his mother (Krull, 1979). Also relevant is the only dream reported in *The Interpretation of Dreams* (Freud, 1900) in which his mother appears in its manifest contents, and it is connected to an error Freud made in writing about Hannibal. The dream in question is the last of his own dreams alluded to in the dream book; it is followed by a pair of short dream fragments from two male patients which bring to a close the dream material for his landmark book.

Much as his lost first dream for the dream book would have had special significance and his last major treatise, *Moses and Monotheism* (Freud, 1939) was a most important death-bed communication, Freud's last dream in his dream book can be expected to convey a special set of encoded messages which undoubtedly touched on his early death-related traumas. This idea is supported by indications that the dream in question was dreamt when Freud was nine-and-a-half years old, soon after his mother's father had died. Freud mistakenly dated this event as having occurred when he was seven or eight years old, which is an age period associated with an incident in which Freud deliberately urinated in his parents' bedroom and his father predicted that he would come to nothing. Another conscious memory from that period of his life is one in which his mother is teaching Freud that we are all dust and return to dust when we die—a lesson from the Bible that alludes to God's punishment of Adam for having violated God's command to not eat from the tree of divine knowledge.

As for the reported manifest dream, Freud sees his mother being carried into a room by two (or three) people with bird's beaks and being laid upon the bed. Freud woke from this dream in tears and screaming; he interrupted his parents' sleep.

Freud's first association to the dream is to the inscribed Phillipson Bible that his father gave him for his thirty-fifth birthday. The dream was funereal and it brought to mind an ill-mannered boy named Phillip with whom Freud played at the time, a boy who introduced Freud to a word for copulation. His mother's face, Freud notes, was like her father's face as he lay in a coma a few days before he died. Freud therefore believes that his mother was dying in the dream and he links the dream to a repressed sexual craving for her.

Several analysts (Balmary, 1979; Krull, 1979; Rizzuto, 1998) have suggested that the dream had other meanings as well. As Freud probably knew, there are links that connect one of the figures in the dream and in the

Phillipson Bible to the Biblical story of David's son Absalom who had sexual relations with his father's concubines in the presence of the father's men who eventually killed him. Absalom, who for his part wanted to murder his father, was Solomon's half-brother. Another figure in the Bible is tied to the treacherous killing of Abner, David's general, and there is an allusion in the imagery to the ferry boat that carries the dead to their last judgment.

Quite telling too is the fact that Freud failed to associate the name of the Bible and of his friend to his half-brother, Phillip—an omission that speaks strongly for the need to repress an actual trauma rather than a fantasied wish. The trauma in question seems best represented by Absalom's having sexual relations with his father's women for which he was punished through death. This is less in keeping with an Oedipal wish than it is with an actual betrayal of the father for which his intrusive, betraying half-brother should be killed— and for which his mother, as portrayed in the dream, should simply die. We again must assume that Freud is to be the executioner of his half-brother and that for some reason, he allows his mother to die in peace (see chapter 8).

As for the final dream in Freud's magnum opus, it was from a man in his late twenties who recalled a dream that he had had sometime between the ages of eleven and thirteen in which a man with a hatchet was pursuing him; he tries to run away but is paralyzed and unable to move from the spot. The patient's associations were to his younger brother whom he had once kicked in the head, drawing blood. His mother said that the patient would be the death of his brother some day. The patient's thoughts then went to overhearing his parents having intercourse and seeing blood on his mother's bed.

The final encoded themes in the dream book deal, then, with wanting to murder a brother and being threatened for wanting to do so—all of it associated with overhearing parental intercourse.

While there are other clues to the conjecture that Freud may have come upon his mother in bed with his half-brother and that whatever actually did happen, to Freud's unconscious belief that Amalie had an affair with Phillip, I will note only two more pieces of evidence. The first is the historical fact that when Freud was about three years of age, the Freud family broke up. This happened around the time of Freud's cupboard memory and the birth of his sister Anna—the child for whom Freud thought Phillip might well have been the father. There are signs of a family scandal and dispute: Jakob was doing well in business at the time and had no discernible reason to leave Freiberg for Vienna. There also was no evident reason for Emanuel and Phillip's move to Manchester England, although there has been some unsubstantiated speculation that they did so because they were involved in Jakob's brother's counterfeiting activities for which the brother was jailed.

The second piece of evidence comes from *The Psychopathology of Everyday Life*. (Freud, 1901). In the chapter on errors, Freud discusses a mistake he made in *The Interpretation of Dreams* (Freud, 1900). In the chapter on infantile material to be found in dreams, Freud recalled one of several dreams he had of being in Rome—the city involved in a travel inhibition that Freud did not resolve until the summer of 1901. In connection with the dream he comments that like Hannibal, one of his childhood heroes, he was fated to not see Rome. In the Punic Wars, Freud had sided with the Carthaginians rather than the Romans; he equated their war with the conflict between the Jews—Hannibal was Semitic—and the Catholic church.

This led Freud to an oft-quoted memory from between ages ten and twelve in which, while walking with his father, the father recalled an earlier incident in which a Christian boy had knocked off his cap, called him a Jew, and ordered him off the pavement. The father did as he was told and then went his way (Rizzuto, 1998). Disappointed in his father, Freud contrasted his father with Hannibal's father who made his son swear that he would take vengeance on the Romans. Freud misidentified the father as Hasdrubal, Hannibal's brother, rather than Hamilcar Barca, Hannibal's father. Freud's error substituted a brother for a father and named the brother as the father—a brother who is stronger than the father and who asks for vengeance as well.

In discussing this error in *The Psychopathology of Everyday Life,* Freud (1901) noted that he had used the brother's name instead of the name of the father and he tied this to his dissatisfaction with his father's behaviors towards the enemies of their people. Freud added that he could have gone on to tell how his relationship with his brother was changed by a visit to England—at age nineteen—which enabled him to get to know his half-brother, the child [sic] of his father's first marriage. Freud then mentioned his half-brother's son who was the same age as Freud, so it is clear that manifestly he was referring to Emanuel and that it is Phillip whom he once more had obliterated. There are indications as well that Freud hardly saw Phillip during that visit and that Phillip was estranged from the Freud family for the rest of his life. Freud then commented:

> Thus the relations between our ages were no hindrance to my phantasies of how different things would have been if I had been born the son of not my father but of my brother. These suppressed phantasies falsified the text of my book at the place where I broke off the analysis, by forcing me to put the brother's name for the father's. (Freud, 1901, pp. 219–220)

Here Freud fantasizes about being fathered by his brother. On the one hand, this fantasy could readily express his unconscious belief that Amalie and Phillip had had an affair which then prompted Freud to create the reactive fantasy as to what it would have been like if Phillip had been his father. The alternative is evident, namely, that Freud believed that Phillip had in fact fathered him. I shall come back to that conjecture in the next chapter.

## SUMMING UP

Was Freud dealing with infantile fantasies or with actual traumatic realities? Because the answer lies with closely guarded family secrets and obliterated, repressed wishes or memories, we can only review the available historical material, carry out as much trigger-based decoding as possible, turn to our knowledge of archetypes, and come to the most likely conclusion.

There are several indicators that speak for obliterated traumas far more than repressed infantile wishes and fantasies. For one, there are convincing indications that Freud's paradigm shift involved a significant, uncalled for flight from reality and that it was in part a symptomatic, defensive turning away from the possibility of accessing his own traumatic past. Because the move was misdirected and thus unconsciously driven, it is more likely to have been a defense against the retrieval of disturbing actual events than a consequence of forbidden fantasized wishes.

Turning to emotion-laden archetypes, it has been found with great consistency that major decisions of the kind made by Freud in 1897 are in fact deeply influenced by prior traumas—that fantasies play a minor role in these pivotal events. In addition, archetypically, the underlying issue, whatever its nature, is not sexually tinged but a matter of life and death; death anxieties, often in all three of its forms—predatory, predator and existential—are the root cause of errant choices and behaviors. This means that even when a trauma manifestly is of a sexual nature, the boundary violations and transgression involved in the situation—in Freud's case, these are matters of both incest and adultery—are viewed unconsciously as acts of murder and as crimes that must be punished, ultimately by death. Other death-related themes accrue to these traumas, as seen for example in the indications that Freud unconsciously viewed Phillip's affair with Amalie as a way of killing Jakob, the cuckolded spouse. As soon as Freud placed himself in the middle of this drama, he was at risk of committing some form of punitive murder and then a reactive suicide, and thus, he was taking himself to the edge of a precipice.

These constellations of obliterated memories, fantasied responses to what actually had happened, and the devastatingly destructive and self-endangering urges that they evoke, are the stuff from which a need to activate strong denial-based, communicative defenses is aroused. In Freud's case, his need for denial of reality was intensified when his father died and at the time of the first anniversary of his death—events that must have re-aroused the unconscious memories of the early-life traumas in which the father had been involved. The danger of recovering the obliterated memories, and with it the impulses to act against the offending parties, was all the greater because Freud had discovered the key to decoding the encoded expressions of these traumas as disguised in manifest dreams. Much as is seen in today's adaptive psychotherapy patients, Freud intuitively seems to have appreciated that the trigger decoded, conscious articulation of even fragments of these actual traumatic events would bring him to the brink of disaster. In his moment of unconsciously experienced danger and despair, Freud came up with an ingenious solution to his problem: The past is not real and is not to be believed or dealt with; instead, life is wrecked by psychologically disruptive, biologically driven fantasies and wishes. Reality is inconsequential; wishes are paramount, especially if they are incestuous—and secondarily murderous. And because this kind of denial of reality is an archetypal unconscious defense against the reality of death and the anxieties this realization evokes, Freud's reality-denying defensive position found great favor among his followers and the world at large. The fame he thought would not be his because he had given up his seduction theory would in fact come to him because he made this shift and offered a fundamental denial of reality that came from and resonated with the archetypal denial of reality needed by all humans—however costly it may be.

The likely existence and death by suicide of Rebekka Freud is at times only thinly encoded and represented in Freud's writings and as such, it may well have constituted one of the forbidden realities to which he dared not return to. The main reasons for this avoidance most probably lay with his unconscious view that his father had murdered Rebekka and Freud's reactive impulse to punish his father in kind for his ill deed. Freud also would have experienced "existence guilt"—a modified form of survivor guilt—which is often seen in replacement children who are born after the death of a sibling. This kind of guilt would be a form of borrowed guilt in that the death of Rebekka paved the way for his father's marriage to his mother, Amalie, and thereby to the bringing of Freud into the world. The inevitable guilt that this would have evoked unconsciously would lead to suicidal enactments, especially when the encoded expressions of this scenario are trigger decoded and bought towards the surface of the mind.

As for the postulated trauma of an affair between Freud's mother and his step-brother, here too indications are that Freud had no conscious awareness of this liaison, but was aware of it unconsciously. There are many encoded clues to this situation and to the threat posed to Freud were he to decode the dreams that touched on it. To cite a few of these clues, there is the allusion to Rebecca and her taking off her gown because she is no longer a bride, that is, no longer a virgin, which means that she has slept with a man other than her husband. Strikingly, the image, which seemed to be a *non sequitor* in the letter, also decodes as indicating that the illicit intercourse took place *before* Amalie married Jakob. This constellation of meanings reflects the remarkable craft and creativity that is characteristic of the highly perceptive and inventive deep unconscious mind. The imagery does not decode well as an Oedipal image—this is premarital rather than post-marital sex. All in all it speaks for an as yet unformulated actual trauma of the kind I shall propose in the next chapter.

Also notable is the cupboard memory in which, in thinly disguised form, Freud is holding his half-brother Phillip accountable for the impregnation of his mother with his sister. Freud's dream of his mother's death also is linked in disguised fashion to her having been sexually unfaithful to her husband with Phillip, even though Freud blocked out the evident association between the Philippson Bible and his step-brother Phillip; the hidden allusion to Absolam also speaks for this possibility. There is as well Freud's confusion between a father and a brother, and his odd comment as to how different his life would have been if he had been his step-brother's child. There also are indications that Freud's unconscious reactions to these traumas included wishes to punish the offenders—that is, his mother, step-brother, and father— and yet a need to restrain himself from doing so because of the murders and suicide that would ensue.

In this context it is well to note that the first anecdote in *The Psychopathology of Everyday Life* (Freud, 1901) is about Freud's forgetting the name of the artist who painted the frescoes, 'The Last Judgment," in the church in Orvieto—Signorelli. The underlying theme is that of condemning sinners to death and to hell. Freud blocking out the name speaks for his struggle against condemning his mother and Phillip for their sins, but also in light of his associations, for condemning his father for his infidelities and for his fantasied murder of Rebekka. In addition, like Hamlet, Freud is reluctant to avenge the symbolic murder of his father by Phillip because doing so will cost him his own life.

Freud seems to restrain himself from taking revenge on his mother; themes encoding such impulses are rare in his writings. He does so in the one dream in the dream book (Freud, 1900) in which she appears manifestly wearing a death mask in the context of associations to sexual infidelity. Freud's mother also is indicted and punished in encoded form through his allusions to the crimes of murder and incest and in the suicides of Lady Macbeth and Rebecca West (Freud, 1916). The incestuous mother is, in these images, brutally condemned to death by suicide, an ending that is tied to the fate of Jocasta, the incestuous mother of Oedipus (see chapter 8). Amalie is portrayed as the victim of the unwittingly seductive son but she is condemned to death nevertheless. In writing about them, Freud repressed the suicides of Lady Macbeth and Rebecca West, another indication of his reluctance to punish his mother much as Hamlet was reluctant to punish his father (see also chapter 8).

The idea that unconsciously, Freud was an unwilling executioner also can be found in his allusions to Don Giovanni (Balmary, 1979) and to his paper on the Moses of Michelangelo (Freud, 1914d)—and as we shall see, to the Oedipus myth as well. The first is the tale of a ruthlessly seductive brother figure, Don Juan, who is condemned to death by a victimized father who sends the seducer of his daughter to hell. The second involves Freud's interpretation of Michelangelo's sculpture of Moses in which he eschews the image of Moses as a vengeful man, replacing it with one in which Moses is trying to stay calm and at peace so as to not punish his Jewish followers for their transgressions. In order to adopt and sustain this position, Freud ignored and denied the Biblical story of Moses' rage against his Jewish followers for having carved and worshiped a golden calf. There is a sense, then, that Freud was tortured unconsciously by his violent responses to those who were involved in his early-life traumas and that he was seriously conflicted as to whether he should avenge their transgressions or let them pass.

Fleeing the entire reality-based mess and entering a detached world of fantasy appears to have been Freud's chosen resolution to his dilemma. As Balmary (1979) so wisely suggested: Freud's paradigm shift relieved the others in his life—his mother, step-brother, and father—from their responsibilities for his emotional woes for which Freud would want to murder them in some way and then kill himself for having done so. As is true of most humans, Freud was prepared to hold himself fully accountable for his emotional ills, restrict his awareness of their causes largely to the conscious realm, and punish himself in some attenuated way rather than experience on any detectable level the vicious impulses that are unleashed when the sins of the father—and others—are recognized as the cause of a person's suffering—a father who must be dutifully avenged and punished as well. Because the self-blame is largely unjustified, we may think of this position as creating a tolerable myth to protect one from the intolerable truths of reality.

As if this was not more than one person could hope to cope with, there is one more extensive set of encoded images and themes that speak for the reality of severe early traumas in Freud's life—a trauma that has been overlooked by previous researchers. Let's turn now to this particular trauma and see what it was about.

# Chapter 8

# The Ultimate Trauma

As I have said, the adaptive study of archetypes indicate that powerful traumas with strong death-related implications lie behind major life decisions that go awry. We may therefore wonder if the two main traumas explored in the previous chapter—the suicide of Rebekka Freud and the affair between Amalie and Phillip—are of sufficient power to have unconsciously driven Freud in such an unreasoned, irrational, and erroneous manner to flee reality and with it eliminate all possibility of decoding and recovering the story of his own early-life traumas. The death and possible suicide of Rebekka, which took place before Freud's birth, did not involve Freud personally. Nevertheless, he would not have wanted to own up to a heritage in which one of his father's wives had killed herself, an event that would have tarnished his image of his father as a fantasized murderer. There also would have been some kind of unconscious survivor guilt in that Rebekka's death paved the way for Jakob's marriage to Amalie and thus to Freud's coming into being. These are not, however, especially compelling reasons to cause Freud to so severely dread dredging up his obliterated past.

An affair between Amalie and Phillip would not have involved Freud directly, unless he was witness to their liaison—an incident that he readily could have obliterated from his awareness. If so, Freud would have seen himself as a party to their illicit relationship and experienced deep unconscious guilt and the urge to punish—that is, execute—both himself and the offending parties. Even if the affair was only a family secret in which Freud was not personally involved, he would not have wanted to recover its details and ramifications which included the soiled images of his mother and half-brother and the degradation of his father. This liaison was a death-related incident largely through the violence inherent to its frame violations and the unconsciously experienced implication that Phillip had gotten rid of and therefore murdered Jakob.

143

As his father's protector Freud would have been inclined unconsciously to punish Amalie and Phillip for their transgression and Freud would then respond with suicidal impulses to the unconscious guilt that this would engender.

All in all, however, these two traumas do not appear to be so personally death-related and terrifying to account for Freud's errant change of paradigms and his inability to later reverse courses. This realization calls for the search for another, even more disturbing death-related trauma that would have overwhelmed Freud unconsciously to the extent that escaping reality was his only means of survival. And it turns out that there is a likely trauma that fits this description, one that has not been given serious consideration or properly documented. The trauma in question is an extension of the conjecture that Amalie Freud did in fact have an affair with her step-son, Phillip Freud, and that this hidden liaison, known unconsciously to Freud, had a powerful personal affect on him because of beliefs or knowledge that extended well beyond the infidelity and betrayal in which they had engaged.

The added trauma in question is that early in his life, Freud unconsciously detected clues that Phillip Freud rather than Jakob Freud was or could have been his biological father. In keeping with the finding that the deep unconscious mind entertains several versions of a given trauma, it can be conjectured that in the course of his lifetime, Freud alternately believed that Phillip was his father; was not sure who his biological father was; doubted that Jakob was his biological father; and found it impossible to determine just who his father was. At no time was he *unconsciously convinced* of the singular idea that Jakob and no one else was his biological parent.

I have then postulated a trauma that strikes at the heart of Freud's identity, one that embodies a host of compelling implications and ramifications. Freud would have been dealing with the unconscious belief that he was an out-of-wedlock child born of incest or at the very least he would have been experiencing a profound uncertainty as to his origins. But most tellingly, Freud's unconscious doubts about who did and did not give him life, maddening in itself, would have constituted a death-related trauma that touched on his very existence—and possible non-existence. Furthermore, if Freud had unconsciously registered evidence that Phillip was in fact his biological father these perceptions would be maddening because of the stark contradictions between the conscious and unconscious stories of his life (see Searles, 1979). In this light, the psychodynamics of the situation would speak for unconscious needs and reactions that were undertaken by Freud to save his sanity. In addition, this is the kind of trauma which, when reactivated, would be likely to evoke panic-stricken acts that would harm both himself and others. In his change of heart letter to Fliess (Freud, 1954, Letter 69,

September 21, 1897, pp. 215-218), Freud saw his flight from reality as causing himself and his children great financial and other kinds of harm—a theme that may well represent far greater damage to all concerned.

The murderous and suicidal impulses that any budding conscious or unconscious awareness of this situation would have evoked in Freud would have been unbearably devastating for him, so much so that with the death of his father and its first anniversary he would be expected to do almost anything to not move in the direction of moving this discovery into focused conscious awareness. Indeed, the death of his father would have put Freud at the edge of a precipice from which he could easily have jumped to his death. In this sense he truly saved his life by abandoning reality and his seduction theory before the principles it espoused and the decoding efforts towards which it would have taken him were engaged in. Freud needed to deny reality and death in order to go on with his life. This is the archetypal response to death-related traumas seen in patients who are given the opportunity to reveal and work over these devastating events in adaptive psychotherapy. It also in all likelihood is the defense-laden archetype that has led psychoanalysts and lay people throughout the world to embrace Freud's second paradigm and to erect an impenetrable wall against possible incursions from the first paradigm which would destroy the life-saving, denial-based defenses that have been put into place.

The evidence for this thesis that can be found in Freud's early family life and most tellingly in his encoded narratives. It is far stronger and integrated than the evidence for the other two traumas that have been explored in the previous chapter. The historical incidents that support this thesis are few and far between, but the encoded indications of Freud's unconscious uncertainty as to his true identity are abundant and quite compelling. Indeed, once an individual begins to dream, make up stories, and tell tales—be they psychoanalytic patients or writers—despite all efforts at defense, they inevitably will reveal in disguised form the secret traumas of their lives. The enormous number of narratives generated by Freud speaks for an overwhelming need of this kind on his part.

I shall cite evidence for Freud's uncertainty about his male parent and then discuss the possible sources of his doubts. However, it is well to be reminded again that archetypally, we are dealing with a core of unconsciously perceived realities—clues detected by the deep unconscious mind of which the conscious mind has no awareness—onto which deductions, fantasies, wishes, speculations, and the like are grafted. It is critical, then, to first identify the trauma in question by decoding the narratives that encode its nature and then treat the rest of the encoded imagery as reactions to the incidents so identified. With this in mind, let's look now at the encoded indications that the identity of his biological father was indeed a most compelling and relentless matter of doubt, chagrin, and danger for Sigmund Freud.

## THE OEDIPUS MYTH

There is no better narrative with which to begin our search for clues to Freud's doubts about his origins than with the very same narrative that Freud used to establish his fantasy-centered paradigm—the myth of Oedipus. To briefly reiterate the sequence of events that led up to his change of heart, Freud had abandoned his seduction theory of hysteria and neuroses in September 1897, a month before the anniversary of his father's death and around the time that he picked out his father's grave stone. One month later (Freud, 1954, Letter 71, October 15, 1997, pp. 221–225), he wrote to Fliess that through his self-analysis he had discovered the universal source of neuroses in the boy's wish to sleep with his mother and do away with his rival, his father. He indicated that he had found that these forbidden, guilt-evoking wishes were disguised in his patients' and his own dreams, and added that these desires and the conflicts that they engender are openly expressed in the story of Oedipus. Indeed, Freud's analysis and use of the myth is based on the belief held by some analysts, including Carl Jung, that myths tend to express human unconscious needs in relatively undisguised form. Balmary (1979) challenged this position and the adaptive approach has found reason to believe that all narratives are on one level the result of encoding mechanisms. This means that while there are evident manifest meanings to these tales, there is another more powerful layer of meaning that is trigger evoked and encoded in these stories—and thus in need of trigger decoding in order to access their deep unconscious personal and archetypal meanings.

The Oedipus myth has a complex pre-story and a striking variety of identifiable manifest themes. Of these, Freud singled out only two inter-related themes: Oedipus' sleeping with his mother and his murder of his father. He set aside the remainder of the story which he thereby more or less neglected.

What do we find however when we look at the entire myth? From an adaptive vantage-point, it is well to think of the myth as a dream-equivalent with manifest and latent-encoded meanings whose triggers need to be determined. In this sense, then, by virtue of his placing the myth at the center of psychoanalysis, I shall treat the story as the equivalent of another first-dream and thus as one of Freud's most important and potentially revealing dream-like stories. I shall then explore its manifest contents for thematic threads, but also shall look for bridging themes—themes that seem to connect the myth to possible obliterated death-related traumas that took place in Freud's earliest years. Next, I will attempt to decode the themes in the myth by using the postulated trigger as the decoding key, thereby accessing the myth's likely latent or unconscious meanings, especially those that seem to be related to the question of the identity of Freud's biological father.

One other aspect of this planned exploration needs our attention. I am postulating that Freud had doubts as to who his father was, that there was in his mind two possibilities, Jakob or Phillip. This means that when Freud was reacting unconsciously to the actions of his father, he might have been dealing with either his familial father or his half-brother—or through condensation, both of them. Not knowing which version of his origins was most meaningful for him unconsciously, we will be obliged to consider all possibilities and to also find aspects of the stories I shall be analyzing that seem to point to one of these two possibilities. This much can be said right off: This seems to be a situation in which both having to know and wanting to not know the truth—the facts, the reality—would be intensely in play. Even though we are focused on Freud's mistaken flight from reality, it is well to appreciate that these profound and possibly irresolvable uncertainties may well have played a significant role in his enormous creativity as well.

It is not known if Freud knew the pre-story of this myth, but he was well versed in Greek mythology and he indicated to Fliess that he had some reading to do in connection with the myth so he could study it in detail. Whatever the uncertainties, the pre-story, which takes place before Oedipus was born, sets the stage for the myth proper; it has some notable themes that provide us with broad insights into the human condition and probably into Freud's unconscious issues as well (Balmary, 1979; Devereux, 1953). As noted in the previous chapter, Laius, Oedipus's father, is the central figure in this prelude which deals with his rape of a brother figure, Chrysippus, the illegitimate son of King Pelops who was Laius's protector. In response to the rape, Chrysippus commits suicide and Pelops puts a curse on Laius.

To comment, there is considerable distance between these themes *per se* and the conjectured traumas in Freud's early life; if there is a link, it is well disguised. The theme of suicide may bridge over to the suicide of Rebekka Freud, but the idea that it was caused by a homosexual assault is a very questionable formulation although it does imply that in Freud's unconscious eyes, Jakob had raped Rebekka and thus caused her to kill herself.

The idea of rape and suicide may however more tellingly encode Freud's unconscious view of Phillip's affair with Amalie as a rape and Amalie's participation in the incestuous act as cause for her committing suicide—a reaction to that purported affair that Freud encoded in several of his other narratives (see chapter 7). There also is a possible bridging theme that links Chrysippus's status as the illegitimate son of King Pelops to the possibility that Freud was born on March 6, 1856 and thus was the illegitimate son of Amalie and either Jakob or Phillip. In addition, given that the story is about the seduction and rape of a brotherly figure, the images, if known to Freud, could have been used to encode a version of Amalie's affair with Phillip in which Amalie is the seducer and in response, Freud imagines that Phillip should react to his allowing himself to be seduced by punishing himself through suicide.

All of these formulations are highly tentative because it is not known if Freud knew the pre-story and unconsciously selected the myth because that part of the tale encoded aspects of his early-life traumas. Coincidence may well play a role here, although the identification of so many possible bridging themes gives pause to thinking that they were in fact one of the unconscious reasons Freud chose this story as a reflection of the essential basis for human neuroses.

As Freud (1926) said about the sources and effects of anxiety, *non liquet*—the facts are not clear. That said, if the pre-story was the only possible encoded evidence for the thesis I have proposed, I would be obliged to view my conjecture as lacking in firm encoded validation. As I have indicated, speculative work of this kind calls for the discovery of encoded imagery that speaks loud and clear for a particular thesis.

There is however one aspect of the pre-story that Freud knew either by implication or through knowledge of its dramatic lines. As I noted in chapter 2, the myth is one of predestination in that the oracle foretells that Oedipus is fated to murder his father and marry his mother—a fate that is connected with the curse that Pelops put on Laius for Laius "murder" of his son. Even if Freud did not know the pre-story, he could not have failed to notice, however unconsciously, that chance in the form of an action taken by his father before he was born had played a key role in the unfolding of Oedipus's life.

Indeed, two death-related archetypes are invoked and pre-ordained in the pre-story—one pertaining to the fate of Oedipus and the other to the fate of his father. Oedipus is destined to play the role of son who will avenge the crimes of his father, wile Laius is destined to be punished for these very same crimes. Each will therefore unconsciously seek to fulfill their destinies—one of the myth's subplots that Freud unconsciously sees himself as destined to fulfill.

As for Freud's introduction of the legend into psychoanalysis, as noted earlier, less than two weeks after he announced to Fliess that he no longer believes his *neurotica,* he lays the groundwork for his proposal that the Oedipus myth plays a key role in emotional life (Freud, 1954, Letter 70, October 3, 1997, pp. 218-221). He indicates that he is engaged in his self-analysis; exonerates his father as a source of his neurosis; mentions the death of his brother, Julius, and his reactive conscious guilt; introduces his nursemaid as someone who washed him in reddish water in which she had previously washed herself and describes her as encouraging him to steal coins for her—the last a theme that Freud associates with his feelings of uselessness as a therapist.

Twelve days later (Freud, 1954, letter 71, October 15, 1897, pp. 221-225), Freud stresses the importance of his self-analysis, describes asking his mother about his nurse and learning of her presence when Amalie was in bed at the time when Anna was born and of her thievery, all of which leads Freud to his cupboard memory and Phillip's arranging for the nurse's disappearance. It is at this point that Freud introduces the play Oedipus Rex and suggests that there is a universal love in the boy for his mother and jealousy of his father. He moves quickly to Hamlet and the inhibition of his wish to kill his uncle who had killed his father and married his mother. As Freud sees it, Hamlet's hesitation stems from the fact that he entertained the same motives against his father as was enacted by his uncle.

Some time later, in *The Interpretation of Dreams* (Freud, 1900, pp. 261–267), Freud offers a pithy, highly selective description of the details of the Oedipal legend and he again links the myth to the story of Hamlet. Noteworthy is Freud's allusion to Jocasta's efforts to reassure Oedipus, which take place when he becomes troubled by recalling that the oracle had told him that he will murder his father and sleep with his mother. Jocasta tells him that many a man dreams of laying with his mother and that he should accept that dream without being troubled by it. Freud mentions that Oedipus blinded himself for his misdeeds, but he makes no mention of Jocasta's suicide. There are strong indications that omissions of this kind are significant for Freud who failed to mention the suicide of Lady Macbeth and the two suicides—of Rebecca West and the man she loves—that take place at the end of Ibsen's play, Rosmersholm. It is here that Freud notes that Oedipus's fate was determined by the gods and sealed before he was born—that his story is a tragedy of human-made destinies. Freud then comments that the story touches on the unconscious infantile wishes of every young child, wishes that evokes horror and self-punishment.

Mindful of the Hamlet story, Freud next indicates that he no longer believes that Shakespeare wrote the plays attributed to him; he also reiterates his view that the Hamlet tale has its roots in the same soil as the play, Oedipus Rex. In the Oedipus play the wishes to sleep with the mother and murder the father are brought out into the open and realized as they would be in a dream. While this contention runs counter to adaptive findings that indicate that such wishes and the traumatic events that have evoked them always appear in disguised form in dreams, Freud does note that in Hamlet these same wishes are repressed.

Freud point out that Hamlet was written immediately after the death of Shakespeare's father—a comment that is made despite his rejection of Shakespeare as its author—and that a son named Hamnet born to Shakespeare had died at an early age. Evidently, Freud was tracing the action of this dream-like play to traumatic events in the life of the writer, but paradoxically, he was doing so in the context of affording the power over emotional life to fantasies and wishes that are detached from such realities. Freud then repeats his thesis that Hamlet was unable to take revenge for the death of his father because his uncle had realized Hamlet's own unconscious infantile wishes—a conflict that is represented in Hamlet's distaste for sexuality as expressed in his conversation with Ophelia. In this connection, we may think of these two stories—those of Oedipus and Hamlet—as reflections of Freud's unconscious, conflicted reaction to the actual Oedipal triumph that he seems to be working over—the one accomplished in reality by Phillip and the other accomplished in fantasy by the young Freud. Oedipus is the victor who actually murders his father and sleeps with his mother, while Hamlet is the fantasizer who inhibits his murderously vengeful impulses until he is forced to enact them.

## THE ENCODED MYTH

I turn now to the various themes in the myth so we can align them with Freud's possible early-life traumas. We are aided in this pursuit by the knowledge that traumatic triggering events activate unconscious perceptions which in turn, become unconscious memories that, when reactivated, are encoded in dreams and other narratives. Because triggers evoke themes and thus themes mirror triggers, treating the myth as if it were one of Freud's dreams enables us to allow the themes of the myth to direct us to their likely triggers. In so doing, we will be looking for clues to both the immediate triggers for this dream-story and its more remote, early-life triggers as well.

Freud placed the incestuous relationship between Oedipus and his mother, Jocasta, at the center of the myth; the murder of his father was seen as secondary to the sexual wish. If we try to decode these themes and trace them to an actual early-life trauma, they would suggest that Freud had seduced or been seduced by his mother and that in so doing, he had done away with his father. This would be the postulated trauma that he was processing unconsciously on the occasion of the anniversary of the death of his father, a trauma, one would add, with dire implications that Freud needed to obliterate and avoid.

All in all, however, stated in terms of realities, this formulation does not seem to be credible. It is extremely unlikely that Freud's mother seduced her son in a blatantly sexual manner or that Freud did real harm to his father so this is a conjecture that is not especially tenable nor does it speak for an unbearable unconscious need to obliterate reality. While Freud does describe a memory of seeing his mother *en nudam* during a train trip from Frieberg to Liepzig when he was about three years old, there are no other encoded clues to a possible incestuous relationship between himself and Amalie.

A look at the broad range incidents and themes in the myth weakens the relevance of Freud's own, fantasy-centered, sexual interpretation of its meanings. There are eight acts of violence—murder, attempted murder, suicide, and other forms of self-harm—as compared to the one act of incest. This suggests that there is an arbitrariness to Freud's selection of incest as the core issue in the tale. Shifting the focus back to obliterated actual incidents, the violent images suggest that there is a traumatic, death-related center to the myth which is in keeping with archetypal expectations; the themes suggest the existence of a set of early-life traumas that involved experiences that did great violence and harm to Freud and probably others as well. This sense of violence far outweighs any suggestion that the myth primarily is a tale of forbidden sexual desires.

These criticisms of Freud's interpretation of the myth are in keeping with adaptive findings that conscious efforts at self-analysis are, by virtue of the evolved design of the emotion-processing mind, always extremely defense-oriented and that they unwittingly serve the human need to deny death and its encumbrances far more than the quest for unconsciously validatable insights. Only the effective use of trigger decoding can enable an individual to go against his or her natural denial-based conscious-system defensive tendencies and arrive at genuinely adaptive insights. Thus, it is to be expected that Freud's efforts to generate interpretations derived from his self-analysis would lead him to either secondary truths or falsehoods. He would have been unconsciously driven to avoid the deeper and more compelling truths and death-related meanings of the Oedipal imagery and its unconscious sources.

All in all, then, at this juncture in his career, Freud provided himself and the world with two basic denial-based defenses: First, the claim that the Oedipus myth was about a universal fantasy and related set of wishes rather than about a reality-based trauma, and second, the interpretation that the tale is primarily about fantasied incest and the consequent murder of a rival, rather than more compelling issues which are described below.

## REINTERPRETING THE MYTH

Whereas Sophocles's play, *Oedipus Rex* (Taylor, 1986), begins with a plague that has devastated Thebes and then retraces the history of the characters who are involved in its occurrence, I shall look at the story in the sequence in which it actually unfolded in "real time" as the basis for my analysis of its meanings. Thus, a major key to the central meanings of the myth of Oedipus lies with the exciting incident that sets off the actions that take place as the drama unfolds. Oedipus is living in Corinth as the purported son of its king and queen,

Polybus and Merope. On the occasion of his eighteenth birthday, he is told by a drunken friend that the king and queen are not his parents as he believes; Polybus and Merope tell him to ignore his friend's remarks. Oedipus consults the oracle about the identity of his parents, but the oracle does not answer his question; instead he tells Oedipus that he is destined to murder his father and marry his mother.

Still convinced that Polybus and Merope are his parents, Oedipus decides to flee to Thebes. It is on this journey that he meets, is provoked by, and unknowingly kills his father, Laius, who, as we later find out, had been warned that were he to have a son, the child would murder him. Having cohabited in a drunken stupor with his wife, Jocasta, who then bore him a son, Laius had pierced the boy's ankles, binded them together, and given the infant to a hunter whom he told to leave the boy to die on Mt. Cithaeron. The hunter did not obey Laius and turned the child over to Merope who claimed him as her own.

Examining the tale to this point, it can be seen that Freud made use of a common archetypal defense, one that he shares with those who try to interpret their own encoded stories: He trumpets a secondary theme and issue while presenting and ignoring the more crucial theme and issue by placing it out in the open where hopefully, no one else will see it. Freud stressed the incestuous element and totally ignored the basic theme of the myth: the misinformation as to who Oedipus's biological parents actually were. Strikingly, as was the case with Freud, Oedipus makes no immediate, palpable effort to find out the truth of his origins, but simply takes flight from the parents he mistakenly believes are his own.

*Unconsciously, but not consciously,* Freud must have known that the myth he chose as the representative of the basic issues in human emotional life is fundamentally about the search for one's biological parents, that is, for one's true identity. Given that this is the fundamental challenge and driving force of the myth, we must hypothesize that Freud had experienced a fundamental early-life trauma that created a profound uncertainty in him as to the identity of both of his parents. In this regard, there appear to be two unconscious versions of his origins other than the "myth" fostered by his family that Jakob and Amalie gave him life. The first belief is that neither Amalie nor Jakob were his parents, while the second belief was that Jakob was not his father. Small wonder that, like Oedipus, there are indications that Freud did not want to know the truth of the matter, that he preferred to escape from the entire situation and sustain the belief that Amalie was his mother and that Jakob was his father even though, as the myth implies and encodes, there were good reasons to think otherwise. In this light, the vengeance taken by Oedipus taken against his assaultive father and the role he plays in the suicide of his mother are reactions to the utter confusion they created in respect to his identity and to their attempt to disown and murder him after he was born.

Given that previous writers have focused almost entirely on the role of the father in both the myth and in Freud's life, it is well to pause to consider the fact that Oedipus's false mother insists that he is her child, while his true mother goes unidentified until the climax of the story at which point she kills herself for having slept with her son. Being uncertain as to the identity of his biological mother may be a reactive fantasy to the central doubts about the identity of his father—was he Jakob or Phillip? It also may a reflection of the unconscious thought, discussed in the previous chapter, that Rebekka Freud was the woman who carried and gave birth to him—and then for some unknown reason committed suicide. That said, while there are both historical and encoded reasons to believe that Freud had well-founded serious doubts as to who had fathered him, there is little evidence to suggest that Amalie had not borne and brought him into the world. Even so, let's keep an open mind and remember that truth is stranger than fiction.

A version of this situation which exonerates the mother but not the father can be found in Freud's (1909b) paper on the family romance where the central theme is that the child believes that he is of royal birth only to realize and accept later on that this is not the case. Freud linked this common fantasy of having parents other than those who brought one up to the story of Oedipus. He also noted that as a rule, the mother is imagined to have had as many affairs as she has had children, while it is the father who initially is disposed of and replaced by an exalted figure. Writing there, Freud pointed out that: "'*Pater semper uncertus est*' while mother is *certissima*.' Paternity always is uncertain while maternity always is most certain" (Freud, 1909b, p. 239). This appears to be one unconscious version of the basic, traumatic truth of Freud's life.

The next action in the story is the meeting of Oedipus with Laius and his entourage at a fork in the road where the roads to Delphi, Thebes, and Corinth meet; the killing of Oedipus's horse when he refuses to make way for Laius; and Oedipus's murder of Laius and all but one of his servants—who, as it turns out later, is the woodsman who had saved the infant Oedipus from death.

How is this interlude to be trigger decoded? We already know that Oedipus has two fathers: The consciously recognized father who is not his biological but an adoptive father and the consciously unrecognized stranger who actually is his biological father. His true father has tried to murder him so the murder of Laius by Oedipus is a talion revenge—a murder that is punishment for an immediate attempt to murder him and for a previous attempt of a similar nature.

Treating the story as his dream, Freud seems to be making use of condensation which allows for two basic, trigger decoded interpretations of this part of the story as it connects to his conception—one tied to the unconscious belief that Jakob was his biological father, the other tied to seeing Phillip in this role. Here, the belief that Jakob fathered him does not seem to organize the imagery—there was no palpable reason for Jakob to try to murder his son, twice over, no less. But if Freud was convinced that Jakob was not his biological father, the themes would fit the reality because Jakob, in not giving life to Freud, did in an unusual manner attempt to murder his son. Even so, this formulation is not entirely in keeping with the story because Oedipus murders his actual father and not his adoptive father. The particular hypothesis may well be in error, but the material may have taken on this cast because of the utter confusion that Freud experienced unconsciously under these circumstances. Furthermore, if Freud believed unconsciously that Phillip was his biological father, Freud would have had reason to punish and murder him for having committed the crime of incest. This would account for Oedipus blinding himself when his incestuous relationship with his mother, Jocasta, is discovered—and for Freud, it would tie to the wish that in her guilt his mother would take her life for having been party to the incest with her step-son.

The theme of murdering the false father appears elsewhere in Freud's encoded writings, especially as we shall see, in Freud's last original book, his treatise on Moses, the father of the Jews (Freud, 1939). In that story, Freud encodes the murder of both of his fathers, true and false—evidently Phillip and Jakob. Thus, Freud's enormous sensitivity to the death of Jakob can be seen to arise in part because his death fulfilled one of Freud's vengeful unconscious reactions to his conception. The Oedipal tale also presages Freud's need for his paradigm shift because it indicates that he did not want to—or could not—know the truth of his origins. The shift to fantasy from reality accomplished just that. Finally, it is noteworthy that in both the Oedipus myth and Freud's version of the story of Moses, the father-figure acts in ways that invite his punishment through murder. This is quite understandable in the case of Laius who has caused a suicide and has attempted to murder—and believes has actually has killed—his own son. The conscious and deep unconscious guilt that these acts create in him will cause him to relentlessly seek his own punishment—something he accomplishes on the road to Thebes.

Another decoded meaning of the murder of Laius would involve Freud's unconscious experience of Phillip's affair with and impregnation of Amalie as a so-called Oedipal triumph. Phillip's triumph over his father, Jakob, is seen as—and is tantamount to—murdering his rival. This is the reality-based Oedipal meaning of the myth which does not point to Freud as the incestuous son, but to Phillip—a point made by Krull (1979) as well. This interpretation does however call for an actual event, unconsciously perceived or imagined by Freud, in which Jakob, as did Laius, had tried in some manner to murder Phillip. Still, given the multiplicity of evident family secrets that seem to pervade the real-life situation, some such incident may yet emerge when the full story of the Freud family is known.

Returning to the myth, Oedipus continues his journey to Thebes and is confronted by the Sphinx who challenges him, at the price of his life, to answer her riddle: "What goes on four legs in the morning, two legs in the afternoon, and three legs in the evening?" Oedipus correctly answers the riddle—it is man—and the Sphinx commits suicide by throwing herself from the parapet of the city. For ridding Thebes of the Sphinx, Oedipus is rewarded with the hand in marriage of the widowed Queen, Jocasta. Time passes, they have four children, but then Thebes is devastated by a plague that prevents the populace from bearing children. The oracle is consulted and he tells Creon, Jocasta's brother, that the plague will continue until Laius's murderer is found and punished. Oedipus begins to suspect that he is that murderer and that he has slept with his mother, while Jocasta tries to minimize the importance of their possibly having committed incest. The woodsman who had saved Oedipus's life is summoned, the truth is revealed and Jocasta commits suicide. Oedipus blinds himself with her hairpin and asks to be returned to Mt. Cithaeron so he can die; instead he is confined to the royal castle to die later on.

In light of the triggering events that Freud seems to be processing unconsciously, the interlude with the Sphinx appears to have several encoded meanings. For one, it is a riddle that involves the basic question of the nature of life as it moves from the cradle to the grave. Oedipus's ability to solve the riddle suggests that those who survive an early threat to their lives and who are wounded for life in the process somehow gain a kind of special wisdom—divine or unconscious—that enables them to survive later threats to their continuing existence (Langs, 2008). This may well be Freud's fantasy, hope, and quest: That his having been permanently damaged by his father, whomever that refers to, he will have acquired the divine wisdom to solve life's emotional problems. The story also adds that he has been or will be only partially successful—he solves a profound universal mystery only to fail to solve another more personal mystery, that of his origins.

This interlude also contains the first reference to suicide in the main body of the myth and it is Oedipus's knowledge of the truth about human life that causes the suicide of this monster-like female. This fate is, of course, repeated near the end of the story when Jocasta kills herself. The encoded message appears to be that Freud sees his mother, Amalie, as the passive victim of the crimes of men yet nonetheless views her as having participated in their wrong-doings and as deserving to be punished by killing herself for having done so. While the myth is unclear as to the role Jocasta played in the attempt to murder Oedipus as a newborn, she did play an unknowing role in the incestuous liaison with her son. For his part, indications are that Freud was reluctant to acknowledge this part of the myth, further evidence that his need to not know the facts of his life was an extremely powerful motive in his life—and paradigm shift. Thus Freud like Oedipus wished to be blind to the truth of the tragedy to which he was an innocent party—and victim.

Oedipus's marriage to Jocasta is incestuous, but what then of her suicide and his self-blinding when the true story of his origins and marriage come out? Freud plainly believed that the punishments that are meted out arose because of their incestuous relationship. But the revealed truth indicates first, that Oedipus had murdered his biological father and that Jocasta probably played an indirect role in Laius's attempt to murder their son. In addition, the self-inflicted punishment that Oedipus brings down on himself is explicitly in keeping with the oracle's call for vengeance against the man who murdered Laius; there is no explicit call for punishment for the incestuous liaison between Jocasta and Oedipus. Notably, too, Oedipus's punishment for own "crime" is through self-harm; it is not placed in the hands of others.

These realizations call for an overview of the tale in order to redefine its primary themes. It is preordained that Oedipus is fated to murder his father. There is no indication that he wishes to do so in order to marry his mother nor is there any biological pressure for this kind of act. It is well known archetypically that the sins of the father fall on the sons, but it also is the case that the sons are given the responsibility to avenge and punish their fathers for having sinned. If Oedipus is destined to kill his father, his father must have committed a crime or sin, and we know from the pre-story of the myth that this is the case: Laius raped Chrysippus and caused him to commit suicide. This act, rather than the incestuous wish, is the evident background unconscious motive for Oedipus's killing of Laius. Yet in becoming the executioner of his father, no matter how justified, Oedipus seems to fated to be punished for his violent deed. The link between murderous enactments against others, however disguised, and suicidal forms of self-punishment, be they blatant or disguised, is archetypal. For her part, Jocasta was fated to die mainly for having committed incest and possibly for aiding and abetting the attempted murder of her son. And Oedipus must die or suffer the equivalent of death because he has avenged the crime of his father in a murderous manner and because he then committed incest—transgressions that, no matter how justified or carried out in all innocence, also must be punished so justice is served.

In this light we must revise Freud's formulation of the myth. There is of course a universal love for the mother seen in every young boy and a wish to possess her totally by getting rid of the rivalrous father. This may in some cases create unconscious incestuous wishes that are the cause of unconscious conflicts, but this does not appear to be the basic universal cause of neuroses. Most importantly, the Oedipus myth only weakly supports such a thesis.

More to the point, the myth is the story of a special issue between a father and son in which the father had committed a prior sin and then twice attempted to murder his son, the second time because of his unconscious guilt and need to see to it that he is punished accordingly. Oedipus responds by punishing his father for his ill deeds, even as he takes on some of the father's guilt by committing murder himself.

In Freud's personal life, the issue of his father's ill deeds may refer to Jakob's infidelities and his not giving life to Freud if Phillip was in fact Freud's biological father. But the ill deeds may also have included Phillip's incestuous liaison with Amalie for which they too must be punished. As the son of this illicit union, it is Freud's mission to carry out this punishment and as disguised in the Oedipus myth, he intends to do so by contributing to his mother's suicide and murdering his father. Freud's reluctance to carry out his preordained mission against the Oedipally triumphant Phillip is implicitly expressed in the Oedipal tale and explicitly encoded, as Freud took pains to note, in the story of Hamlet's reluctance to avenge the murder of his father by his uncle. Freud's unconscious attraction to Shakespeare's story appears to be based on its themes of an ill-gained liaison between a brother figure and a wife which appears to be another encoded version of Phillip's affair with Amalie. In the play, Hamlet is killed once he has accomplished his mission—again, the justified executioner dies nonetheless. We can see why Freud was reluctant to know what he knew because of where it would take him—to a precipice from which he would be pushed to his death.

In sum, then, it seems to have been these very real and grim, albeit unconscious impulses towards murder and suicide that seem to have unconsciously caused Freud to flee from reality and the dreadful drama that his father's death was moving him towards. Freud was at a precipice and his life was at stake; without drastic action he would not survive the reincarnation of the drama of his personal life. Justified vengeance was Freud unfinished business in life and taking actions to carry it out when reminded of his mission by his father's death would have had in some form disastrous consequences. Unconsciously, Freud chose the Oedipus myth because it fit the trigger-evoked story that Freud had to tell the world and enact. He was under as much pressure to tell his tale of woes as to not tell it. Telling it in encoded form was his solution and once he told it that way, he told it again and again. Yet he could only tell it as we have seen in the guise of an unreal fantasy and under the condition that he pretend that the issues reflected in the dream-like tale did not exist in reality. Both were measures designed to save his life and that of his mother.

It seems then that decoding his dreams and recalling the traumas of his early life would have been the end of Freud. On the other hand, as a fantasied tale that never really happened, he could live on and attract a universe of followers who shared—and still share—in his denial-based needs for hidden unconscious reasons of their own. The problem is that this kind of denial obliterates but does not resolve conflicts; indeed, its use constitutes a failure to deal with the very realities that are driving one's work—and life. The underlying memories, guilt, and impulses to murder and commit suicide do not go away, but remain within the psyche as a most disruptive force which causes many untoward and self-destructive enactments—and many false denial-based premises for those who practice psychoanalysis. As is true of all humans, Freud—and his followers—have paid dearly for their denial of death and death-related realities. The same is true of the world at large.

The implications of the Oedipus myth appear, then, to be far more profound than a boy's wish to sleep with his mother and eliminate his father along the way. The archetypal grounding of the myth lies with the question of the nature of one's origins—who am I and from whom did I come? For Freud, this appears to have been a very special issue, far more than a family romance fantasy but a vital question regarding who had fathered him and brought him into the world—and who had not. Indeed, the myth begins with birth and ends with death; it is, as the riddle of the Sphinx reminds us, the fated story of a journey through life. It entails the painful realization that our lot in life is largely determined before we are born, much of it by the complex circumstances of our birth and the sins of our parents. The faults of others set the path for our lives even before we have exited the womb. Only the most fortunate experience fateful circumstances and acts of others that support a relatively satisfying life; sad to say however, the way the mind is designed, harmful fateful moments carry far more power than those that are enhancing. Much work needs to be done to afford the latter moments the greater influence over our lives.

When Oedipus comes of age, doubts are cast as to who his biological parents are. His response, supported by the adoptive mother who brought him up and who then lies to him about his origins, is an encoded representation that bridges over to Freud's unconscious experience of his mother's telling Freud who his father was—her lying to him it would seem. Oedipus and thus Freud want to accept their mothers' pronouncements. While Oedipus does pause to consult the oracle as to his origins, when the oracle fails to answer that question, Oedipus accepts his mother's word and gets on with his life; for a long while, he makes no further effort to determine the truth of the matter. In a fashion linked to Freud's theories of neuroses, Oedipus makes a brief attempt to discover the deepest truths of his life, but when the effort seems to fail he goes on his way bathed in ignorance. He tries to flee the new dangers that he is facing in that the oracle has shifted the nature of his basic challenges from origins to patricide and incest. Not until many years have passed and a plague has overcome Thebes—a blight that descends on the city largely because in Oedipus' ignorance he has murdered his father—does Oedipus begin to wonder if he is the son of the murdered king and of his wife, Jocasta, as well.

This cutting short of an initial search for the most vital truths of his life is a critical element of the Oedipal story. In encoded fashion, it speaks for Freud's preference for ignorance over knowledge, but it also speaks for the denial of death and its cost in human suffering in that Oedipus murders his father as a result—his sexual transgression follows from that essential act. Evidently Freud did not heed the wise voice of his own deep unconscious mind and as a result, his disguised dream-like narrative tells him of the dire consequences of his avoidance of death and death-related issues—the results of his having skipped over the message that it is death anxiety that causes sexual boundary violations like acts of incest.

This aspect of the myth supports the thesis that his paradigm shift was a flight from reality and humankind's and his own most compelling truths, and that he has chosen to be preoccupied with lesser truths so as to obliterate those truths that are far more profound and influential in human life. This is a critical feature of all of the forms of second-paradigm psychoanalysis to this very day. And it explains why Oedipus does not commit suicide, but blinds himself at the end of the tale—his blindness has been the cause of his ruin and that of many others. His psychological blindness is one of his most grievous sins and the reason for his eventual punishment in kind. This too indicates that Freud probably knew unconsciously that in embracing his second paradigm he was closing his eyes to the most painful realities from which a person can suffer—or benefit.

There is however one moment of untainted insight in the myth. It occurs when Oedipus saves his life and frees the city of Thebes from captivity by solving the riddle of the Sphinx. The man who as a child survived an attempt to kill him has the wisdom to survive another such attempt after he has come of age. He has already survived a fresh threat to his life when he murdered Laius, but that was done in blind ignorance. With the Sphinx, knowledge was recruited in the face of a predatory enemy who had activated his predatory death anxiety—endangered, Oedipus saved his life and caused the universally endangering, female-like Sphinx to commit suicide.

The implication here is that a person may survive death-related threats either through denial and ignorance or knowledge and wisdom. Freud chose ignorance regarding the question of his origins which then left him vulnerable to violent acts of unknown causes—the psychological blindness he chose in shaping his second paradigm was a terribly costly choice. On the other hand, had he chosen knowledge and drawn on the wisdom of the deep unconscious mind to combat death's greatest challenges, the outcome would have been far more healing and salutary. Oedipus is not punished but rewarded for defeating and destroying the life endangering Sphinx, but he is punished for the inadvertent murder of his father. There are wise, death- and knowledge-related archetypal messages here.

As for the Sphinx, the encoded message is that mother figures who cause harm to others or commit transgressions in other ways are fated to kill themselves—Freud comes back to that theme repeatedly through his writings. But at this point in his story, Oedipus's flash of wisdom does not open him to his larger personal truths, and so the tale wears on unresolved. In the end it becomes a story of punishment for crimes—past, present, and future. Attempted murder, murder, and incest are the main transgressions and death and death anxiety loom large as experiences that Oedipus tries to obliterate; in so doing, he dooms himself to harming others and himself as well.

The final message of the myth seems then to be that as awful as the truth may be, it can be healing; blindness and ignorance are far more costly options that lead eventually to utter devastation. Freud seems to have known this unconsciously, yet he evidently feared that knowing the truth of his origins and of the many violent impulses those truths would evoke in him would be far more unbearable than not knowing. The threat of murder and suicide must have been so intense that obliteration and blindness were, he believed, his only recourse for saving his life. The disastrous consequences of his paradigm-shifting flight into darkness regarding the essence of human life have yet to be appreciated. Much as Freud evidently had no conscious awareness of the underlying nature and consequences of the terrible choices he was making—and why he was making them—psychoanalysts to this day remain similarly unaware of the underpinnings of the theories and practices they so cherish. They are awash in theories and practices that involve trivialities rather than cardinal issues, and far more blindness than vision.

Finally, in respect to the thesis regarding Freud's uncertainty as to the identity of his father, the myth he selected as the foundation for psychoanalysis appears to reflect the foundational issue that unconsciously dominated his personal life. The most relevant features of the Oedipus story encode Freud's unconscious realizations that his purported father, Jakob, attempted to murder him, evidently by not giving him life; that Freud was given false information regarding the identity of his parents; that he did not know and did not want to know who his biological father was even though that issue was the driving force of his life; that Freud's biological father was not the father whom he thought was his father; and that Freud's unconscious intentions to wreak vengeance against all concerned for having abandoned and harmed him would cause him to punish himself unmercifully.

The support for the thesis is striking. That said, let's delve now into other encoded narratives that are relevant to these issues to see if they support the formulations made on the basis of analyzing Freud's investment in the story of Oedipus Rex.

## THE DOUBLE DREAM

I turn first to the dream that Freud had either the night before or the night after the death of his father. The first version of the dream is presented in a letter to Fliess written some nine days after his father had died (Freud, 1954, Letter 50, November 2, 1896, pp. 170–171). Freud calls it a very pretty dream and indicates that it was dreamt the night after his father's funeral. In the dream, he finds himself in a shop where there was a notice saying: "You are requested to close the eyes."

The same dream as described in *The Interpretation of Dreams* (Freud, 1900) is a double dream:

> During the night before my father's funeral I had a dream of a printed notice, placard or poster—rather like the notices forbidding one to smoke in railway waiting-rooms—on which appeared either
> "You are requested to close the eyes"
> "You are requested to close an eye."
> I usually write this in the form:
> $$\text{"You are requested to close } \begin{array}{c} \text{the} \\ \text{an} \end{array} \text{eye(s)."}$$
>
> (Freud, 1900, pp. 317–318)

Because it was triggered by his father's death, the dream and Freud's associations to it should enable us to glean some clues as to how his loss affected Freud unconsciously. In so doing, we should keep in mind that the dream actually preceded his turn to the Oedipus myth by more than a year. It therefore presages rather than follows the myth and must be understood in that light.

As for the first version of the dream, Freud recognized the setting as the barber shop to which he went the morning of the funeral. He was delayed there and arrived late at the house of mourning, which displeased his family. He had arranged a simple funeral and his family agreed that that was the best choice.

Freud states that the phrase on the notice-board had an implied double meaning, both involving the idea that "One should do one's duty towards the dead," his doing so twice over in the form of an apology as though he had not done his duty and that his conduct needed overlooking and in carrying out the actual duty itself. The dream according to Freud therefore was a dream of self-reproach.

These are the kind of vague and naïve self-interpretations that are characteristic of Freud's attempts at self-analysis. Only the theme of two meanings has a possible bearing on the issue of two fathers regarding whom Freud should close his eyes; the connection, while viable, seems weakly implied.

The second version of the dream is somewhat more revealing. The theme of "twos" pervade the dream: The double dream with two simultaneous images in this rendering; being told twice to close the eyes or eye; attributing the timing of the dream to two different nights; and the offer of two versions of its contents.

In his dream book, Freud presented this dream to illustrate how two versions of the same dream tends to lead to two different trains of associations. However, Freud did not make clear the nature of these two trains of though except to say in this presentation that some members of his family had objected to his having arranged a simple funeral; they thought that they would be disgraced in the eyes of those who attended the services. Freud indicates that one pathway reflected in the dream asked these visitors to close their eyes in order to overlook this simplicity.

There is then no power or depth to Freud's views of the two versions of this dream. Nevertheless it is worth noting that closing the eyes of the deceased is a son's responsibility, a way of showing his respect. But the dream also has other likely implications. As a double dream dealing with the death of Freud's supposed biological father, it may well encode Freud's unconscious realization that he must close his eyes to the behaviors of not one but two possible fathers—this may well have been the missing second, unconscious train of thought. Freud may also have been working over the death of each father, adoptive and actual, each of whom had died in some manner—Jakob physically and Phillip by moving to England. Alternatively or simultaneously through condensation, the dream may have encoded the need for Freud to close his eyes to two transgressions carried out by Jakob—perhaps his possible infidelities and the suicide of Rebekka Freud, or two other ways in which Jakob had hurt Freud. On yet another encoded level, the dream also may allude to overlooking two ways in which Phillip, who at the moment is being thought of as Freud's biological father, had damaged Freud as well. As Freud notes in introducing the dream, through condensation, at least two of these possibilities may have been represented by this double dream. Most assuredly, the dream indicates that with the death of his father, two issues—two fathers or two transgressions—need to be overlooked.

Most striking is the theme of closing the eyes, to not seeing. As I suggested in connection with the Oedipus myth, this too speaks for the likelihood that the death of Freud's father had activated a set of early traumas in which Jakob played a significant role, and that Freud did not want to open his eyes to these events and their ramifications. The dream, then, reflects Freud's strong preference for blindness over vision and bears further testimony to the defensive aspects of his paradigm shift. Here too we sense a conflict in Freud between seeing the nature of his early-life traumas and his need to not see them at all—with a preference for the latter.

The theme of respect for the dead—in this case for his father, whomever he was—suggests that Freud did have a love and respect for one of his fathers, most likely Jakob who, if Phillip was Freud's biological father, had taken on the role of his life-saving adoptive father. In the Oedipus myth, the loving father whom Oedipus evidently loves in return seems to be represented by King Pelops, the king of Corinth. However, this love is overshadowed by Oedipus's hatred of his true father, Laius, who has sinned as a seducer, caused a suicide, and twice tried to murder his son. The images speak, then, for a limited amount of unconsciously wrought love in Freud for Jakob and for a great deal of hatred and murderous intentions towards Phillip as Freud's true father. Some of this rage is expressed in the story of Don Giovanni (Balmary, 1979), who was a seducer of women and the murderer of the father of one of his intended victims. There is the ultimate punishment via a descent into hell for Don Juan which is, for Freud, connected with the forgetting—another form of blindness—of the name Signorelli who painted the Last Judgment frescoes that Freud saw in Orvieto.

As discussed in the previous chapter, these encoded themes may allude to the possibility that Freud knew that Jakob had committed adultery or that he saw his father as having seduced and harmed his second wife, Rebekka. There is, however, a great deal of speculation in these proposals. Thus, a more likely pair of early traumas related to this encoded imagery would have been Phillip's seduction of Amalie and his being Freud's biological father. There would then be strong reasons for Freud to close his eyes to these realities and their recollection because of the extraordinary pain they would have caused him. That said, Freud's blatant communicative resistances, which are reflected in his failure to provide narrative associations to this important dream, has certainly deprived us of a more definitive interpretation of this dream. As such, it is supportive of my thesis but there is a need for further evidence in its favor.

## THE REBECCA STORY

We come next to Freud's *neurotica* letter to Fliess and his association late in the letter to Rebecca taking off her wedding gown (Freud, 1954, Letter 69, September 21, 1897, pp. 215-218). As noted in the previous chapter, the story pertains to the Biblical tale of Rebecca's marriage to Isaac. It alludes to commentaries by the Rabbis who believed that when Rebecca came to marry Isaac he inspected her hymen and found that it was not intact. Rebecca was able to convince Isaac that she was still a virgin and that she had cut herself on a bush, but doubts about her virginity remained.

The theme of this story is that a woman who has come from another land to be married is not pure in body, but has transgressed sexually and thus cannot be a bride. Balmary (1979) proposed that Rebecca is a stand-in for Rebekka Freud, but this conjecture does not account for the rest of the story, especially the theme that prior to her marriage the woman in question has had sex with someone other than her future husband.

In contrast, the themes support the conjecture that these encoded themes allude to Amalie Freud and that her premarital transgression of a sexual boundary was known unconsciously to Freud early on. Thus, the story, which is linked to Freud's emerging paradigm shift, appears to encode in a thinly disguised manner Freud's unconscious perceptions that his mother, who traveled from Vienna to Frieberg—that is, who had come from another land—had had premarital sex with Phillip. It also seems to support the conjecture that it was then that Freud was conceived—a thesis that accounts for Freud's March 6th birth date and the family's need to conceal it. Indeed, the theme of not knowing is implied in the story in that Jacob sees something disturbing but is willing to accept a questionable story that goes against what he has seen with his own eyes.

The jury is still out on the question of whether the birth date that the family gave Freud was correct because several municipal records, which some writers believe could have been in error, record date of March 6, 1856 rather than May 6th of that year. When Freud was once asked about it, he shrugged off the question with a joke, saying that he didn't want anyone to make him any older than he is. Nevertheless, the May date makes Freud a honeymoon baby—Jakob and Amalie were married on July 29, 1855—while the March 6th date makes him a bastard child and raises the question as to who had fathered him.

There is considerable difficulty in trying to sort out the few known historical facts about the Freud family situation in order to confirm or cast doubts on the conjecture about Freud's uncertainties regarding his birth date and biological father. We know almost nothing about how Jakob met and married Amalie, nor do we have much information about Phillip's whereabouts during the years 1855 and 1856. We do know that Jakob transferred his business to his son Emanuel in December 1853 while he himself was away in Vienna and that Emanuel took charge of the business in January 1854. If it was Jakob who impregnated Amalie two months prior to their marriage, it would mean that they had had premarital sex and arranged to be married after Amalie discovered that she was pregnant. This is one possible scenario but it is not well supported by Freud's encoded themes; it also does not seem to have enough traumatic impact to serve as the source of a basic and enduring flight from reality. While the plague suffered by the Thebans rendered them sterile—yet another birth-related theme—there is no issue in the Oedipus myth of an out of wedlock impregnation.

The other possible scenario is that Phillip had an affair with Amalie in 1855 and impregnated her. For some reason, Amalie and her parents were opposed to their getting married, so Jakob stepped in and proposed that she marry him. The wedding arrangements were made as quickly as possible; we do not know if Phillip was in attendance. This version of what happened would explain the marriage between the much older Jacob and much younger Amalie in the absence of logical reasons for their decision to wed. It also is in keeping with the rupture within the family that built up over the next few years and took place soon after the birth of Freud's sister Anna, when Freud was approaching three years of age. It appears that Phillip was frozen out by the rest of the family and that conflicts tied to this chain of events may have been the reason for this unusual happening.

All in all, it seems that Freud's need to close his eyes on these traumas, supported by his eye-closing paradigm shift, has successfully prevented us from seeing more. Nevertheless, Freud's seemingly odd and out-of-place comment in his renunciation letter seems to add further encoded support to the thesis I have been advocating.

## LEONARDO DA VINCI

In 1910, Freud published his first and only large-scale biographical study, one that was focused on one of his subject's childhood memories (Freud, 1910a). As another first of its kind from Freud, I should have investigated the story, but did not do so because there was so much other material for me to sort out. Balmary's (1979) book had had alerted me to Freud's comment on studying the lives of famous people with which he began this treatise and I quoted it at length at the beginning of chapter 6. I did not look further, however, until quite recently when I found a quote from Rorty (1989) that indicated that Freud had ended this study with some pithy comments on the role of chance in human life. These comments were entirely unknown to me and they therefore were not introduced in chapter 2 of this book where I proposed a fourth trauma for humankind, that of realizing that fate and chance govern so much of our lives. The chapter had been completed and edited and the book was nearly finished so I decided to insert these comments here, in the final chapter.

I hastily investigated the situation. I found out that this is Freud's only comment on fate and chance as external factors in human life, that his only prior remarks on chance, which were made in *The Psychopathology of Everyday*

*Life* (Freud, 1901) address the ways in which seemingly chance actions are actually based on unconscious fantasies and needs. I also quickly learned to take seriously the saying repeated often during my psychoanalytic training that whatever you discover today, somewhere Freud said it first (even if it was, to use one of his already cited images, a flirtation rather than a serious, elaborated on statement).

Freud mentions Leonardo in one of his letters to Fliess (Freud, 1954, letter 98, October 9, 1898, pp. 267-268), referring to his being left-handed and not known to have had any love-affairs. In 1907, Freud listed a study of Leonardo as one of his favorite books and in 1909, in a letter to Jung, Freud indicated that he became interested in Leonardo because he was seeing a patient who has the same constitution as the artist without his genius (Freud, 1910a). There are reasons to be suspicious of this rationale because Freud wrote about fictional patients, friends, and acquaintances who actually were stand-ins for himself.

A far more suggestive feature of this paper, however, are its bookends: An opening comment in which Freud justifies the study of famous people and a closing summary that encodes one version of Freud's postulated early-life traumas and a striking commentary on the role of accidental circumstances on human life. These aspects of this very long paper suggest that Freud's unconscious mind was intensely working over aspects of his early-life traumas as he wrote this treatise. Freud also made a critical error in writing the paper; substituting one bird for another as he explored an early memory of Leonardo's, but the editors of the English translation of the paper suggest that this may have arisen from a comparable error made in most of the books he used for source material. Still, Freud was a meticulous observer, and errors of this kind on his part were not uncommon whenever he entered the narrative world where his past traumas were encoded. There is, then, no point in trying to make too much of this error, especially since there are other striking clues, most of them encoded, to the issues Freud may well have been working over unconsciously in this paper.

The early memory with which Freud was concerned here is traced back by Leonardo to a time when he was in a cradle. He recalled a bird visiting him there, opening his mouth with its tail, and striking its tail many times against his mouth. Freud identified the bird as a vulture, but scholars are in agreement that the bird was a kite, which is a hawklike predator. In any case, the memory is considered to have been fateful for Leonardo's future career and life.

Focusing solely on material that is relevant to my hypotheses regarding Freud's early and pre-life traumas, much of Freud's analysis is based on the contention that the memory involved an incident that occurred during Leonardo's suckling period and that the vulture was a substitute for the infant's mother. Freud cites mythical and other historical material to make the point that vultures were conceived as solely female in nature and that the early Egyptians believed that there were no males of the species—that they were impregnated by the wind. Whether Freud's ideas also apply to kites is not relevant to our pursuit in that Freud either chose a memory of a bird which unknown to him fit the myth about vultures or he was invested in this myth because it was another story that was much like a dream of his own, one that encoded the story of his early-life traumas he needed so badly to tell.

For Freud, then, Leonardo was a child who was aware of his father's absence and that he was alone with his mother. Indeed, it is well known that he was an illegitimate child who was not received into his father's house until he was five years old. His father's wife was unable to conceive so the father impregnated a peasant woman who may have been a slave from the Middle East; she then brought him up for his first five years.

In commenting on this memory, Freud notes:

Our aim in dissecting a childhood phantasy is to separate the real memory that it contains from the later motives that modify it. In Leonardo's case we believe that we know the real content of the phantasy: the replacement of his mother by the vulture indicates that the child was aware of his father's absence and found himself alone with his mother. The fact of Leonardo's illegitimate birth is in harmony with his vulture phantasy; it was only on this account that he could compare himself to a vulture child. . . .

An inevitable effect of this state of affairs was that the child—who was confronted in his early life with one problem more than other children—began to brood on this riddle with special intensity, and so at a tender age became a researcher, tormented as he was by the great question of where babies come from and what the father has to do with their origin. (Freud, 1910a, pp. 90–91)

Commenting further, Freud suggests that the vulture was a representation of the real content of Leonardo's memory. Freud also proposes that these early-life circumstances set an irreversible tone to how Leonardo reacted to the world and that their importance could not be modified by later experiences. The years spent alone with his mother were of decisive influence for his inner life.

Although we know that Freud owned a biography of Leonardo for many years, we do not know when and to what depths he began to carefully study this material. That said, one other seeming coincidence that may have influenced Freud's choice of subject is reflected in two errors that Leonardo made in penning his father's death notice. The first is quoted by Freud in the text of his paper: It is an uncalled for repetition of the time of the day that his father died. The second, which Freud considers to be a greater error, is placed in a footnote where Freud points out the Leonardo also gave his father's wrong age in the notice, saying he was 80 years old instead of 77 when he died. A third error of Leonardo's, which Freud notes soon after these comments, involves the number of children his father sired after Leonardo's birth.

The first two errors have their parallels in Freud's double dream on the night before or after his father's funeral and in Freud's slip about Hannibal in which he confused a brother for a father. Two dates and two ages certainly echo the theme of two fathers. In Leonardo's case, this may have alluded to his having had two mothers in his earliest years—his biological and an adoptive mother, the wife of his father—or to having had two fathers—again one biological and an adoptive father in the form of his grandfather. Much of this undoubtedly was known to Freud. In addition, the questions pertaining to his origins—Leonardo's certainty as to who his mother was, yet his being uncertain about the identity of his father—touches on and may well encode Freud's uncertainties about his own origins. The fact that his father's wife was unable to conceive may encode Freud's view of why Rebekka disappeared after evidently having married Jakob—there are those scholars who believe, in the face of much skepticism, that Jakob divorced her because she was barren. It is characteristic of the deep unconscious mind to generate clues to actual traumas in the most unexpected narratives.

Freud's comments imply that an early trauma may well be encoded in an early memory (and by implication, in other narratives as well). He also affords these actualities a powerful role in a person's life. Oddly enough, he also noted that these early-life incidents affected Leonardo's love for the truth and his thirst for knowledge, but they also marked him for failure—a point very similar to the main arguments of this book in respect to the life and work of Freud himself.

In sum, then, Freud may well have chosen Leonardo da Vinci for his first—and only—biographical study because of significant resemblances between the early traumas and life histories of the two men. This means that unconsciously, Freud had come to realize that story of the early-life traumas suffered by Leonardo encoded a number of his own significant early-life traumas. It seems more than coincidence, as Freud noted in his book on *The Psychopathology of Everyday Life* (Freud, 1901), that there are such strong parallels between the two lives. Rather than seeing this hidden correspondence as Freud did in terms of unconscious phantasies, I see them largely in terms of corresponding early-life traumas. As such, I take Freud's turn to the story of Leonardo's infancy as further support for my conjectures that Freud did not know who his biological father was, that he believed at times that he had two fathers—one biological and the other adoptive—and that he was conceived before or outside of Jakob's marriage to Amalie. The material does not, however, support the speculation that Freud may have thought at times that Amalie was not his biological mother, but it does suggest that the early traumas Freud experienced in the hands of his family had diminished his view of his mother.

Finally, there is Freud's conclusion to his paper in which he returns to the theme of the influence of accidental external circumstances on the career choices and life of Leonardo—and on the fate of humans in general. He then notes, "If one considers chance to be unworthy of determining our fate, it is simply a relapse into the pious view of the Universe which Leonardo himself was on the way to overcoming when he wrote that the sun does not move" (Freud, 1910a, p. 137).

How strange, and yet telling, that Freud cites the surrender of the death-denying, earth-centered theory of the universe in a discussion of the role of chance and fate in human life (see chapter 2). He then goes on to say:

> we are all too ready to forget that in fact everything to do with our life is chance, from our origin out of the meeting of spermatozoon and ovum onwards—chance which nevertheless has a share in the law and necessity of nature, and which merely lacks any connection with our wishes and illusions. The apportioning of the determining factors of our life between the "necessities" of our constitution and the "chances" of our childhood may still be uncertain in detail; but in general it is no longer possible to doubt the importance precisely of the first years of our childhood We all still show too little respect for Nature which (in the obscure words of Leonardo which recall Hamlet's lines) "is full of countless causes [*ragioni*] that never enter experience." Every one of us human beings corresponds to one of the countless experiments in which these "ragioni" of nature force their way into experience. (Freud, 1910a, p. 137)

According to the editors of the English edition of this paper, the allusion is to Hamlet's familiar words "There are more things in heaven and earth, Horatio/Than are dreamt in your philosophy."

In much-deserved respect to Freud, I could not have summed up one of the essential messages of this book more poetically—and clearly. For one moment, Freud acknowledges the power of early-life realities over our inner wishes and fantasies and gives chance and fate their deserving due; he also alludes to the influence of laws and necessities of nature, and thus to archetypes and universals. I am moved to say again that truth in the sense of reality is in so many ways and on so many levels stranger—and more intriguing and affecting—than fiction. In terms of this book, this is another way of saying that inner-mental theories of the mind and the observations that they promote are relatively clichéd, uninteresting, and uninformative, while reality-centered theories and where they take us in respect to life and human nature will never cease to amaze—and inform. As for the thesis that Freud did not know who his biological father was, the unconsciously driven aspects of his selection of Leonardo for study and his emphasis on the lasting effects of the circumstances of his birth—his illegitimacy and the absence of his father—again seem to provide encoded evidence that supports this line of thought. It begins to look like every time Freud takes on the writing of a new book or a new psychoanalytic investigation, he unconsciously experiences a strong need to work over the story of his personal origins.

## DIE RICHTERIN

One other last minute discovery that I made after completing the working draft of this book also involved a first effort by Freud. In this case, it was his first application of psychoanalysis to a work of literature—the novel, *Die Richterin,* published in 1895 (Freud, 1954, letter 91, June 20, 1998, pp. 255-257). We are not told what attracted Freud to the novel, whose plot is not outlined in the letter; instead, Freud offers a random set of comments regarding the plot.

The story involves the death of a Count Wulf and the confession of his wife, Stemma, sixteen years after his death, that she had poisoned him because she loved another man who had fathered her daughter. After making her confession, she poisons herself and dies. There is a subplot in which the Count's son by a previous marriage falls in love with his half-sister.

Freud's begins his commentary on the book by stating that it is a defense against the writer's memory of an affair with his sister. Freud ties this idea to a version of the family romance that is generated as a defense against incest: If your sister is not your mother's child, you are relieved of guilt. He wonders about the source of so much adultery and illegitimacy in creating these romances and accounts for them through the behaviors of lower class female servants. He then adds that in all analyses one comes upon the same story twice over—once as a fantasy related to the mother and the second time as a real memory of the servant. This is what happens in the novel as applied to *die richerin*—the female judge who is the mother (that is, Stemma). Mistress and maid end up lying dead side by side. It is the mother who is surprised, unmasked, and con-demned, but the maid also is punished. The sister's anorexia, which is caused by an infantile seduction, is not laid to the brother's door but to the mother's. The sister ends up dashed against the rocks. The father's murder is carried out because he stands in the son's way. Hostility towards the mother is expressed in making her a step-mother. Freud patients create these revenge-and-exoneration romances about their mothers as if they were boys.

In a separate final comment in the letter, Freud notes that his psychology is going curiously, as if in a dream.

To comment, we may note again the stress on themes of adultery, illegitimacy, murder, and suicide. Freud traces this dream-like novel to an actual trauma, incestuous in nature, in the life of the writer—implying, it would seem, that his interest in writing about this novel is derived from an actual trauma in his own life. Notably, Freud indicates that an affair between a half-sister and half-brother is rendered non-incestuous because they do not share the same mother. This is a striking unconscious commentary on the likely affair between Phillip and his step-mother Amalie. The unconscious view of their affair as expressed here is to the effect that it is not truly incestuous because Amalie was not Phillip's mother. The denial of the incestuous element in this view of their liaison helps to account for the scarcity of vengeful, murderous wishes against Amalie because of her role in the liaison with Phillip—and possibly in Freud's illegitimacy as well. On the other hand, given that the unfaithful wife murders her husband, Freud seems to be holding Amalie accountable for the symbolic murder of Jakob Freud in her having an affair with Phillip. In is on this account that the mother figure commits suicide in the novel, although in addition, the daughter who falls in love with her half-brother also ends up dead as well.

It seems reasonable to conjecture that Freud was attracted to this book because a contemporary triggering event had unconsciously re-aroused the early life traumas connected with an affair between Phillip and Amalie. Adaptive studies have shown that traumas of this kind are first unconsciously perceived as such and then subjected to a wide range of fantasied possibilities as to the underlying causes and consequences. All in all, once again a first venture by Freud brings up themes of adultery, incest, illegitimacy, murder, and punishment suggesting an early life of trauma and chaos.

## MOSES AND MONOTHEISM

I come now to the last major piece of encoded evidence for my main conjectures: Freud's (1939) *Moses and Monotheism.* There are strong reasons to believe that this book, the last of his creative works and thus another likely dream equivalent, was his final encoded commentary on the early traumas in his life. Freud experienced considerable inner pressure to write and finish this book, much of it from unconscious sources. He himself, as well as others (Yerushalmi, 1991), have seen the book as a kind of last will and testament.

The historical evidence used by Freud for the main ideas presented in the book are quite debatable and much of his thinking is unfounded. In addition, his reasoning is arbitrary and his presentation often self-contradictory. Freud had first thought of the book as a novel, and for purposes of analysis I shall treat it as such without discussing the conscious rationale for his ideas. The book, then, may be thought of as another dream equivalent replete with encoded, trigger-evoked messages, a story that seems, once more and for the last time, to touch on the hidden family secrets that Freud was unconsciously compelled to tell the world before he died. Because he embellished the story with many side comments and irrelevancies, I shall concentrate on the main themes in the tale as he told it and attempt to determine if the imagery decodes readily around the thesis that Freud lived to the end of his life believing among other possibilities that he had had two fathers—one of them biological and the other in name only, adoptive.

The fundamental story as Freud tells is that there were two Moses and that the first Moses was the father of the Jews, but he was not a Jew—he was an Egyptian and thus an interloper. This Moses taught the Jews that they were the favored people of a monotheistic God and presented them with the practice of circumcision, which according to Freud, was an Egyptian custom. This Moses was a harsh leader and eventually, in a manner similar to the events hypothesized by Freud in *Totem and Taboo* (Freud, 1913b), his sons rebelled and murdered him. Eventually the Jews found another leader, also named Moses. He also preached in the name of a monotheistic God, but this God was different from the sun god of the first Moses, and this leader was kinder than the first Moses.

According to Freud, there were, then, two founding Moses in the history of the Jews and the two figures eventually were fused into one. Disavowing that they had sinned and murdered the first Moses, the Jews carried within them the guilt of the deed, a burden that contributed to their emphasis on instinctual renunciation—sexual renunciation in particular. The second monotheistic religion called for a prohibition of making an image of God and thus advocated the worship of a God whom one is forbidden to see. Circumcision was the weapon used by the powerful father figure to subdue his followers; going against his edicts resulted in its equivalent—castration. Finally, there could be no direct expression of the murderous hatred of the father in Moses's religion, only a reaction against this hatred and an underlying sense of guilt for having sinned and continuing to sin against God. This state of affairs laid the groundwork for the Christianity that Paul created in which original sin and redemption through the sacrifice of a victim served as its foundation stones. Freud sees this as embodying an admission of the murderous sin against the first Moses and an acceptance of the punishment it calls for through the emergence of a Messiah, Jesus Christ, who led his followers to redemption through his death as the son of God.

Freud stresses the presence of several dualities in this story: The two Moses; the existence of two families in the history of the first Moses, one royal and the other common; two groups of people—Egyptian and semitic—who came together to form one nation; two monotheistic Gods and two names for this God; the foundations of two religions—the first one repressed but the second emerging victoriously behind it; and two reactions to the murder of the first Moses—one traumatic and the other an escape from the trauma.

Freud also focused on the relationship between the father and his son which involved the son's murder of the father and the son's eventual punishment for the crime through the crucifixion of Jesus. The sins of the fathers are brought down on the sons, but the sons also are assigned the task of punishing the fathers for their crimes.

It seems reasonable to theorize that for Freud, the story of Moses encodes the story of his relationships with his two fathers—one of them repressed and obliterated and the other known consciously. This situation repeats the part of the Oedipus myth in which the father is murdered by the son as a punishment for the father's sexual misdeed, the rape of Chrysippus. Oedipus eventually punishes himself for the murder of his father by blinding himself. In the Moses tale, the son's punishment for the crime of murdering the violent father is death.

That said, we need to ask again: To whom does Freud see himself as his son and who is the father who has committed the sinful crime that Freud must avenge? In the Oedipus myth, the avenged father has been a transgressor, a rapist, while in the story of Moses, the avenged father is a foreigner—a transgressor in another sense of the word. This points to Phillip as the father who has sinned because he was a transgressor in his liaison with Amalie and in his giving her a bastard child. Jakob may be represented as the care-taking, adoptive father, King Pelops in the Oedipus story and as the more benign second Moses who takes over the Jewish religion after the death of the first Moses. But Jakob also is Phillip's passive victim of his son's involvement with Amalie. This view of Jakob may have been encoded in the story of Jakob and the Christian boy—another interloper—who humiliated him by knocking off his hat and forcing him to walk in the street. Freud made no effort to treat this incident, told to him by his father when Freud was nine or ten years old, as an encoded narrative, that is, as having anything more than manifest meaning. His biographers have taken a similar approach and the likely unconscious meanings of this trauma seem to have been overlooked.

As a last will and statement, Freud's study of Moses seems to strongly encode his unconscious belief that he had two fathers—and that while he was uncertain as to who was who, the most likely scenario would have Phillip as his first, biological father and Jakob as his second, more benign adoptive father who taught him his Judaism. It also can be said, as Freud himself has claimed, that it is highly unlikely that his repetitive allusions to themes related to this issue were without intense unconscious sources. Adaptive studies have shown that a single early-life, death-related trauma will indeed, without let up, evoke a wide number of encoded versions of what happened and what it meant. Repetitive themes that bridge over to the nature and meanings of the trauma are legion. Such seems to have been the case with Freud and the mystery of who had fathered him—and when.

## Freud's Fainting Episodes

By bringing up Egyptian history in his last major narrative message to the world, Freud reminds us that he fainted twice—in 1909 and 1912—in the presence of Jung, his heir apparent, or as Freud put it, the Joshua to his Moses (Donn, 1998; Gay, 1988). In both situations, Freud believed that Jung was expressing murderous wishes against him, much like a son towards his father. In the first conversation, which took place in Bremen on the eve of their journey together to America, Jung was speaking of the discovery of some mummified prehistoric human corpses, and as he kept dwelling on the fate of these bodies, Freud fell into a faint. Freud's self-interpretation of the incident is that it involved latent homosexual feelings towards Jung and had a connection to the death of his brother Julius—implying some kind of unconscious guilt over having murdered his sibling. For his part, Jung was convinced that Freud believed that the story indicated that he—that is, Jung—entertained death wishes towards him.

In the second incident, Freud had been reconciled with Jung after some months of tension and at an informal meeting prior to a Congress of psychoanalysts, a discussion came up regarding Abraham's paper on the Egyptian Pharaoh, Amenhotep. Freud remembered that after Amenhotep's death, his son had erased his name from all of the existing monuments. Jung then added that Amenhotep's son was the first monotheist among the Egyptians—a claim that Freud made use of in his Moses book—and that he was a great genius, very human and quite individual, and that he should not be dismissed for having scratched out his father's name. Freud felt that Jung was referring to a son who had symbolically killed his father and Freud seemed to link this to Jung's recent behavior with himself. Freud fell into a faint and when he recovered, he looked up at Ernest Jones, who was present, and said "How sweet it must be to die" (Donn, 1988).

As I have indicated, adaptive studies have shown that fantasy-based self-interpretations of the kind made by Freud regarding these incidents always are defensive and off the mark; they tend to use a grain of evident truth to cover over a deeper layer of less evident and far more painful truths. Thus, Freud failed to see that his relationship with Jung basically fit the father–son prototype even though the second story is openly of that ilk. In that connection, Freud evidently identified himself with the father whom the son wishes to murder—or actually does murder in a symbolic manner. For his part, in fainting, Freud symbolically fell dead. The fainting indirectly speaks, then, for an anxiety-provoking situation in the past in which a son actually murdered his father in a symbolic manner. This fits with one of the unconscious beliefs that Freud seems to have entertained regarding Phillip's replacement of Jakob in the latter's marital bed—casting him out of the bed is tantamount to killing him off.

## SUMMING UP

All in all then, Freud's first and last work-related encoded narratives deal largely with a son's conflicted relationship with his father. In the Oedipal myth, which is driven by the search for his biological parents, Oedipus is responsible for the death of both of his parents. In the Moses myth, as we might call it, the Moses who is believed to be the father of the Jews is not a Jew but an outsider, but there also is another Moses who was a Jew. The first Moses is murdered because he is too harsh and harmful to his followers and we know from the Bible that the second Moses—the Moses of the bible—is punished by God, probably because, as a young man, he had murdered an Egyptian man who was taunting another Jew. This Moses is not allowed to enter the promised land—only his apprentice, Joshua, is given that blessing. But in addition, the murder of the first Moses by his sons is avenged through the sacrifice of a later-day son, Jesus Christ, whose crucifixion was meant to pay for the violent sins of his brothers and fathers.

It appears then that a trauma that was perpetrated before Freud was born unconsciously played a significant role in the evolution of his psychoanalytic thinking and although not explored here, in setting the course of his personal life. Freud first considered doing law and dealing with questions of justice, but he gave up that pursuit in favor of seeking the underlying psychological reasons why people behave and suffer emotionally as they do. But given the ways in which the answers to these questions would have endangered him personally, Freud opted to leave the path that would have taken him to the most basic truths about his own emotional life and about human life in general. Instead, he unwittingly selected a path laced with defense and denial. He gave up his counter-archetypal position regarding death and death anxiety, shifted to an archetypal, denial-based theory, and the world willingly followed him in his exodus from the devastating realities of life—and death. Even though Freud and his followers subsequently have illuminated many aspects of human emotional life and set the stage for selected and limited researches into the human psyche, Freud gave psychoanalysis a foundation of neurotic defenses, misconceptions, and misdirected leads that ignores or barely acknowledges the most basic challenges humans are called on to face in their journey from birth to death—dealing with death and the three forms of death anxiety it engenders.

The accumulated decoded evidence suggests that Freud was compelled to tell the encoded story of the most painful aspects of his early life because he deeply needed to expose and punish those who had harmed him even if it meant punishing himself for carrying out his duty as a son to see that justice was done. But because the conscious realization of the horrors to which he had been subjected to would have brought him to a precipice where both murder and suicide in some attenuated form were real possibilities, the over-riding need to move to safer ground took over. So one minute Freud was attempting to discover the hidden story of his life so he could make peace with his smoldering traumas, but the next moment he was inclined to mete out justice at all cost. As a result, he backed away from doing his archetypal duty and beat a retreat from reality. In the course of his struggle to reveal and conceal, communicatively, Freud ingeniously, albeit unconsciously, found a way to tell his story in a form that was so well camouflaged that no one using his second paradigm of emotional life has been able to detect the most compelling hidden truths it embraces. Only a trigger decoder committed to Freud's first paradigm could see through the mist and describe the situation for what it really was.

Freud had to abandon reality before he could show the world how to decode an emotionally charged, narrative message. And by the time he was ready to explain his method, it was centered on how to find lesser meanings and miss the greater ones. Freud was like a detective who has discovered a new, foolproof way to identify someone who has committed a crime but keeps testing it out on innocent parties. Freud's descendants have continued this tradition. And because at bottom Freud's inner-mental focus serves the human need to deny death and its encoded representations, his version of psychoanalysis has been widely accepted.

Although it may be said that eventually, the truth must prevail, from the look of things, this will not be an easy achievement. As Bion (1977) so wisely put it, when it comes to death, there is only one truth but countless lies. The truth is forbidding and the lies enormously appealing; innumerable lives have been lost in the vain attempt to sustain these lies. Thus the wall erected by second-paradigm advocates to steel themselves against penetration by Freud's first paradigm is riddled with lies masquerading as purported truths. These same lies protect psychoanalysts and their patients from the risk of experiencing the intolerable urges and madness that comes with dealing with death and its attendant anxieties. All concerned prefer to accept a more tolerable form of madness—death and its anxieties do not rest easy when they are obliterated from awareness—conspiring to pretend it is not a form of madness at all. With this as the true state of matters, I expect that it will take a very long time before the truth of emotional life and the life of Sigmund Freud are fully known and adaptively processed—and his version of psychoanalysis suitably modified.

In a previous book (Langs, 2008), I suggested that psychoanalysis had failed religion by not providing it with the psychology it needed to flourish in a way that it could truly serve as a voice of peace and love rather than as a divisive belief system that has caused —and still causes—so many individuals to suffer so badly. This book shows that this failure is a much broader one in that, because it is grounded in Freud's second paradigm, psychoanalysis has not made its necessary contributions to human psychology in general and thereby to personal and world peace. As the only viable form of depth psychology, it has an implied mandate to do so, but because it is so steeped in the denial of reality, it has not as yet answered the call. Indeed, a denial-based psychology cannot offer effective solutions to the world's seemingly unending problems with violence and death nor can it offer humankind the insights it needs to live as best it can emotionally.

Sigmund Freud is the founder and is still the spiritual leader of our efforts to understand the emotion-processing mind and the basic challenges of life it has evolved to face. We can only wonder why a band of sons, psychoanalytic followers of Freud, have not as yet banded together a la Totem and Taboo to challenge the oppressiveness and lack of freedom with which Freud's psychoanalysis has chained them. Clearly, death and death anxiety, especially their pervasive *unconsciously experienced forms*—unconscious death anxiety is the psychological plague of humankind—evoke such an intense unconscious sense of dread that humans naturally prefer some form of denial far more than some form of emotional truth—and the freedom and mental health it brings with it. And the situation is all the more difficult to resolve because the deep unconscious wisdom subsystem, the locale of the resources we need to resolve these issues, has an accurate but devastatingly grim picture of ourselves and those around us—and of our ultimate fate in death. The conscious mind simply cannot bear to face the truths known to its deep unconscious counterpart, yet it must do so if we are to survive the holocausts that lie ahead for us personally and collectively.

This book has been offered as another of many efforts that I have made to move psychoanalysis in this direction. I like to believe that if Freud were alive today, despite his unconscious dread of reality, there is enough of an argument here to have moved him to at least reconsider how he fashioned psychoanalysis and begin to wonder if the time has come for an overhaul of psychoanalytic thinking. He no longer can do so, but there are those who can. May they step forward now

# A Personal Note

As reluctant as I am to reveal personal information, this book would be badly out of balance were I to not briefly present my own early death-related traumas and also offer a few words on why as a psychoanalyst I ended up committed to Freud's trauma-centered theory while he ended up committed to his fantasy-centered paradigm. Both of us suffered from significant early traumas and yet we went in opposite directions. As the saying goes: "Some ships sail east, some ships sail west, by the self-same wind that blows." Trauma was the wind that pushed Freud and me in opposite directions. Why this is so is one of the many unsolved mysteries identified by the first-paradigm-related, adaptive approach. I shall therefore describe my remembered traumas and offer some tentative ideas about my differences from Freud.

## MY EARLY TRAUMAS

When I was about three-and-a-half to four years old my mother had a miscarriage at home. My uncle, who was an obstetrician, and my father, who was a general practitioner, were in attendance. My bedroom was next to my parents' bedroom and my sole conscious memory of the incident is of my uncle and father scurrying about in the hall outside of my bedroom. I knew that something urgent and terrible was happening, but I had no idea what it was. I have no conscious memory of when and how I later learned what the episode was about.

When I was about five or six years old, my father built his medical office in the basement of our home. With the help of a male colleague, he performed tonsillectomies there. The recovery room was in our flat. I have conscious memories of instruments being boiled in large pots on our stove and I vaguely recall that when I was somewhat older—this work went on for some ten years or more—I saw patients' blood somewhere. In my mind, all of these patients were young boys.

When I was ten years old the father of one of my neighborhood friends reminisced to me about my father's first marriage, adding that my father lived with his wife across the street from where we lived now. I had no prior conscious awareness of any of this and I kept it a secret from my siblings and parents. When I decided to go into personal analysis, I asked my parents about this information and they told me that my father did indeed have a first marriage and that his wife had died in the influenza epidemic of 1919. A few years after this conversation, when my father died, I learned that my two siblings both knew about his first wife, but had never uttered a word about it to anyone.


## MY COMMITMENT TO A TRAUMA-CENTERED THEORY

As to how and why I developed and stayed with a trauma-centered theory of emotional life, the answer begins with a nagging feeling I had throughout my psychoanalytic training that the role of reality in neuroses was being under-played in the classical psychoanalytic teachings I was receiving. I was fairly certain that my own early traumas had affected me directly, that my reactions to these events were not based so much on how I perceived and fantasized about them but on the inherent anxiety and psychological harm they had caused me. As a result, while I was practicing psychoanalysis as I had been taught—that is, focused on fantasies, transferences, and resistances—I also keyed into what was happening in reality between myself and my patients. I began to realize that the material from my patients that I was formulating in terms of transferences from past relationships did not materialize as projec-tions from within their psyches; it was being triggered by the interventions I was making. This was a novel idea at the time. Thus, it was no coincidence that my first psychoanalytic paper (Langs, 1971) was entitled 'Day Residues, Recall Residues and Dreams: Reality and the Psyche.' It was a study of the interplay between reality and the inner mind, that is, between the incidents that led to the recall of a repressed dream and the psychological meanings of the recovered dream imagery. At the time, I had no idea that this paper fore-told my future as a psychoanalyst—and in a way, as a human being as well.

As this was happening, several other factors played a role in my continuing concerns about the role of reality in psychical events and in the analytic experi-ence and the process of cure. In the early nineteen sixties, I became a research fellow at the Research Center for Mental Health at New York University. The staff there was winding up a series of laboratory studies of subliminal perception (Silverman, Lachman, and Milich, 1982). Impressed by their finding, I carried the concept over to my clinical work where I supplemented my investigations of patients' conscious perceptions of and reactions to my interventions with a search for perceptions and reactions that were subliminal and thus unconscious—encoded for example in their responsive dreams. It became clear that much of this imagery bridged over and was linked to my comments and behaviors and much to my surprise, I began to see that unconscious perceptiveness was an extremely common clinical and general phenomenon. I was struck too by the extent to which, properly decoded, these encoded narratives provided me with highly reliable, quite consistent information about the qualities and nature of my therapeutic efforts, including, remarkably enough, the extent to which they constituted valid, healing efforts. I had the sense that I was discovering and entering a new world of human experience and tapping into an unconscious system of the mind whose wisdom far exceeded all conscious capabilities—including my own. Continuing these pursuits became irresistible.

Another fortunate happenstance was the fact that my analytic work with patients was being supervised by Jacob Arlow who was a staunch believer in the existence and importance of disguised unconscious fantasies in mental life. As a result, he taught me how to decode manifest dream images—that is, to deconstruct their symbolic meanings in order to access the unconscious fantasies and wishes he believed they camouflaged. This gave me a way of analyzing dreams that was far more incisive than the method Freud employed during his formative years. Freud's efforts mainly involved direct readings of the manifest contents of dreams and theory-driven speculations as to the implications of these same surface contents. The approach I was taught was much more a process of actually decoding a dream image. Most importantly, in time on my own I began to carry out the decoding in light of the triggering event that had evoked and fit with the disguised manifest themes I was deciphering. The recognition of evocative triggers put the decoding process on solid ground and served as a guide and key to undoing the disguises inherent to the narrative imagery. The discovery of the role of these triggering events—*adaptive contexts,* as I first termed them (Langs, 1978b)—gave my decoding efforts a sensibility and consistency that was lacking in Freud's more random approach to dream material. This consistency made me feel somewhat secure regarding the many new insights I began to develop; the ways in which they fit together kept me on their trail.

Another helpful situation lay with my doing a great deal of teaching and supervising of psychotherapy trainees at a local mental health facility. The interventions that these fledgling therapists made often were flagrantly and undeniably erroneous. As a result, they evoked strong encoded images from their patients and this enabled me to see in bold relief the extent to which patients who *consciously* ignored or excused blatant errors—for example, therapists' missing sessions, checking up on patients who missed their sessions, becoming verbally abusive of their patients—*unconsciously* were unforgiving of their therapists' lapses. I saw too, as revealed by their responsive encoded images, that unconsciously they were extremely wise about the sources of these errors and about the dire consequences, unconsciously transmitted, of these harmful interventions. More and more I could see that the encoded responses from patients to their therapists' interventions included a highly accurate assessment of their correct or erroneous, helpful or harmful qualities. The deep unconscious system from which this wisdom was emanating appeared to be a reliable guide to doing effective psychotherapy and investigating the emotion-processing mind. I had lucked into an invaluable aid and was not about to let go of it.

The discovery of criteria for the presence or absence of encoded, unconscious validation was a turning point for me because I was facing fierce criticism and opposition from my colleagues who were co-teaching with me at my psychoanalytic institute and hearing about my teachings from the trainees whom they were analyzing. They had no compunctions about telling me the awful things their analysands were saying about me, and they warned me that I'd better stop what I was doing, that I was destroying my career, and that I'd soon be dropped from the Institute and ostracized by my colleagues—all accurate predictions of what lay ahead. (Ironically, my new approach had advanced sufficiently for me to know that their patients' stories about the supposed awful and assaultive qualities of my teachings actually encoded their valid unconscious perceptions of just how awful and assaultive my colleagues were in their psychoanalytic work with these student-analysands. You can be sure I didn't point that out to my fair-weathered friends; I wasn't suicidal.)

In the midst of these pressures to call a halt to what I was doing, I would go back to my office and listen to my patients' encoded responses to my interventions. When they were in keeping with my reality-centered adaptive approach I obtained unconscious validation, but when I reverted to intervening based on my classical psychoanalytic training the responses uniformly were non-validating in nature. My patients' deep unconscious minds kept telling me that I was on the right track, and they were imploring me to stay the course. I had no choice but to listen to their wise deep unconscious advice. I could not have lived with myself had I copped out. Now that I was attuned to unconscious messages, I would not be able to handle my patients' valid encoded perceptions that my non-adaptive efforts were harming them more than I was helping them. My guilt, self-criticisms, and self-loathing would have been unbearable.

All in all, then, the empirical data was so solid and consistent—archetypal, as I came to realize—and so freshly illuminating and surprisingly sagacious that I had no choice but to stay on track. And I did so even though it was causing me harm and suffering—financial, social, and otherwise—at the hands of my dismissive fellow analysts. I also persevered in the face of the unrelentingly grim death-related imagery that working with narrative material was evoking, much of it reverberating consciously and unconsciously with my own most painful issues. This was not the case with Freud. Despite the occasional desertion of a student or colleague, his way of listening was highly intellectualized and relatively easy to attend to, and for him personally, it opened the door to referrals and world recognition. In contrast, the more I advanced and expanded my thinking and wrote about it, the fewer the students and colleagues that came along. I did not relish the isolation, but all it did was goad me on.

In addition to these practical differences between Freud's fate and my own, there were several elusive, both realistic and psychodynamic, factors that seem to have played a role in the professional paths we chose to take. Freud's most compelling trauma seems to have been a singular incident with several aspects to it—his possible illegitimacy and being fathered by his half-brother, Phillip. While these traumas touched on his very existence and identity, and thus involved him directly, they seem to have been kept secret from him and probably had been obliterated early-on from his conscious awareness. In a few words, whatever his early-life traumas were, they seem to have been remembered unconsciously rather than consciously, and they affected him accordingly. In contrast, both of my earliest traumas were suffered by others. And both of them were bloody, talked about openly by my parents, and consciously registered by me, however replete they were with unconscious meanings.

It would appear then that the secreting and obliteration from awareness by Freud of his early traumas set the stage for his turn to denial mechanisms; there were few if any conscious clues for him to deal with and his deep unconscious, encoded recollections were easily subjected to denial. On the other hand, the inescapable openness of my early-life traumas rendered their denial all but impossible. I knew full well the horrors of these incidents and thus, in principle, the emotional pain that is caused by such realities; these were not matters I could pretend to have been inconsequential. I do in fact recall my use of forms of denial to deal with them, but none of them involved a belief that what I knew to have happened never happened.

Beyond this there must be a host of other, as yet unknown to me, factors in the difference in the basic choice that Freud and I made. Possibilities include other features of the early traumas that each of us suffered; family attitudes towards dealing with grim and death-related realities (paradoxically, my parents were far more deniers than truth tellers); cultural influences; biological genetic factors; unconscious determinants of our particular learned ways of coping with death and death-related traumas; and last but not least, the effects on each of us of the evolved archetypes of the emotion-processing mind. The role of this last factor is most intriguing because Freud went from counter-archetype to archetype while I went from archetype to counter-archetype. It is a mystery well worth solving, one that reflects some of the rewarding beauties and promises of the adaptive approach: No sooner have you solved one mystery than another unsolved puzzle comes forward to take its place. This also is one of the signs of the vitality of the trauma-centered paradigm and one of many reasons I shall remain committed to its principles for the rest of my living days. After all, the discoveries I made and solidified gave me a way of working with patients and living my life with others that is akin to a divine gift. Painful as it has been, there is no way I could ask for more.

Robert Langs, M.D.
October 2009

# References

Abbott, Edwin. *Flatland: A Romance of Many Dimensions.* New York: New American Library, [1884] 1984.

Anzieu, Didier. *Freud's Self-Analysis.* Madison, CT: International Universities Press, [1959] 1986.

Balmary, Marie. *Psychoanalyzing Psychoanalysis: Freud and the Hidden Fault of the Father.* Baltimore, MD: John Hopkins University Press, [1979] 1982.

Bion, Wilfred. *Seven Servants.* New York: Jason Aronson, 1977.

Breuer, Josef, and Freud, Sigmund. *Studies on Hysteria.* Standard Edition 2:3–311, 1893–1895.

Chertok, Leon. "The Discovery of the Transference: Toward an Epistemological Interpretation." *International Journal of Psycho-Analysis* 49 (1968): 560–576.

Clodd, Edward. *Pioneers of Evolution: Darwin and Wallace.* Whitefish, MT: Kessinger Publishing, 2005.

De Duve, Christian. *Vital Dust.* New York: Basic Books, 1995.

Devereux, George. "Why Oedipus Killed Laius—A Note on the Complementary Oedipus Complex in Greek Drama." *International Journal of Psycho-Analysis* 34 (1953): 132–141.

Donn, Linda. *Freud and Jung: Years of Friendship, Years of Loss.* New York: Macmillan, 1988.

Ellenberger, Henri. *The Discovery of the Unconscious: The History and Evolution of Dynamic Psychiatry.* New York: Basic Books, 1970.

Freud, Sigmund. "Further Remarks on the Neuro-Psychoses of Defence." Standard Edition 3:159–188, 1896a.

——. "Heredity and the Aetiology of the Neuroses." Standard Edition 3:141–158, 1896b.

——. "The Aetiology of Hysteria." Standard Edition 3:189–224, 1896c.

——. "Sexuality in the Aetiology of the Neuroses." Standard Edition: 3:261–285, 1898a.

185

——. "The Psychical Mechanism of Forgetfulness." Standard Edition 3:287–298, 1898b.

——. "Screen Memories." Standard Edition 3:301–322, 1899.

——. *The Interpretation of Dreams.* Standard Edition 4 and 5, 1900.

——. *The Psychopathology of Everyday Life.* Standard Edition: 6:1–289, 1901.

——. "Fragment of an Analysis of a case of Hysteria" Standard Edition 7:1–122, 1905a.

——. *Jokes and their Relation to the Unconscious.* Standard Edition 8:3–243, 1905b.

——. "Three Essays on the Theory of Sexuality." Standard Edition 7:146–243, 1905c.

——. *Delusions and Dreams in Jensen's Gradiva.* Standard Edition 9:1–96, 1907.

——. "Analysis of a Phobia in a Five Year-Old-Boy (Little Hans)." Standard Edition: 1–147, 1909a.

——. "Family Romances." Standard Edition 9:235–241, 1909b.

——. "Notes Upon a Case of Obsessional Neurosis." Standard Edition 10:151–318, 1909c.

——. *Leonardo Da Vinci and a Memory From His Childhood.* Standard Edition: 59–138, 1910a.

——. "The Future Prospects of Psycho-Analytic Therapy." Standard Edition 11: 141–151, 1910b.

——. Psycho-analytic Notes on an Autobiographical Account of a Case of Paranoia (*Dementia Paranoides*). Standard Edition 12:1–82, 1911.

——. "The Dynamics of Transference." Standard Edition 12:97–108, 1912a

——. "Recommendations to Physicians Practising Psycho-Analysis." Standard Edition 12:109–120, 1912b.

——. "On Beginning the Treatment (Further Recommendations on the Technique of Psycho Analysis, I.)" Standard Edition 12:121–144, 1913a.

——. *Totem and Taboo.* Standard Edition 13:131–161, 1913b.

——. "Observations on Transference Love (Further Recommendations on the Technique of Psycho-Analysis, III.)" Standard Edition 12:157–171, 1914a

——. "On the History of the Psycho-Analytic Movement." Standard Edition 14:1–66, 1914b.

——. "Remembering, Repeating and Working Through (Further Recommendations on the Technique of Psycho-Analysis, II.)" Standard Edition 12:145–156, 1914c.

——. "The Moses of Michaelangelo." Standard Edition 13:209–238, 1914d.

——. "Thoughts for the Times on War and Death." Standard Edition 14:274–302, 1915.

——. "Those Wrecked by Success." Standard Edition 14:316–331, 1916.

——. "Introductory Lectures on Psycho-Analysis: Part III. General Theory of Neuroses." Standard Edition 16:243–496, 1917.

——. "From the History of an Infantile Neurosis." Standard Edition 17:1–122, 1918.

——. *Beyond the Pleasure Principle.* Standard Edition 18:7–66, 1920.

——. *The Ego and the Id.* Standard Edition: 19:3–66, 1923.

——. "The Dissolution of the Oedipus Complex." Standard Edition 19:173–179, 1924.

——. *An Autobiographical Study.* Standard Edition 20:1–74, 1925.

——. *Inhibitions, Symptoms and Anxiety.* Standard Edition 20:75–172, 1926.

——. *The Future of an Illusion.* Standard Edition 21:1–56, 1927.

——. "Analysis Terminable and Interminable." Standard Edition 23:209–254, 1937a.

——. "Construction in Analysis." Standard Edition 23:255–270, 1937b.

——. *Moses and Monotheism: Three Essays.* Standard Edition: 23:3–137, 1939.

——. *An Outline of Psycho-Analysis.* Standard Edition:23:139–208, 1940.

——. "Project for a Scientific Psychology." Standard Edition 1:283–397, [1895] 1950.

——. *The Origins of Psycho-Analysis. Letters to Wilhelm Fliess, Drafts and Notes: 1887–1902,* edited by Marie Bonaparte, Anna Freud, and Ernst Kris. New York: Basic Books, 1954.

Gay, Peter. *Freud: A Life for Our Time.* New York: Norton, 1988.

Gilder, Joshua, and Anne-Lee Gilder. *Heavenly Intrigue: Johannes Kepler, Tycho Brahe, and the Murder Behind One of History's Greatest Scientific Discoveries.* New York: Doubleday, 2004.

Gleick, James. *Isaac Newton.* New York: Vintage, 2004.

Good, Michael (ed.) *The Seduction Theory in its Second Century: Trauma, Fantasy, and Reality Today.* Madison, CT: International Universities Press, 2006.

Heimann, Paula. "On Countertransference." *International Journal of Psycho-Analysis* 31 (1950): 81 84.

Isaacson, Walter. *Einstein: His Life and Universe.* New York: Simon and Schuster, 2007.

Jung, C. "Analytic Psychology: It's Theory and Practice." In *The Tavistock Lectures.* London: Routledge & Kegan Paul, 1968.

——. "The Personal and the Collective Unconscious." In: *Two Essays on Analytical Psychology.* Princeton, NJ: Princeton University Press, 1972.

Kohut, Heinz. *The Analysis of the Self.* New York: International Universities Press, 1971.

——. *The Restoration of the Self.* New York: International Universities Press, 1977.

Krull, Marianne. *Freud and His Father.* New York: Norton [1979] 1986.

Kuhn, Thomas. *The Structure of Scientific Revolution.* Chicago: University of Chicago Press, 1962.

Langs, Robert. "Day Residues, Recall Residues and Dreams: Reality and the Psyche." *Journal of the American Psychoanalytic Association* 19 (1971): 499–523.

——. *Technique in Transition.* New York: Jason Aronson, 1978a.

——. *The Listening Process.* New York: Jason Aronson, 1978b.

——. *The Psychotherapeutic Conspiracy.* New York: Jason Aronson, 1982.

——. "The Irma Dream and the Origins of Psychoanalysis." *Psychoanalytic Review* 71 (1984): 591–617.

——. *Madness and Cure.* Lake Worth, Fl: Gardner Press, 1985.

——. *Empowered Psychotherapy.* London: Karnac Books, 1993.

——. *The Evolution of the Emotion-Processing Mind, With an Introduction to Mental Darwinism.* London: Karnac Books, 1996.

——. *Death Anxiety in Clinical Practice.* London: Karnac Books, 1997.

188 References

—— (ed.). *Current Theories of Psychoanalysis*. Madison, CT: International Universities Press, 1998a.

——. *Ground Rules in Psychotherapy and Counselling*. London: Karnac Books, 1998b.

——. *Freud's Bird of Prey*. Phoenix, AZ: Zeig, Tucker, 2000.

——. *Fundamentals of Adaptive Psychotherapy and Counselling*. London: Palgrave-Macmillan, 2004.

——. *Love and Death in Psychotherapy*. London: Palgrave-Macmillan, 2006.

——. *Beyond Yahweh and Jesus: Bringing Death's Wisdom to Faith, Spirituality, and Psychoanalysis*. Lanham, MD: Jason Aronson, 2008.

Langs, Robert, Anthony Badalamenti, and Lenore Thomson. *The Cosmic Circle: The Unification of Mind, Matter and Energy*. Brooklyn, NY: Alliance Publishing, 1996.

Langs, Robert, and Harold Searles. *Intrapsychic and Interpersonal Dimensions of Treatment: A Clinical Dialog*. New York: Jason Aronson, 1980.

Little, Margaret. "Countertransference and the Patient's Response to It." *International Journal of Psycho-Analysis* 32 (1951): 32–34.

Lothane, Zvi. *In defense of Schreber: Soul, Murder, and Psychiatry*. London: Analytic Press, 1992.

Maciejewski, Franz. "Freud and His Wife, and His Wife." *American Imago 63* (2006): 497–506.

Masson, Jeffrey. *The Assault on Truth: Freud's Suppression of the Seduction Theory*. New York: Farrar, Straus and Giroux, 1984.

Masson, Jeffrey (ed.). *The Complete Letters of Sigmund Freud to Wilhelm Fleiss, 1887–1904*. Cambridge, MA : Harvard University Press, 1985.

Mitchell, Stephen. *Relational Concepts in Psychoanalysis: An Integration*. Cambridge, MA: Harvard University Press, 1988.

Nietzsche, Friedrich. *Beyond Good and Evil*. translated by R.J. Hollingdale. London: Penguin Books, 2003.

Pine, Fred. *Diversity and Direction in Psychoanalytic Technique*. New York: Other Press, 2003.

Poetzl, Otto. "Experimentell Erregte Traumbilder in Ihren Beziehungen Zum Indirekten Sehen." *Zeitschrift Fur die gesamte Neurologie and Psychiatrie* 37 (1917): 278.

Rabow, Jerry. *50 Jewish Messiahs*. Jerusalem: Gefen Books, 2003.

Racker, Heinrich. *Transference and Countertransference*. London: Hogarth Press, 1974.

Rangell, Leo. *The Road to Unity in Psychoanalytic Theory*. Lanham, MD: Jason Aronson, 2006.

Rizzuto, Ana-Maria. *Why did Freud Reject God?* New Haven, CT: Yale University Press, 1998.

Roazen, Paul. *Brother Animal: The Story of Freud & Tausk*. New York: Alfred A. Knopf, 1969.

Rorty, Richard. *Contingency, Irony, and Solidarity*. New York: Cambridge University Press, 1989.

Rosenbaum, Michael. *Dare to be Human: A Contemporary Psychoanalytic Journey*. London: Routledge, 2009.

Schur, Max. "Some Additional 'Day Residues' of the 'Specimen Dream of Psychoanalysis.'" Pp. 45–85 in *Psychoanalysis—A General Psychology,* edited by Rudolf Loewenstein. New York: International Universities Press, 1966.

——. *Freud: Living and Dying.* New York: International Universities Press, 1972.

Scott, Eugenie. *Evolution vs. Creationism: An Introduction.* Berkeley, CA: University of California Press, 2005.

Searles, Harold. "The Patient as Therapist to His Analyst." Pp. 95–151 in *Tactics and Techniques in Psychoanalytic Therapy, Vol II. Countertransference,* edited by Peter Giovacchini. New York: Jason Aronson, 1975.

Searles, Harold. *Countertransference and Related Subjects: Selected Papers.* New York: International Universities Press, 1979.

Shengold, Leon. *Soul Murder Revisited: Thoughts About Therapy, Hate, Love, and Memory.* Yale University Press, 2000.

Silverman, Lloyd, Frank Lachman, and Robert Milich. *The Search for Oneness.* New York: International Universities Press, 1982.

Sobel, Dava. *Galileo's Daughter.* New York: Penguin Books, 2000.

Stolorow, Robert, Bernard Brandshaft, and George Atwood. *Psychoanalytic Treatment: An Intersubjective Approach.* Hillsdale, NJ: The Analytic Press, 1987.

Sulloway, Frank. *Freud: Biologist of the Mind: Beyond the Psychoanalytic Legend.* New York: Basic Books, 1979.

Swales, Peter. "Freud, Minna Bernays, and the Conquest of Rome: New Light on the Origins of Psychoanalysis." *New American Review,* 1 (1982): 1–23.

Szasz, Thomas. "The Concept of Transference." *International Journal of Psycho-Analysis* 44(1963): 32–443.

Taylor, Don (trans.). *The Theban Plays: Oedipus the King by Sophocles.* London: Metheun, 1986.

Vitz, Paul. *Freud's Christian Unconscious.* New York: The Guilford Press, 1988.

Winnicott, Donald. "Hate in the Countertransference." Pp. 194–203 in *Collected Papers: Through Pediatrics to Psycho-Analysis.* New York: Basic Books, [1947] 1958.

Yerushalmi, Yosef. *Freud's Moses: Judaism Terminable and Interminable.* New Haven, CT: Yale University Press, 1991.

# Index

Abbott, Edwin, 66, 71, 185
adaptive approach, xi, 19–20, 53–60,
    94–95, 180–84
  unique insights of, 56–60, 70, 78–79,
    103, 108–110, 112, 143
anxiety, death-related.
  *See* death anxiety
Anzieu, Didier, x, 108, 185
archetypes, vii, x, xi, 7, 10–11, 41–42, 58,
    63–64, 71–73, 88, 96–99, 109–111,
    115, 117, 120, 138, 139, 143, 145,
    148, 151, 152, 156, 160, 175, 183
  communicative. *See* communicative,
    archetypes
  death-related, 11, 58, 61, 94–95,
    96–99, 103, 110–11, 119, 138,
    139, 143, 145, 151, 156, 175
  denial-based, 15, 20, 21, 24, 25, 109,
    117, 175
  Freud's counter-response to, 10,
    28–29
  and ground rules (frames), 59–60,
    67, 104, 106
  in Jungian thinking, 10, 66, 71
  Langs's counter-response to, 96,
    183–84

and paradigm shifts, 11, 15–30, 61,
    63–64. *See also* paradigms;
    paradigm shifts
Atwood, George, 51, 66, 189

Badalamenti, Anthony, 26, 96, 188
Balmary, Marie, x, 2, 4, 28, 31, 32, 33,
    35, 63, 81, 85, 88, 92, 94, 95,
    117, 118, 121, 126, 128, 131, 135,
    141, 185
Bible, the. *See* religion, and the Bible;
    traumas, Freud's (verified and
    conjectured)
Bion, Wilfred, 84, 185
boundaries. *See* ground rules (frames)
Brandshaft, Bernard, 51, 66, 189
Breuer, Josef, 33, 46, 68, 69, 78, 100,
    104, 185

chance (fate) versus self-determination,
    13–15, 148, 158, 165–66, 169–70
Chertok, Leon, 68, 69, 185
church, Catholic. *See* paradigms,
    biological; paradigms, of the
    physical universe; religion
Clodd, Edward, 22, 185

communicative
  approach. *See* adaptive approach
  archetypes, 76–77, 82–85, 91, 96–99
  conflicts (revealing vs. concealing),
    xi, 80, 82, 91–92, 97, 108, 125,
    147, 157–58, 163, 176
  defenses (resistances), xi, 79–80,
    82–85, 91, 97, 115–17
  style, Freud's, 79–80, 82–85, 91–92,
    99–101, 106, 111, 111–13, 134,
    138, 152, 163
conscious system. *See* mind, emotion-
  processing, conscious system of

death
  awareness of, 60, 71, 105
  denial of, 15–27, 42, 60–61, 66, 71,
    72, 80–81, 105, 145, 175
  death anxiety, 59–60, 71, 87–88, 138,
    175–77
  existential, 15–28, 41, 60, 67, 88, 138
  forms of, 11
  predator (guilt-driven), 60, 88, 111,
    119, 138, 139, 143
  predatory, 60, 87–88, 138, 159
  unconscious, 71, 177
decoding, narrative messages.
  *See* narratives, decoding of
  (trigger decoding)
De Duve, Christian, 23, 185
deep unconscious system.
  *See* mind, emotion-processing,
  deep unconscious system of
defenses, communicative.
  *See* communicative: defenses
  (resistances)
denial. *See* mind, emotion-processing,
  denial, used by
Devereux, George, 122, 185
Donn, Linda, 174, 185
dreams
  adaptive discoveries regarding, 54,
    77–79, 84, 109–110

Freud's discoveries regarding, 3, 45,
  76–80, 83
Freud's (personal), 80, 103–108,
  135–36, 137, 146, 161–63

Ellenberger, Henri, 12, 185
emotion-processing mind. *See* mind,
  emotion-processing

Freud, Amalie
  purported affair with Phillip Freud.
    *See* trauma, Freud's (verified or
    conjectured), Phillip's affair with
    Amalie
  seen nude by Freud, 3, 132, 150
Freud, Anna, birth of, 133, 134–35, 140,
  149, 165
Freud, Jakob
  death of, 3, 4–5, 27, 29–30, 32, 35,
    75, 79, 80, 99, 102, 107, 117,
    121, 125, 138, 145, 146, 150, 154,
    157, 161–63
  first anniversary, of his death, 29,
    75–76, 102, 110, 112, 139, 145,
    146
Freud, Julius. *See* traumas, Freud's
  (verified or conjectured),
  death of Julius
Freud, Phillip, purported affair with
  Amalie Freud. *See* traumas,
  Freud's (verified or conjectured),
  Phillip's affair with Amalie
Freud, Sigmund, vii, viii, 1, 3, 4, 12,
  13, 16, 19, 29, 32, 33, 34, 35, 36,
  37, 38, 39, 40, 41, 45, 46, 47, 48,
  50, 51, 60, 68, 69, 76, 78, 80, 83,
  87, 88, 89, 91, 93, 100, 102, 103,
  104, 107, 108, 112, 113, 117, 121,
  123, 124, 125, 126, 128, 129, 132,
  133, 134, 135, 137, 140, 141, 144,
  146, 148, 149, 153, 154, 161, 163,
  165, 166, 167, 168, 169, 170, 171,
  185–86

dreams of. *See* dreams, Freud's
  (personal)
early traumas of. *See* traumas,
  Freud's (verified or conjectured)
fainting episodes of, 174–75
reality, personal dread of, 83, 118,
  127, 138–39, 144–45, 150, 157
self-analysis of, 1, 3–4, 101, 107,
  108–110, 126, 132, 133, 134,
  146, 148–49, 151
as subject, 92–93
*See also* communicative, defenses
  (resistances); communicative,
  style, Freud's

Gay, Peter, 94, 118, 187
Gilder, Anne Lee, 16, 18, 187
Gilder, Joshua, 16, 18, 187
Gleick, James, 25, 187
God
  and creation, 20–22
  creationism, 21–25
  intelligent design, theory of, 21
  and paradigms, 18–19, 20–25, 26
  *See also* religion; paradigms;
    paradigm shifts
Good, Michael, ix, x, 2, 3, 19, 34, 37,
  41, 46, 63, 66, 69, 187
ground rules (frames), 46, 67–68,
  104, 106, 109, 119. *See also*
  archetypes, and ground rules
  (frames)
guilt, deep unconscious. *See* death
  anxiety, predator (guilt driven)

Hamlet, 126, 132–34, 140, 141,
  149–50, 157, 169
Heimann, Paula, 46, 187

immortality, 141–42
  human, issues with, 4–6,
    31–33, 46
Isaacson, Walter, 26, 27, 187

Jung, Carl, 10, 66, 71, 187

Kohut, Heinz, 46, 51, 66, 187
Krull, Marianne, x, 80, 81, 88, 90,
  94, 102, 107, 117, 121, 129, 131,
  135, 187
Kuhn, Thomas, 9, 187

Lachman, Frank, 96, 189
Langs, Robert, vii, viii, ix, xi, 2, 6, 11,
  20, 22, 24, 28, 41, 45, 46, 53, 56,
  59, 60, 62, 66, 67, 71, 76, 81, 82,
  84, 96, 102, 103, 109, 119, 120,
  155, 177, 180, 181, 187–88
  traumas of, 179–84
Little, Margaret, 46, 68, 188
Lothane, Zvi, 41, 188

Maciejewski, Franz, 125, 188
Masson, Jeffrey, 19, 28, 29, 32,
  35, 72, 188
memories, screen, 89–90, 137, 173
Milich, Robert, 96, 189
mind, emotion-processing, viii, 56–59
  conscious defenses (resistances) of,
    viii, x, 45, 61–62, 79, 82, 97–98,
    109, 110–13
  conscious system of, viii, 6, 41, 52,
    56–57, 58, 61–64, 108–109, 117
  deep unconscious system of, vii, viii,
    x, 6, 55–59, 108, 112, 117
  denial, used by, 41, 58, 98–99,
    138–39
  models of, Freud's, vii, viii, 47–53,
    64–66
Mitchell, Stephen, 46, 66, 188

narcissism. *See* trauma, as blows to
  human narcissism
narratives
  decoding of (trigger decoding), xi,
    57, 76, 83–84, 91, 98, 99, 101,
    108–109, 139, 146, 151–61

narratives (*continued*)
    as encoded messages, xi, 54–55, 76–80,
        90–92, 97, 99, 101, 145, 150–51
    Freud's, xi, 87–90, 100–101
    resistances against. *See*
        communicative: defenses
        (resistances)
    *See also* dreams
neuroses, causes of. *See* theories,
    of neuroses; traumas, in general:
    role of in neuroses
Nietzsche, Frederick, vii, 188

Oedipus, myth of, ix, 1, 4–5, 13–14, 36,
        91, 94, 120, 121–25, 126, 132–34,
        136, 140–41, 146–61, 173, 175
    adaptive interpretation of, 103,
        151–61
    complex, 36–37, 45, 51, 71, 73,
        85, 108
    Freud's interpretation of, 1, 4–5, 103,
        113, 132–34, 146–50
    pre-story in, 121–22, 147–48, 163
    violence in, 5, 94, 103, 120, 151–61

paradigms, vii, 9–10, 11–30, 31–42,
    59–60
    and archetypes. *See* archetypes, and
        paradigm shifts
    biological, 12, 20–25
    and denial of death, 14, 15–27, 42,
        66, 81, 177
    and existential death anxiety, 15–27
    first (initial), in principle, 16, 20–22
    first, of Freud, ix, x, xi, 2, 19, 32–34,
        44–45, 59–60, 61–64, 67–68,
        70–73, 98–99, 127
    of the physical universe, 12, 15–27
    of psychoanalysis, 23–24, 31–42,
        43–75
    psychological, 12, 15
    second (Freud's), ix, 2, 4–5, 15, 19,
        21–22, 34–42, 45–53, 59–60, 61–
        64, 62–73, 98, 113, 122, 127, 177

second (revised), in principle, 12,
    15–20, 22–25
paradigm shifts, ix–x, 6–7, 9–13, 15–27,
    28–30, 31–42
    Freud's, ix–x, 5, 6–7, 28–30, 31–42,
        61–64, 68–73, 83, 95, 116–18,
        122, 126, 138, 141, 148–49
    missing material regarding, 102–108
    and murderous impulses, as defense
        against, 110–13, 138, 140, 141,
        157, 160, 176
    reasons offered for, by Freud and
        others, 4–6, 38–42, 76–82, 89–90,
        101–102, 116
    resistances against making, 9–10,
        14–15, 16, 24
    resources available for propositions
        about, 101–110, 116–17
    and suicidal impulses, as a defense
        against, 110–13, 127, 132,
        138, 140, 141, 143, 144,
        157, 160, 176
    *See also* archetypes, and
        paradigm shifts
perception, unconscious (subliminal),
    viii, x, 40–41, 57–58, 65, 70, 76,
    96, 116
Pine, Fred, 3, 44, 46, 66, 188
Poetzl, Otto, 41, 188
psychoanalysis
    creation of, 1, 12–23, 32–42
    unconscious, defined in, 48–53

Rabow, Jerry, 24, 188
Racker, Heinrich, 46, 188
Rangell, Leo, 3, 44, 46, 66, 188
reconstructions, trigger decoded, 83, 89,
    91, 115
religion, 88, 102–103, 117, 123
    atheism, 21
    and the Bible, 126–28,
        135–36, 140
    and paradigms, ix, 4, 16–19
    theism, 21

*See also* God, and paradigms;
paradigms; paradigm shifts
resistances, communicative.
  *See* communicative, defenses
  (resistances)
Rizzuto, Ana-Maria, x, 89, 103, 117,
  118, 131, 135, 137, 188
Roazen, Paul, 120, 188
Rorty, Richard, 43, 62, 72, 188
Rosenbaum, Michael, 3, 44, 46,
  66, 71, 188

self-analysis, Freud's. *See* Freud,
  Sigmund, self-analysis of
Schur, Max, x, 107, 108, 121,
  132, 189
Scott, Eugenie, 21, 189
screen memories. *See* memories, screen
Searles, Harold, 41, 46, 55, 188, 189
seduction theory. *See* theories, seduction
Shengold, Leon, 41, 189
Silverman, Lloyd, 96, 189
Sobel, Dava, 16, 17, 189
Stolorow, Robert, 51, 66, 189
Sulloway, Frank, x, 4, 29, 33, 38, 189
Swales, Peter, 125, 189
Systems, of the mind. *See* mind,
  emotion-processing
Szasz, Thomas, 68, 189

Taylor, Don, 5, 13, 189
theories
  abandonment of, 3–6, 29, 31,
    38–40, 80–81, 126
  adaptive, 19–20, 180–84.
    *See also* adaptive approach
  of evolution, 22–25
  fantasy-centered, 13, 36–37
  inner-need (drive) centered, 36–37,
    45–47
  mind-centered (inner-mental), 37, 51
  of neuroses, 66–68, 121, 130
  reality-centered (trauma-centered),
    14–15, 32–34

reality versus fantasy, as primary
  emotional issue, 2, 5–6,
  31–42, 138
seduction, ix, 1–2, 13, 29, 33–34,
  80–81
  *See also* paradigms; paradigm shifts;
  traumas, in general
Thomson, Lenore, 26, 96, 188
transference, 3, 33, 45–46,
  52, 68–71
traumas, in general
  as accidents of fate, 13–15,
    148, 158
  as blows, to human narcissism,
    11–15
  conscious obliteration of, 97–98
  death related, 13–18, 97–99,
    115–16
  early life, 46–47, 90–92
  lasting effects of, 78–79, 116
  role of, in neuroses, 6, 46–47
  unconscious beliefs
    regarding, 119–20
traumas, Freud's (verified or
  conjectured)
  and the Biblical Rebecca
    story, 126–28, 163–65
  biological father, uncertainties
    regarding, 81, 95, 118, 125,
    144–77
  date of birth, uncertainties regarding,
    81, 118, 129, 147, 164, 168
  death of half-siblings and
    cousins, 81, 118–20
  death of Julius, x, 3, 81, 90, 119,
    120, 124, 132, 148
  death of Sally Kanner, 81
  and Die Richterin, 170–71
  and Don Giovanni, 123–24, 163
  Freud, Jakob, infidelities of, 81,
    117–18, 125, 157, 162–63
  and Freud's dreams, 161–63
  in general, ix, x, 78–82, 89–90, 95,
    112–13, 118, 125, 144–77

traumas (*continued*)
  and Leonardo Da Vinci, 165–70
  and the Oedipus myth, 146–61
  Phillip's affair with Amalie, 81, 106,
    118, 123–24, 125, 129, 131–38,
    139–40, 143–44, 164, 170–71
  and Rebecca West (Ibsen), 128–31, 140
  and the story of Moses, 154, 171–75
  suicide of Rebekka Freud, 81, 95,
    118, 120–31, 139–40, 143, 147,
    162–63, 168

trigger decoding. *See* narratives,
  decoding of (trigger decoding)

validation, unconscious (encoded), x,
  5–6, 55, 58, 77, 92, 95, 97,
  115–16
  failures of, 104–105
Vitz, Paul, x, 103, 131, 189

Winnicott, Donald, 88, 189

Yerushalmi, Yosef, 103, 189

## ABOUT THE AUTHOR

**Robert Langs,** M.D., is the author of forty-seven books written on the basis of his innovative approach to the human mind and to psychotherapy, psychoanalysis, and the human condition. His focus on the unconscious experience of and adaptations to reality and its death-related traumas places him in a unique position to retell the interrelated stories of Freud's early-life traumas and the psychoanalysis he created with a freshness that brings new insights and wisdom to both biographical investigations and the broad field of dynamic psychology.